REASONABLY HAPPY

FINDING SERENITY THROUGH CHALLENGE AND CHANGE

Terry Ellis

The Lisburn Press
www.TheLisburnPress.com

THE LISBURN PRESS
3115 OLD FORGE DRIVE
BATON ROUGE, LOUISIANA 70808

REASONABLY HAPPY
Copyright © 2021 by Terry Ellis

PUBLISHED IN THE UNITED STATES OF AMERICA

Visit our website at TheLisburnPress.com.

First edition published 2021

Cover design by Sarah Powell
Text design by Kim Springfield

Library of Congress Cataloging-in-Publication Data is available.

ISBN: 978-0-578-98920-4

For information regarding special discounts for bulk purchases, please
contact The Lisburn Press Special Sales at info@TheLisburnPress.com.

Printed in Canada

This book is printed on acid-free paper.

"Everyone seeks happiness." – St. Thomas Aquinas

"I have forgotten what happiness is."
Jeremiah in Lamentations 3:17

The Serenity Prayer (long version)

God grant me the serenity to accept the things I cannot change,
Courage to change the things I can,
And wisdom to know the difference.

Living one day at a time,
Enjoying one moment at a time.
Accepting hardships as the pathway to peace
Taking, as Jesus did, this sinful world as it is, not as I would have it.
Trusting You to make all things right if I surrender to Your will.

That I may be reasonably happy in this life,
And supremely happy with you forever in the next.

DEDICATION

Above all, of course, I dedicate this book to my good and loving God who never turned His back on me and through grace will never allow any experience to be wasted. I once was lost, but now I'm found. Jesus was always to be the center of my life and now is again. Thank You for finding me in the darkness and leading my back to the light of Your grace.

This book is also for every searching sufferer I've encountered in four decades of walking with hurting people. I hope The Prayer and the words of this book will encourage you to keep trusting that God does indeed save the crushed in spirit (Ps. 34:18). He is near. He is listening. He will help.

This book has been shaped also by a vast, caring, and wonderfully varied anonymous community that has taught me things they really can't teach you in seminary. You all inspire me. I'm very glad to walk the road of recovery with you. Thank you for teaching me, and my prayer is that this book will shed some light on a God that I deeply believe in but that some of you may not. I've always loved the reverence, respect, and hope my skeptical brothers and sisters display when they, with me, bow their heads at the close of a meeting and whisper these words.

Special thanks also for the many people who've encouraged this work and who have supported me through it. Many of you have been with me since the beginning of Chrysalis Interventions, and together we've seen hundreds of people walk out of the darkness of addiction and into the light of recovery. Bill Hamm, you were the first that said "Go." I did. Look what God hath wrought!

And Leslie…sine qua non. Thank you for not giving up on me. I would not have recovered without you, and I'm so glad for the chance to live the rest of my life with you. Together we will always be reasonably happy.

CONTENTS

PROLOGUE

The following results are from a survey I conducted that consisted of me thinking at my desk and a call to my Catholic daughter. It's not scientific and may very well generate more discussion than anything in the rest of the book.

As far as prayers that are familiar to and memorized by the general American public, The Lord's Prayer would be number one. The Hail Mary, the Saint Michael Prayer, and the Guardian Angel Prayer are whispered by hundreds of thousands of worshipers, mostly Catholics, daily. Many families have a familiar grace-at-the-table prayer. Many people know parts of the St. Francis Prayer, but few have memorized all of it. The Shema is certainly up there. Other religious traditions also have cherished prayers in their liturgy, of course.

Somewhere in the top five, however, is The Serenity Prayer, or The Prayer as I refer to it in this book. Go into any of the literally thousands of AA meetings and you are likely to hear The Serenity Prayer at the beginning or end of the gathering. Many people not in this program are also familiar with this three-line prayer. It is very well-known.

My reasons for writing this book are three-fold. I am a Christian minister with two post-graduate degrees and about four decades of experience in churches and many religious institutions. My faith is very important to me, and my religion is a positive, central, organizing principle of my life. The Long Version of The Serenity Prayer is simply a very beautiful and powerful prayer that I've felt led to pray and now study and write about. It's theologically deep and practically relevant. The Prayer is life-changing, and especially for anyone facing change and challenge, The Prayer offers a powerful and refreshing way to understand God and life.

My second reason for writing is for another group of people whom I hope may benefit from it. I am a recovering alcoholic and will relate some of my story in the following pages. When I first entered the rooms of AA, I was intrigued that most everybody recited the familiar first three lines of this prayer even though AA is careful to be non-sectarian and does not even require a belief in God. But the prayer begins with "God." Even doubters and thoroughgoing agnostics recited The Prayer because it gave them comfort and hope. I was moved by their respect and their honest interest in something transcendent. The Prayer is Christian in its origin and language, so I hope to communicate its meaning and explain the powerful and elegant theological concepts it expresses.

Third, The Prayer addresses the idea of happiness, a very popular and important topic. Part of my initial intrigue with The Prayer was that it aimed at making us reasonably happy. The fact that happiness appears in such a theologically rich text may surprise many people who think of God and spiritual matters as very serious, perhaps even morbidly so. That's simply not the case. God would not create us with the capacity to be happy and then wish to shut down our interest in it. In an age where many people think the way to happiness is to jettison any belief in traditional theological doctrines, The Prayer is an endearing example of how a clear mind for spiritual matters warms the heart.

The Prayer has a wide appeal because people perceive that the world is increasingly out of control. Whether that's true or not is impossible to accurately assess. What is clearly true, however, is that we've lost some common foundations and vocabulary that formerly enabled us to discuss and come to some fairly reasonable shared understandings. At the very least, we live in an angry world. Throw in a pandemic and social unrest, and you can understand why so many people feel tremendous and uncertain shifts. I believe The Prayer will help bring peace, perspective, and challenge to anyone who wants to recover and maintain a solid foundation of faith and practice. Ironically, acceptance, which is the main theme of The Prayer, is control.

I've included seven summary points at the end of each chapter. These are intended to highlight the main take-aways for each phrase of The Prayer. I hope they will provide an extra layer of clarity, for we will be wading into some rather deep theological waters.

Finally, a word about prayer, perhaps aimed mostly at my doubting friends. Prayer certainly has no effect if you do not engage in it. Often the questions about prayer silence our prayers before we begin. How does prayer work? Why does something happen sometimes when I pray and not other times? Does God change His mind? These are all wonderful questions and have some very intelligent responses that settle the matter for many people. Other people less so. Keep searching and asking. Good theology invites questions and requires searching. When it comes to the practice of prayer, however, don't wait until you have all the answers. It's simply too mysterious. Pray because you need help and comfort from a Power greater than yourself.

One final, final word concerning my references to God. Throughout this book, as in all my writing for decades, I use masculine pronouns for God. I understand this practice creates some issues for some readers, but I assure you that I'm not implying God is masculine or that men have a superior place in God's creation. God is, in classic theological understanding, a genderless Spirit. My use of a particular set of pronouns is merely my nod to tradition as well as a matter of a simpler sentence construction in many situations. I also capitalize these pronouns in keeping with the very ancient tradition of *nomina sacra* (sacred name) in which names are treated with a special reverence in written texts.

I encourage all readers to memorize The Prayer in its full version. Pray it daily for three months and see what happens to you internally during that time. The results will likely surprise you, because God as I understand Him listens to all our prayers and responds because He loves us. I trust The Prayer will stir your spirit deeply as it did mine.

CHAPTER ONE

A LIFE OUT OF CONTROL

"Parts of me covertly rebel, and just when I least expect it, they take charge. I've tried everything and nothing helps. I'm at the end of my rope."
Romans 7:23-24 (The Message)

"You made us for Yourself, and our heart is restless until it rests in Thee."
St. Augustine, Confessions.

Everyone has had the experience of waking up too early, looking over at the bedroom windows, and noticing the first feeble light of dawn beginning to creep through. You haven't slept well enough or long enough. With a muffled sigh you realize the day is about to begin. You haven't had the restful sleep that you wanted, but you heave yourself out of bed and get going.

Now imagine that same scenario, but instead of a resigned sigh, you feel a depression so dark that you regret having woken up at all. In fact, you dread the dawn, for what you really wanted was not the rest that eludes you night after endless night. What you really want is to never wake up again.

It's a terrible thing to greet the dawn with a curse, but that's where I was during an active addiction to alcohol so severe that I wanted most of all to go to sleep at night and not wake up, ever. This book is about a prayer that saved my life and set me on a new road that I could never have imagined or really even wanted. My journey from the darkness of despair to the light of hope and joy began in a treatment center for addiction.

Little by Little, and All at Once

In rehab, everyone has bad days. No one arrives at a treatment center on a winning streak, but you'd be surprised how many are still convinced treatment is a massive overreaction. We'll quit on our own or make changes or find a different doctor. The walls of denial are thick and breaking them down is going to mean some hard days. One of my worst came in week four of my ninety-day inpatient treatment for alcoholism.

Thinking of yourself as unique is not a recipe for recovery from alcoholism. If you consider your problems unsolvable, your intellect too profound, your past nefarious, your virtues unassailable then you may begin to assume that treatment and counseling won't work for you. You're a special case! It's a common obstacle to recovery.

Having said that, I'll venture that my profile as an alcoholic entering treatment was unusual to say the least. I was a Baptist minister for over three decades. I'd served six churches as pastor over those years, all of them in the Deep South. A Southern Baptist by birth, I was in church the second Sunday of my life and seldom missed a Sunday morning, Sunday evening, or Wednesday night thereafter.

That was the rhythm in our family tradition. I learned Bible stories from caring teachers with flannel boards on Sunday mornings, heard good sermons in worship, then returned in the afternoon for another round of discipleship, choirs, and evening worship. Wednesday nights meant supper in the fellowship hall and mission studies when I was a child and youth group as a teen.

The Ellis generations were deeply rooted in the soil of that vigorous denomination, and I felt right at home. In my family, before I knew much of anything else, I learned about a good, loving, and smiling God. The phrase "smiling God" is something I picked up from a sermon from St. Augustine who described God that way. I liked it and realized that was what my parents and my extended family modeled for me, even though they had never studied Augustine. Everyone gets their first theology from their parents. It's inescapable, for good or bad. Mine was good.

Mamaw, who often spent her Sunday afternoons engaged in "visitation" (in her finest dress with white gloves), gave me a book of Bible facts and quizzed me when I was about 12 or so. Even though I loved God and loved the church, a Bible study book is about the last thing most 12-year-olds want to read. A confession here: I lost that book fairly soon after Mamaw gave it to me. It was not intentional on my part. I still don't know what happened to it. I'll swear that to this day on a stack of Bibles. Interestingly, Mamaw's memory had begun to fade already, but she never neglected to ask me if I had read that book. Her zeal to make sure no grandchild went to hell on her watch was unwavering, and she carried with her to the grave a deep commitment to making sure we could pass any quiz at the gates. We were a faith-filled family. It was the Ellis way, and I rarely rebelled against those good family traditions and intentions.

When I walked the aisle of Porter Memorial Baptist Church in Lexington, Kentucky in 1967, it was to say yes to God, not out of a fear of hell, but because it felt right and good and familiar. A lot of good people had told me that God cared for me. It made sense to get closer to that kind of God. That simple, childlike trust was based on some pretty solid theology.

Helping people was an extension of our faith, and it had always given me a special warmth even in my childhood. I think I was in 4th grade when my teacher asked me to help a classmate named Bobby who had failed a test on math facts. I coached and quizzed him on the multiplication tables. In my mind, I can still see his smile and his surprise at getting a good grade on the retest. I was hooked.

It was a natural fit when, a handful of years later, I felt a calling to become a minister as a nineteen year old. My calling to ministry was one of those "hold onto that" moments, when I *knew* that God had reached out to me in a special way and whispered His will to my soul. I thought literally, "this is why I have been born." I was destined to be a minister. I've never doubted that since that late August evening in 1977. God wanted me to learn the Scripture, share its insights, encourage people, and help as many as I could.

Following my graduation from the University of Kentucky with a degree in psychology, I went to seminary in New Orleans and felt right at home. I vividly remember sitting in my first theology class and thinking, "I'm exactly where I'm supposed to be."

I remember with equal clarity picking up my first Greek New Testament in the campus bookstore and thinking without a shade of doubt, "I will read this." I fell in love with that beautiful language. Layer upon layer of nuance and meaning unfolded for me in my studies. The Greek tenses became something like musical notes. The language and imagery of the Scripture was akin to a theological symphony. I'd found the truth that echoes through all of creation. I eventually earned a Master of Divinity (the most grandiose degree title conceivable) in Biblical Studies and a doctorate in Greek New Testament.

I taught New Testament and Greek while a graduate student, pastored a small Mississippi country church on the weekends, and generally felt all was right with the world. That rhythm of study, writing, teaching, preaching, and serving worked well for me for the next 30 years or so. I led churches and for a long period of time was on television and radio weekly. I wrote more commentaries on biblical books, articles on biblical ideas, and Sunday School lessons than I can recall. It was a busy and generally fulfilling career.

As I look back on it now, I realize that I operated on a pretty basic equation that worked well for me. A kind of $A + B = C$. A and B are what I control, the choices surrounding the events, engagements, and commitments of my life. If the A and B are solid, then the outcome should be fairly agreeable. I had invested my life in very solid ideas, and, for the most part, avoided a lot of the destructive ideas and actions that make life more difficult than necessary. Life's hard enough without our adding to it, and that insight, wherever it came from, worked well for me.

In one particularly relevant area, this meant that I did not drink alcohol. Now part of this was certainly an expression of religious conviction. Southern Baptists, by and large, are not drinkers. I know as well as anyone that many, and more today, of them do, but I didn't. And I didn't for years and years. I heard the early warnings, and combined with the well-established teetotalling Ellis history, I didn't drink mainly because it just didn't make sense to do something that could be potentially so harmful. It simply was not on my radar.

In the interest of total transparency, I did have three occasions in the first 50 years of my life when I tasted alcohol. The first was when I was about 13. I was with half a dozen guys passing around a green bottle of beer. I took an obligatory taste and thought it must be spoiled. I literally wondered how anyone could voluntarily drink that. I had a similar experience around age 18 or 19 with some vodka and orange juice. I thought the vodka ruined the orange juice. Some 20 years later I tasted beer after a day of skiing with some friends and remember saying, "I just don't get it." They handed me the keys, and I ordered a Coke.

I share this not to establish my religious credentials, but to simply relate the facts of the matter. In the first 50 years of my life, the amount of alcohol I drank would not fill a Dixie cup. Alcohol was not a part of my A + B. Consequently, my sober "C" was fairly positive and productive.

That began to change around age 50. Some disappointments and hard blows started adding up. No one is immune, yet we all act surprised and stunned when trouble comes our way. Churches can be difficult and complicated, just like families. I had challenges in both arenas but nothing particularly dramatic until that phone call.

In the World You Will Have Trauma

You know how you can remember exactly where you were when you got some bit of really bad news? My parents' generation could recall with precision where they were when they heard on the radio that Pearl Harbor had been bombed. JFK's assassination, Martin Luther King's, the space shuttle explosion, and 9/11 all leave the same mark.

One of those moments for me was when I was traveling on Goodwood just west of its intersection with Airline Highway in Baton Rouge. Woman's Hospital was on my right, an Assembly of God Church on my left. The phone was in my right hand. My good friend Leon was driving us to a Rotary meeting. My sister Carol called, and through her sobs I thought I heard her say, "Ken is dead!" I stammered something along the lines of "Carol, I need you to calm down a little so I can understand you. Did you say something happened to Ken?" "Yes. He's dead. He was shot and killed."

Those words were like a jolt to my mind and heart, kind of like a mental tectonic shift when the landscape changes dramatically and aftershocks continue to rattle around for God only knows how long. He had been murdered in his home. Two young men, aged 19 or so, believing Ken wasn't home, knocked on the door thinking to make an easy grab of some valuables. When he answered, they shot him twice.

Ken was eight years older than me, and just about everything a big brother should be. One of his children asked him one time if he ever picked on me, and he replied "Endlessly." Honestly, I don't remember him like that at all. The age difference was too great for us to be buddies, but Ken filled an important void in my life. Dad came down with multiple sclerosis when I was four and simply was not able to run and throw and wrestle with a young son the way he would have wanted to. Ken did all those things.

He taught me to throw every kind of ball. How to tackle without breaking my nose. How to bat, field, run bases, wrestle, bowl, shoot a gun and a bow and arrow, and how to be tough. He was a good big brother.

We grew apart as adults, though not due to any particular friction. Whenever we talked, he was always pleased I called, expressed pride in me and appreciation for my taking care of our aging parents, but the effort to stay in touch was always one way. Ken was hardly a constant presence in my life but now he would never again show up for holidays or answer my calls. Maybe that's why I underestimated the impact of his senseless death.

I'd been in treatment for alcoholism for about three weeks before I mentioned Ken's death to my small group. "Wait, is this the first time we're hearing about this?" Phillip, my lead therapist, asked. "Well, I suppose so," I replied. We processed this huge bit of news for a few minutes and Phillip asked when I had started drinking. It was about month after Ken's death. I had never drawn the connection.

We all tend to underestimate the amount of stress we're under and its impact. I certainly had in a number of ways. Ken's death was simply one of a string of blows life landed on me. Therapists talk a great deal about trauma. "Small t trauma" is the paper cuts and minor abrasions of life, everything from a fight with your spouse to a fender bender.

More serious trauma is call "big T trauma." These get the headlines in our autobiographies. They are divorces, major accidents, cancer, the death of a loved one, losing a job, and, yes, addiction. Addiction is unique in many ways, and one of them is that it both causes a huge amount of trauma and is the result of trauma. It gashes the life and soul of the addict, and it inflicts perhaps even more damage on the people around the addict, and that damage can be generational.

Look closely into the life of the addict you know or perhaps love, and you'll find trauma. Don't assume "they should just get over it." It's not that simple. The human capacity to deal with trauma varies among individuals and even oscillates within a single life. Some people handle certain trauma well, yet another challenge proves their undoing. Survey your life honestly, whether you've faced addiction or not, and you'll find that to be true. Sometimes we do well and serve as stalwart and inspirational examples to family and friends. Other times the trauma results in an inner collapse and possibly a lashing out that harms the people we love. Resist the temptation to compare your trauma or your response to trauma to someone else's experience. Trauma is a fact of life for us all, and none of us is so immutable that we can avoid it or its prolonged impact.

Responses to trauma reflect the heart of human striving. Here we find the tension between life as we want it and life as it is. When the difference between these two is too great or unexpected, the potential for very bad outcomes increases dramatically. These responses are the key to understanding the spiritual component of addiction.

Doing the Bad You Hate

A little honest self-evaluation is in order here. You might not struggle with drug or alcohol addiction, but you've seen the process at work in you. How do you handle trauma? Most of it you handle well. Perhaps you pray, talk to a friend or a counselor, consciously avoid over-reacting. These responses are healthy and necessary.

But what negative responses give you some sense of relief or release? Many people find comfort in food, and the rising rate of obesity indicates that they're willing to pursue comfort at the risk of their health. The same is true of smoking, pornography, shopping, gambling, etc. These are called "process addictions," and they're all attempts to escape some degree of disappointment or unhappiness. Are these addictions? The word sounds harsh, but if you've ever tried to give up sugar, for example, you know something of the struggle of a true addict. In many of its neurological impacts sugar is similar to cocaine, but of course you don't get a DUI for driving under the influence of a donut.

What if we changed the word from "addiction" to "attachment?" That helps many people to understand more of what addiction is like, for we're all attached to some unhealthy habits or unhealthy thoughts. We've tried repeatedly to stop. We make the same New Year's resolutions year after year. The attachments are very hard to break, and the neurological processes for those more innocent attachments are, in fact, identical to addiction.

I don't intend this brief foray into the roots of addiction to be an excuse for the awful behaviors associated with addiction. Feeling sorry for the addict is not my goal either. I do want to help explain one important part of both the experience of addiction and the everyday experience of life for anyone. Compassion, in the literal sense of the word, is my goal. We must "feel together" for that is truly divine. Trauma hurts, and it hurts us all to the point that we can become both victims and perpetrators. Even Paul wrote that he did not understand why he could not do the good he wanted but instead did the evil he hated (Rom. 7:15). He wasn't writing about addiction specifically, of course, but a more general problem that every human being understands in moments of honesty. We don't always act in our best interests. We all struggle with unhealthy attachments.

I began drinking to escape the effects of trauma, the death of my brother and other big-T and small-t traumas. Many other healthier avenues were available to me, but I didn't consider them. Drinking, I thought, was merely a private way of quieting the dark thing inside of me that often felt like it was trying to claw its way out of my chest.

Toward the end of my relatively brief but intense experience with active alcoholism, darkness overtook me from the inside. My wife Leslie would later say that I was unraveling. It's a good description, though I couldn't see it. Upon later reflection, I said I was hollow. The performance of my pastoral duties deteriorated. I was acting simply on a kind of muscle memory. The inner shadows began a slow extinguishing of any external light.

One morning, the same Leon who was driving when I heard about Ken's death called to ask if he could come by my office to see me. When he arrived promptly at 10 a.m., he pulled his chair around to the side of my desk, leaned forward and said, "Terry, we need to get you well." Leslie had called him the night before and told him I was killing myself. She was right and didn't realize that was my goal.

I knew what Leon meant, and I knew why he was there. I felt caught, guilty, ashamed, and hopeless. I used to say that a sliver of my old self heard that call to get better, that a part of me wanted to get well. As I've reflected over the years, though, that's really not true. There was no fight left in me. I'd given up on life and longed for death. So, when cornered, I didn't feel anger or resistance but more of a despairing resignation. "Go with me tomorrow to a doctor that I've chosen, and do whatever he says," Leon continued. I agreed, but again not because I wanted to get well. That new doc recommended I go to Palmetto Addiction Recovery Center. I agreed and left the next day.

Now Back to My Bad Day in Treatment

As I've said, all addiction patients have bad days. Treatment is equal measures challenge and comfort. If you're not uncomfortable, the addiction counselor is not doing his or her job. Every addiction wants to survive, so denial is its front-line defense. It's a neurological issue in which the "impulse" part of brain supplants the "wisdom" part of the brain. It's fascinating science but a miserable experience. The initial focus of treatment, therefore, is trying to break through the multiple defenses and walls of denial the addiction has set up to protect itself. So, because the addiction will fight for its life, the first month especially can be rough.

I don't recall the specific event that day, but I do recall pacing the floor of the therapist's office like a caged animal. Anger, resentment, and probably a good dose of fear swirled in my mind and soul. Enough of "me" had returned to care, and I didn't know if I wanted to stay in ministry or marriage or anything else for that matter, or even if the options were mine. I remember the therapist saying, "I'm going to step out for a few minutes and let you have some time." I continued pacing.

And that's when I saw it, a framed version of The Serenity Prayer hanging on the wall. I knew the first three lines. We recited those in the AA meetings every night at the facility. This was the long version, and I had never seen it before. Each line spoke to me. Paul had the scales fall from his eyes in Damascus, and my experience in that office was something like that. The

Prayer just made sense to me. It touched me deeply and resonated with my soul. Each line revived a spiritual memory or opened a new window. I copied it. Committed it to memory. I said that prayer daily for years, and still to this day regularly.

Jacques Cousteau was one of my childhood heroes. I watched his programs and asked my parents for the series of books he published, *The Undersea World of Jacques Cousteau*. After suffering serious injuries from a near fatal plane crash, he swam daily to try to regain his strength. One day, an officer gave him a pair of diving goggles to keep the saltwater from stinging his eyes. That gift changed his life. In his 1953 book *The Silent World*, he wrote, "Sometimes we are lucky enough to know that our lives have been changed, to discard the old, embrace the new, and run headlong down an immutable course. . . . It happened to me on that summer's day when my eyes were opened to the sea."

It happened to me in that office when I first saw The Prayer. It gave me a new way to look at all of life. I was finally able to let go of some things that were dragging me down and embrace some new ways of looking at myself, the world, and God.

My life, from my earliest memories, revolved around God, and I had preached and taught and written for many years that God has a way of showing up in our suffering. Frankly, I simply had not faced real suffering. The gravity of my own chaos, however, drew me into a darkness I'd never experienced before. I learned things in that treatment center they simply can't teach you in seminary. For the first time in my life, I had a desperate need for God, and He showed up in The Prayer. With those words I limped into a circle of light and sat down with Him. I wanted to live again. I welcomed the dawn.

The Point of The Prayer (and the aim of this book)

The key to The Prayer is the phrase "reasonably happy." I believe God taught me what that meant, and I believe it's basically what every person wants, and they have a sense of it. They want happiness but have often given up the quest. Don't give up! I'm absolutely certain that God wants every one of His children to be reasonably happy, and He's given us the means. It's possible, and indeed a divine birthright.

Our shared, and nearly universal, problem is that we want and expect to be *unreasonably* happy. We want happiness all of the time. We come to expect it. This distortion taints so much of our life-view that any reasonable *unhappiness* leaves us feeling wronged, disappointed, devoid of gratitude, and full of complaint. Left unchecked, it can lead to despair, and that was the experience that led to my alcoholism.

I don't suggest for a moment that the expectation of being unreasonably happy will lead to something as dramatic as an addiction. What I do suggest is that the search for unreasonable happiness inevitably leads to disappointment. In trying always to live on Cloud Nine we miss the reasonable and attainable happiness available to us on Cloud Five. Unhappy people overshoot the real goal in life.

For this reason, even though "reasonably happy" is in the next to last line of The Prayer, I want to focus on it first. It's the goal in the here and now: "that we may be reasonably happy in *this life.*" Everything that precedes that phrase supports it. The Prayer is the means of becoming reasonably happy, and it contains some of the very deepest currents of Christian theology. As such, this is not an easy self-help book, and reasonable happiness is not the result of some basic life skills like making your bed or creating a daily to-do list. Reasonable happiness in this life comes through knowing deeply the One who ultimately grants us eternal joy.

The Prayer "works" in all situations in life but is especially important in the out-of-control times. Of course, the prerequisite for being reasonably happy is realizing the limits of our control and the fact that we live on the threshold of genuine chaos every moment. The Prayer keeps us aware.

My hope is that you will find the same comfort and challenge in The Serenity Prayer that saved my life and restored my soul. If you're reading this book, then you have some interest in happiness, and chances are you've struggled with the very distortion I briefly described in the previous paragraphs. It's time to accept life as it is and embrace a truly miraculous way of understanding God's plan and purpose for you in this life. Uninterrupted bliss is a fantasy on this side of the veil. Reasonable happiness, however, is an achievable and sustainable goal. The Prayer shows us the way.

_____

Toward reasonable happiness:

- Everyone gets their first theology from their family of origin. If we are loved and celebrated, it is much easier to believe in a God who loves and rejoices in us.
- Our outlook on life, belief in God, the ability to trust is formed over time. It is seldom, if ever, an immediate result of a single decision. We become who we are, for better or worse, little by little.
- Believing that we can control the outcome of life is a common misconception. We can do everything right and still encounter trauma.
- Everyone does harm to themselves and others as the result of the combination of trauma and bad decisions. Even St. Paul wrote that he often did the thing he hated even though we wanted to do what he knew was good and right.
- We all struggle with unhealthy attachments that lead us away from the fullness of life. We miss happiness.

- Everyone needs an intervention, a point in time when someone or something alerts us to the possibility of a better life.

The Serenity Prayer, daily prayed over a months-long period, will bring you into the stream of God's grace. You will find through it the reasonable happiness God created you to enjoy.

C H A P T E R   T W O

THAT WE MAY BE REASONABLY HAPPY IN THIS LIFE, AND SUPREMELY HAPPY WITH YOU FOREVER IN THE NEXT

"I have come that they might have life abundantly."
John 10:10

"All men seek happiness. This is without exception."
Blaise Pascal

In the beginning of his book *Orthodoxy*, G. K. Chesterton writes that he'd long fancied writing a book about an English yachtsman who had the glorious dream of sailing from England to discover new islands in the South Seas. Not being very adept at navigating, however, he sails around for quite some time and ends up landing in Wales where he plants a British flag.

The modern search for happiness is much the same. By all accounts, we appear to want happiness very much. We're willing to invest ourselves in all manner of endeavors to get there, but we're so poor at navigating that we end up back at the same place we left some months earlier.

The pursuit of happiness is endowed by our Creator, as our Declaration of Independence rightly puts it. Do an internet search about happiness and you will likely be overwhelmed by the results of how people are engaging in this pursuit. You'll find articles by reputable authors in well-known journals that will promise happiness if you exercise more, eat better, sleep more soundly, have better sex, burn candles, save money, worship in this way, etc. And most all of the suggestions work, for a while.

People have a tendency to find something that makes them happy for two minutes to two months, but as a permanent, ongoing state, the pursuit often seems without a final destination. I've known unhappy people who complain about the previous pastors of churches to which I've been called and tell me how thrilled they are that I have arrived. Sometimes, it doesn't take six months for them to decide that I too am a major disappointment. Most of us have an expensive but idle exercise machine somewhere in our homes that now serves as a clothes hanger. Our bookshelves sag under the weight of self-help and happiness books. Our histories are littered with relationships that ended up being more hormonal than enduringly satisfying.

We all want happiness, but we're very poor at finding it.

Thomas Couture took three years to complete the painting *Romans During the Decadence* that hangs in the Musée d'Orsay in Paris. This massive painting (approximately 25 feet by 15 feet) depicts a couple dozen Roman revelers engaged in an orgy. They're obviously wealthy, for the get-together is in a columned room with ornate statues, fine marble flooring, and comfortable furnishings. In the center is a lovely woman in repose. She is still clothed, though her robe hangs provocatively off her right shoulder. Most arresting, however, is her face. She has the exhausted vacant eyes of someone who is totally bored. Even the statues that recall the great figures of Roman history appear to be scowling at the debauchery before them.

Aquinas said there are four common substitutes for God: wealth, power, pleasure, and fame. The painting depicts people who have all four in abundance, but the woman in the middle clearly renders the verdict on whether these excesses have brought real and lasting happiness. The answer, as always, is a sad "no."

What Couture explored on canvas, Johann von Goethe explored on paper. He took nearly 60 years to complete his classic about Faust, a scholar and alchemist who believes he has exhausted all knowledge. In despair that even his great learning has not brought him lasting satisfaction, he's about to commit suicide when Mephistopheles, the devil, offers him a bargain. He will serve Faust for 24 years, making every whim possible, in exchange for his soul. The real crux of the wager is that he will deliver to Faust a sublime moment of wondrous transcendence in which Faust would hope to abide forever. So desirous is he of this moment of pure happiness that Faust accepts the offer and forfeits his soul.

Some of the greatest men and women who have ever lived have been exploring this same theme of our never-ending search for happiness. Yet, with all of this warning, assurance, inspiration, and direction, we're still like teenagers standing in front of an open refrigerator convinced that something in there has to fill us up. We just can't find it.

I do not believe the God who created us to yearn for happiness would make too hard a bargain for us to attain it. The very good news is that we don't have to make a deal with the devil. The Prayer contains eternal and accessible principles that enable us to be reasonably happy now, and eternally happy with God forever. And that's the destination we're all really looking for.

Beginning at the End

As I mentioned in the opening chapter, I'm going to start this book at the end of The Prayer. The last lines of The Prayer read "that we may be reasonably happy in this life, and supremely happy with You forever in the next." That's where the whole prayer is heading. Happiness. Happiness is likely what attracted you to this book in the first place, which will now join the endless search results when someone types in "how can I be happy?" The Prayer is the key. Let that sink in for a moment. You can pray a prayer that has the potential to bring you reasonable and supreme happiness. And you don't have to sell your soul.

Everybody wants to be happy, so The Prayer addresses a fundamental desire and pursuit of every human being. The need is obvious and great. A lot of people seem very unhappy, and all of us face unhappiness regularly. What if we could ask God to help us become reasonably happy?

Well, we can. In fact, it's not that complicated, though it can be very hard to put into practice.

Let's do a quick overview. The Prayer opens with three requests. We ask God for serenity, courage, and wisdom. That's a great start. We need serenity to recognize our limits. We need courage to recognize our possibilities. We need wisdom to keep from becoming egomaniacs who try to control everything and everyone around us.

The Prayer then shifts to outline the attitudes and commitments we make to reach reasonable happiness. We are to become aware (Living one day at a time and enjoying one moment at a time). We are to recognize the role of suffering in our lives (Accepting hardships as the pathway to peace). We stop fighting, succumbing to, or complaining about this broken world (Taking this sinful world as it is). We decide to put our faith and trust in the only place that makes sense (Trusting You to make all things right).

Armed with these gifts and attitudes, we can properly address the notion of happiness. We can be happy in this life, *reasonably* happy in this life. We can also live with the hope of a happiness that extends into eternity. These are very powerful ideas that call clearly to the human heart. The main problem we face, of course, is that we're trying to attain the goal without first really understanding what it is or having any real idea of how to get there.

Complicating the search is the oft-raised objection that the search is too shallow and insignificant. I heard a minister one time say with firm assurance that "God is not interested in your happiness!" We'll explore this more deeply, but I firmly disagreed with that minister then and do even more now. I think happiness is important and too vital an issue to be haughtily dismissed.

It's true that if someone says, "I just want to be happy," they may sound shallow and self-centered, and perhaps they are. It can sound like a whine. On the other hand, happiness is one of the great themes of some of the loftiest philosophers and greatest theologians. People can go through a Bohemian chapter in their lives, making the pursuit of happiness look like a recreation of *Romans During the Decadence*. Clearly, that's a waste of time. On the other hand, the pursuit can fulfill a genuine longing for the *summum bonum* of life and produce some of the finest qualities of character and genuine inner peace and satisfaction. The search, therefore, can either be for the cheapest or the deepest.

Whether the search is ennobling or hopelessly self-centered depends on the destination each seeker has in mind. Unlike the hapless sailor, we have to have the end in sight along with the means to get there, and we must have them in that order. Is happiness a thoroughly individualized goal? Or is it a God-ordained and God-centered purpose that can only be discovered in and through Him? What exactly did our Creator endow us to pursue?

So, What Is Happiness?

Happiness today often has a smiley face quality about it, accompanied by unicorns, rainbows, and puppy dogs. "Just be happy!" is a reigning motto. A quarter of a century ago, famed minister and author Robert Schuller wrote *The Be (Happy) Attitudes* about the Beatitudes in the Sermon on the Mount. Schuller had a talent for marketing and turn of phrase, but while the book was very popular, many serious-minded critics regarded it as spiritual pablum cleverly crafted for a happy-hungry audience. It fed into the notion for some people that happiness is frivolous and beneath the regard of the high-minded who seek a deeper spirituality.

What has really happened, though, is that our clever and constantly churning marketing machines have glitterized a very important subject. If we dig down beneath the fluff, we find a limitless lode of deeply valuable ideas that can profoundly alter our lives. Happiness, for all of the contemporary trivial glam, is actually one of the main topics of the greatest philosophers and theologians for the last 2,500 years. What we'll find is that Schuller wasn't all right with the light-sounding title of his book, but neither was he all wrong.

Socrates (d. 399 BC) is credited with being one of the founders of Western philosophy and the first moral philosopher. His star pupil was Plato (d. 347 BC) who is responsible for establishing the Academy in Athens, the first institution of higher learning in the West. In turn, Aristotle (d. 322 BC) was a student of Plato at the Academy in Athens and is chiefly responsible for synthesizing some of the greatest philosophical ideas from his great teachers. Socrates, Plato, and Aristotle form the great trinity of classic Greek philosophy. These are extremely heavy hitters.

How delightful then to discover that Aristotle, the final link in this marvelous chain, devoted more space to happiness than any writer prior to recent times, and he did so as a natural extension of the great minds that shaped his. We'll see that Aristotle exerted a powerful influence on Western thought even to the present, except when it recently became fashionable to view him as an impediment. We might even say the lighter and frothier ideas of happiness grew from that neglect.

In his pivotal work the *Nichomachean Ethics*, Aristotle presented a theory of happiness and how one can be happy. The Greek word he used, *eudaimonia*, is translated as happiness and literally means "a good spirit."

Far from being an unimportant addendum to life, Aristotle maintained that happiness is the central purpose in life. It was not something bestowed by the gods, rather happiness depends on oneself, a very appealing idea to the do-it-yourself modern ear. Happiness, however, is far from being an emotion we create via controlling our environment. It's much deeper than that.

Happiness is the result of a lifelong cultivation of virtues. It is directly connected to virtuous behavior, and Aristotle devotes a great deal of space to describing virtues such as courage, generosity, friendship, justice, and others. The Golden Mean prevents a distorted excess in any of the virtues. Finally, contemplation, or the exercise of reason, is also mandatory. Happiness depends on a clear and deeper thought-life.

We may well imagine that one of those disapproving statues in Couture's *Romans During the Decadence* was Aristotle. The displayed excesses of sexuality and other pleasures by obviously wealthy and influential aristocrats was the complete opposite of the lifelong cultivation and exercise of virtue. In fact, Aristotle maintained you couldn't pronounce a life "happy" until the end, when you could look back over the decades of conduct and see a coherence between professed beliefs and practice. No wonder the young woman in the painting looks despondent. She's run headlong down a path that can only produce unhappiness.

We'll return to look more closely at the teachings of Jesus and the idea of happiness in the New Testament in the next section, but let's now see how Aristotle's ideas played out in the Christian world. There was much more interplay than some might imagine. The early Church Fathers and later Christian thinkers "baptized" much of what Aristotle taught. He was a genuine seeker of truth, and it's quite natural that those who followed the One who claimed to be the truth would find reflections of Him in any genuine seeker. That is still the case, by the way.

Augustine's (d. 430 AD) influence on Christian thought is immense. He's particularly remembered for his formulation of the doctrines of original sin and, especially in a later chapter of his life, for his ideas on predestination. As such, he is quite a theological hero for both Catholics and Protestants, especially those Protestants who embrace double predestination.

One might imagine that such a weighty theologian would have little to say about happiness, but that would be a mistake. One of his greatest works, *Confessions*, is both autobiographical and theological, and he devotes quite a bit of space in one of the chapters to the idea of happiness. In this way, he follows the great philosophical traditions that preceded him and that he drew on.

Like Aristotle, Augustine believes the desire for happiness is universal. We all want to be happy. It's a vitally important quest. He would also agree with Aristotle that we consistently love the wrong things, believing they will bring happiness and then wondering why we experience even deeper unhappiness when we obtain those things. Finally, Augustine very much reflected Aristotle by asserting that full and complete happiness is an ultimate end-product, only truly experienced in the bliss of heaven.

Not surprisingly, Augustine, because of his much more developed doctrine of a personal God, believed that happiness can only be achieved in and through and with God. Love is the key. We are to love God and be grounded in Him. Only then can we begin to hear the echoes of the ultimate happiness that awaits us.

This God-centered search for happiness is quite distinct from Aristotle's idea that you depend on yourself for happiness. For Augustine, it's vital to realize that "you are not your own." We belong to God and always sense a restlessness until we find our rest in Him, an idea that is on the very first page of his *Confessions*. Happiness is a gift from God, not a product of a well-ordered life.

Occasionally, I hear people describe Christianity as very dour and joyless. St. Augustine himself is often viewed as particularly heavy, due especially to his views on predestination. While that's a complicated doctrine on which pallets of books have been written, we need to give him credit for his searching thoughts about happiness. One of the true and undisputable pillars of the church was very much into happiness.

Skipping ahead another 800 years, we find another great voice of the Church devoting even more space to the idea of happiness. Thomas Aquinas (d. 1274) sought to synthesize Aristotelian ideas with Christian theology. So great was his regard for Aristotle that he simply referred to him as The Philosopher. Aquinas wrote prolifically, and his most influential work *Summa Theologiae* is still widely read and studied.

Aquinas, of course, is in compete agreement with Augustine that happiness cannot be enjoyed apart from union with God. Like his philosophical hero Aristotle, he also maintained the importance of the exercise of virtue. A good man living well has the potential for happiness both here and ultimately in the hereafter. Two of Aquinas's major contributions to the idea of happiness are his insistence on dual agency and his use of two words for happiness.

Dual agency refers to the idea that we are in voluntary cooperation with God in many of the actions we perform. It's a very finely tuned argument, but while Aquinas insists on God's sovereignty he also, unlike Augustine, leaves room for our cooperation with the divine prompting. This nuance is especially important when it comes to his views on happiness. The way we think affects the things we experience. Thus, a certain degree of happiness is due to the right application of our divinely endowed ability to reason. He reflects and combines both of his great heroes. The Philosopher insisted that happiness is the full responsibility of the individual, and Augustine regarded happiness as a gift from God. Aquinas insisted on both.

Both Augustine and Aquinas wrote their monumental works in Latin, and the word they used for happiness is *beatitudo* from which we get the word Beatitudes at the beginning of the Sermon on the Mount, (So, honestly, Schuller, much to the chagrin of the highbrow critics, was not entirely wrong in calling them the "be-happy attitudes."). *Beatitudo* means the ultimate experience of heavenly bliss. Remember, Augustine wrote that happiness was only a heavenly experience. *Beatitudo* is what he had in mind. So, what about our quest for happiness in the here and now, and not just in the hereafter?

Aquinas offered a second word, *felicitas*, also translated as happiness. It refers to the experience of any positive feature of everyday life. According to Aquinas, we don't have to wait until heaven to be happy, though that experience will certainly be all-surpassing. We can experience *felicitas* here, and to an important degree our experience of happiness is up to us.

Before looking at what the New Testament says about happiness in the next section, it's important to contrast the definitions of happiness with what we typically find on the scene another 800 years after Aquinas. Today, a significant portion of the culture has rejected any prevailing belief in a transcendent reality, so God doesn't have anything to do with this life according to many people. Morals are relative, so there is no overarching set of virtues to which we all adhere, much less a God who will help us get there. Finally, with the hyper-focus on the self, everyone is on their own, so they seek happiness through the shallowness of exercise, shopping, pills, eating, appearance, etc. To return to Chesterton's illustration, we have a vast number of people today who are not only confused about the destination but have discarded the vessel designed to get them there.

Is God Interested in Our Happiness?

Remember the minister I mentioned who said God wasn't interested in our happiness? Let's look a little more closely at his claim. It's an important question. Is happiness important to God? Are we wasting time talking about happiness? Aiming too low? Isn't our focus really supposed to be on our purpose and eternity and things above, not things below? Did Augustine have it right? Or did Aquinas come closer to the truth?

The New Testament was written in Greek, the language of Aristotle. So, we can start by looking at the number of times the Greek word for happiness, *eudamonia*, is used in the New Testament. The answer? Zero. The traditional Greek word for happiness is not in the New Testament. Not one single instance. That would seem to be a point for the preacher.

But let's expand our understanding of happiness a bit more. The word "happy" is derived from the Middle English root "hap," which simply means one's luck, lot, an occurrence, or a happening. The word "happenstance" draws on this meaning. We have many "haps" throughout the day. Our days are full of haps. Some good. Some bad. If I'm healthy, that's a good hap. If my plane is on time and my luggage arrives with me, that's a good hap. A delicious meal is a good hap. The opposites of any of these are bad haps.

Of course, God is interested in the highest and best for us. Our eternity is supremely important, but that doesn't mean our present is unimportant or inconsequential. I believe God is interested in our happiness. In fact, I think He enjoys surrounding us with good haps as a way of reminding us that we're not alone and that we are loved by a very good and joyful God. Let's take a look at some of the evidence from Scripture.

In the Sermon on the Mount, Jesus said that God makes the sun to shine on the evil and the good and the rain to fall on the just and the unjust (Matt. 5:45). Jesus was exhorting us to love even our enemies, and He used God as the exemplar. He's saying that God simply delights in making good things happen. God likes giving good haps to all sorts of people. So, we ought to love all sorts of people.

One of Jesus' most familiar teachings actually focuses on this understanding of happiness. If I ask the general population to complete the sentence "His eye is on the _____ " even secular people are likely to know the answer. It's sparrow of course (Matt. 10:29).

The background is very interesting. Jesus was trying to convince us that God really cares for us, and He pointed out God's careful attention to the sparrow, saying "a sparrow does not fall to the ground without your Heavenly Father noticing." Thus, His eye is on the sparrow (I bet you sang that just now).

If a sparrow falls to the ground, that sounds like it died. So, God notices the death of the sparrow. But how cheerful and reassuring is that? Now here's where the teaching gets really interesting, at least to me. The New Testament, as I mentioned earlier, was written in Greek, but Jesus almost certainly spoke in Aramaic, the common language of the streets in Israel in the first century. Sometimes it really helps us to understand what Jesus meant by trying to get back to the way He said it in Aramaic.

In this case, the Aramaic word translated into Greek as "fall" can also be translated as "land," as in a sparrow lands or lights upon the ground. This gives us an entirely different insight into God's care for the sparrow. He not only notices it when it dies, but when it lights upon the ground for food or a twig to build its nest. God has provided all of these things so the sparrow can be reasonably happy. In other words, God is interested in the moment-by-moment life of the sparrow. Likewise, because we are of much more value than the sparrow, God is intensely interested in our moment-by-moment life. He's interested not only in our eternity, but also our present. He's interested in our "haps" and has provided enough good ones so that we too may be reasonably happy.

Here is another example from the Sermon on the Mount. This time, Jesus used parenting as an example, humorously suggesting that we would never give a child a stone when he asked for bread, or a serpent if she asked for fish. We know how to bless our children. In fact, it's quite natural for us. Then Jesus brought home the point, "If you, who by comparison to God are evil, then how much more will God long to give good gifts to those who ask?" (Matt. 7:11).

Elsewhere in the New Testament, we find Paul telling us to make all of our requests known to God. As a pastor, I was often asked "Is it all right for me to ask God for _____?" They were afraid of being trivial or even offensive if they asked God for something in particular. I think God answers all prayer. No exceptions. Sometimes He answers yes, sometimes no, sometimes not yet, and sometimes "I have something better in mind."

The point is, we can and should, as God's beloved children, ask Him anything we wish. In your intimate and prayerful relationship with God, let Him guide you. Perhaps what you want is not really important. Work it out with God. Don't fall silent before Him because you think He's not interested in your opinion or desires or your happiness. You can ask for the equivalent of bread and fish. The Scripture is quite clear. God is interested in your "haps."

Is happiness really the most important goal in life? If we're speaking of temporal happiness, Aquinas's *felicitas*, then the answer is of course no. God is most interested in shaping us for eternity, and my luggage arriving on time at an airport has no bearing on that. But just because something is not the most important (i.e., happiness), it doesn't mean we're shallow or misguided to have an abiding interest in it. James wrote, "Every good and perfect gift comes from above, from the Father of lights" (James 1:17). God obviously delights in giving us gifts, and one of those gifts is happiness. We have a God who is clearly on our side, and in a very real way has stacked the deck to enable us to be reasonably happy on a day-to-day basis.

In fact, we have become rather adept at using this advantage to create a very safe, comfortable, and pleasant life. We're good at limiting chaos. Traffic lights keep us from crashing into each other. Electricity runs our TVs and blow driers and air conditioners. You can drink water out of almost any faucet in the country and not worry about contracting a gastrointestinal illness. (If you've ever traveled to less developed countries then you would know what an incredible blessing this is.) By and large, just about everything in our country runs with an astounding reliability.

During a trip, I had a layover in one of the busiest airports in the world. I chose a chair that allowed me to look out over the parked planes, taxiways, runways, baggage carriers, etc. Behind me, crowds of people scurried in opposite directions. Some stopped at stores that offered everything from a bag of chips to a pair of elephant skin boots. Most people were on their phones or looking at a screen of some sort with a bewildering selection of choices for entertainment and information. It was a typical day in an incredibly busy airport.

I've traveled enough to have my share of disappointments and even outrages. My luggage has not arrived with me. I've run between flights and rushed up to gates to watch them close the door and not allow me on. I've sat on tarmacs inhaling the noxious fumes of jet-engine exhaust for what seemed like an interminable time. I've had headaches and leg aches and dry eyes from all the usual activities attending air travel.

Here's what struck me as I sat and watched all the goings-on that day: it's a wonder any of us get where we're supposed to be with what we're supposed to have. Think about it. I can get on a plane, as I recently did, in Seattle at noon and be in West Palm Beach before the day ends. How long have *homo sapiens* existed? About 250,000 years? Only in the last 50 years have we had this capability, and to the point that it's really not that unusual. We might say, "Well, you've had a long day." But no one says, "Wait a minute…you just traveled from the northwest corner of the third largest country in the world to the southeast corner in less than one day?!?!?!?!?!" Lewis and Clark hacked their way across a half a continent over a span of several years. We get to recline in a cushioned seat and cover over 2,500 miles in about five hours.

Yes, it is a wonder that any of us get to where we're supposed to be with our luggage. Even more remarkable is that it not only happens thousands of times per day, but mistakes and glitches are extraordinarily rare. Yes, I've missed flights, had luggage delayed, and gotten cranky because things didn't run smoothly. But I've never been forsaken by an airline, permanently lost luggage, or been taken out and beaten by disgruntled airline personnel. By any reasonable standard, this whole travel thing works incredibly efficiently.

In this one arena of life, and one that gets a lot of criticism, the data indicate that I should be reasonably happy. Yet ask most people about air travel and you'll be met with groans and stories of time things didn't work out. Interestingly, the overwhelming number of good haps creates the expectation that life should only be good haps, and in *every area of life*. We just can't seem to handle the bad haps, and in fact have a very stubborn tendency to focus on them.

So, with all of the divine advantages we have and with the success we've had in implementing those advantages on a technical and day-to-day level, why is unhappiness even on our radar? It turns out that the real battle is not with the world and its problems. The real battlefield is in our brain and mind.

Wired for Happiness...and Fear

If we search for reasons why we struggle to deal with challenges, we need look no further than the brain that enables you to read this sentence. It turns out that we are wired for both fear and for happiness. Understanding something about the way our brains work in this regard is important in our lifelong wrestling match for happiness. More importantly, this information also is critical in confronting one of the chief spiritual challenges of our time: addiction.

We tend to focus on the failures because we are hard-wired to do so. Literally. The primal, survival part of our brains uses fear to keep us alive. The amygdala, an almond-shaped structure deep inside both hemispheres, constantly looks for threats. It actually responds much faster to new and dangerous information than our higher areas of brain function. Have you ever had someone pull over in your lane on the interstate? Your amygdala sensed a danger and immediately took over. It tends to be fearful and, in many situations, over-reactive. You jerked your steering wheel to avoid a collision. You survived. In a real sense, fear saved you. The amygdala has done its job. Interestingly, once fear is engaged, anger soon follows. So, though you might be perfectly safe now as you drive down the road, you have a compulsion to perhaps "aggressively gesture" toward the offending driver.

What's more, fear-based experiences form memory constructs much more quickly and deeply than pleasant circumstances. We're more likely to remember fearful events. After all, you want to avoid a repeat. We've had this God-given wiring from the beginning. It's kept us alive through very dangerous periods in human history.

The problem is we still have this wiring in an environment that is safe to a degree our ancestors could never have imagined. But we can't turn it off! We tend to focus on unpleasant events, like missing a flight. That primal part of our brain equates that, in some important ways, to avoiding a predator.

This may sound outlandish to you, but it's true. Anger, you see, is always a secondary emotion. The underlying and primary emotion is fear. What do I fear when a miss a flight? Not getting home on time. Missing a scheduled meeting. Not getting to bed at a reasonable hour. Do these constitute fear? In the primal part of the brain the answer is a resounding YES! When you're angry, look beneath the anger and you'll find some form of fear. It may be nothing more than the fear of not getting your way, but in our modern experience that is the neurological equivalent of running from a hungry tiger.

What does this all have to do with happiness? Unfortunately, we're hardwired for complaint. When something, anything, doesn't go as we expect or desire, then we mark that event. Thus, I never tell you about all the flights that left and arrived on time, the nice flight attendants who took care of me, or the luggage that was waiting for me on the carousel. Give me half a chance, though, and I will tell you about the relatively few instances where things didn't go as I wanted them to.

Again, we tend to give vastly disproportionate attention to the exceptions of life. We live by them. We're unhappy, but usually for no good reason. In fact, what we want is *unreasonable* happiness, uninterrupted good haps. No one gets that option.

Fortunately, we're also wired for happiness. The authors of the Declaration of Independence called it a self-evident truth that we are endowed by our Creator with an unalienable right to pursue happiness. It turns out God did not give us the desire without also giving us the physical means to enjoy it.

Every enjoyable event in your life activates the Pleasure Pathway in your brain. A small release of dopamine, the pleasure neurotransmitter, accompanies a wide array of experiences. Exercise, a nature walk, a good meal, sex, a favorite song, time with grandkids, a starry night, on and on and on. God has created a world that can make us feel pleasure and happiness.

Here's the challenge: our brains tend to give greater weight to what we fear than to what makes us feel pleasure. It's a survival instinct. Obviously, it's more important that we stay alive than we simply have a good time. The result is we tend to overreact to the danger whether it's real or imagined and underestimate the importance of the blessings that literally surround us.

What does this have to do with addiction? All addictions involve the artificial manipulation of the "Pleasure Pathway." Alcohol and certain drugs and other substances create a flood of dopamine, more than the brain was ever intended to accommodate. The survival part of your brain, where the pleasure and fear impulses originate, registers that influx of the drug as an unparalleled event. Repeated use of the drug creates a neurological anticipation and then an expectation of the next flood. The fateful step is when this primal part of your brain equates the drug with survival. That is addiction. That is why your loved ones who suffer from addiction do such irrational things. They are driven by a distorted sense that the drug is necessary for them to live. They cannot envision facing the bad haps of life without having the drug to lean on. This mental obsession with the drug is a truly miserable experience for the addict, though when in active addiction they will often not see it that way.

My lead therapist in treatment was Phillip. He'd been counseling alcoholics and addicts for 35 years. He knew every evasion, argument, justification, defense, and denial a patient could bring. One day early in treatment, he was not impressed with my progress. He pointed a finger at me and with a very serious look said, "You have to figure out how alcohol became lord of your life." It was a "sobering" moment.

He'd framed addiction as a spiritual issue, and I had not thought of it in those terms. Upon reflection, as with nearly everything else he told me, he was right. I was relying on alcohol to give me peace, to help me rest, to blot out feelings and memories that I wanted to erase. All of these challenges are God's business. He is the Author of peace. He is the Bringer of joy. He is the Presence in our pain. Alcohol blocked every spiritual resource that God offered me. I didn't realize the terrible spiritual bargain I'd made. In a sense, I'd made a Faustian bargain and sold my soul.

Essentially, the bad haps had piled up in my life, and at a fundamental level I was unwilling to be patient and let God work in those situations, provide solutions, and help me grow stronger. I short-circuited and manipulated the divinely appointed brain processes and was slowly losing my life. I'd certainly lost my spirit.

I devote space to this topic because we see this problem everywhere and fail to recognize it. About 24 million Americans are suffering right now from an addiction to drugs or other substances. Additionally, another 15 million American adults have an addiction to what are called process addictions, such as pornography, gambling, shopping, and eating. Phillip's question could apply to each sufferer. "How did _____ become lord of your life?"

Addiction is the clearest indicator of the spiritual disconnection in our culture today. We excel at developing and marketing addictive drugs and behaviors. They differ in expression, but neurologically they are very much alike. Spiritually they are all identical. That's why recovery is the spiritual endeavor of reconnecting with the God who created us, gives us an abundance of good haps, and helps us profoundly during the inevitable bad haps.

Chasing Happier Than Happy

In 1978, Scott Peck opened the first chapter of his book *The Road Less Traveled* with these words: "Life is difficult." Many people treated that simple line as a profound and new revelation. It is not. Two thousand years ago Jesus said, "You'll have trouble in this world" (John 16:33). That great truth that we will "suffer various trials" is sprinkled throughout the New Testament. Buddha, about 500 years before Jesus was born, said the first noble truth is that life is suffering. Before Buddha, Aeschylus wrote that "wisdom comes through suffering." The greatest men and women who've ever lived have been trying to tell us the same thing, yet we're still surprised to hear that life is hard.

The hardest part of life is our refusal to accept that life is hard. That is the core of unhappiness. Life doesn't turn out the way we want in every particular, and we're sometimes stunned by that. Why? Our ability to construct a relatively pleasant life in most respects creates the illusion that we should be able to create happiness in *all* respects. That is unreasonable.

Life plainly is a mixture of what we want and what we get. There are no exceptions. No one is wealthy, healthy, smart, or powerful enough to avoid this fundamental truth. We all hurt, and the expectation that we can avoid pain creates its own pain. In fact, when Buddha said, "life is suffering," he didn't mean that we would daily face blinding pain and illness or big T trauma. The word for suffering, *dukkha,* actually means more of a striving or yearning. It implies that we're straining for something we cannot attain. We're straining for unreasonable happiness. The strain creates unrealistic expectations and leads to unhappiness when those expectations are unmet. Giving up that striving brings a new level of peace. This is called acceptance and is the focus of the next chapter.

I can't overstress the importance of this idea. Life *is* hard. Resisting that truth leads not only to unhappiness but to a tremendous amount of confusion about God and the way He works in the world. People either end up treating God like a cruise ship concierge whose duty is to fulfill our every whim, or when that inevitably fails, they fling themselves away from God. All because they're trying to be happier than happy.

This search for unreasonable happiness is nearly universal. Among a particular strain of religious people, the failure to find this unreasonable happiness leads to a truly terrible crash of faith. I see this among many of my fellow Christians who've followed a misguided notion that if they pray in a particular way, or perform some activity, or give an amount of money, then God will give them what they want. This is plainly a form of trying to control and manipulate God, and is, in fact, a violation of the very first commandment. You can't worship a God you're in charge of directing.

This distortion is particularly puzzling because the Founder of our faith died on a cross after having been nearly beaten to death. He didn't try to avoid suffering. He accepted it, and by doing so completely transformed the equation and turned our shallow view of life upside down. Suffering leads to joy and is actually the only way to joy. More on that in a later chapter.

The chief spiritual challenge of our time is a poor or absent theology of suffering. Part of the problem is uniquely American. We are so very good at creating both comfort and the attending expectation that life is all comfort. Luxury surrounds us, touches us, and we access it in many ways. Consumerism convinces us to consume as many goods, services, and forms of entertainment as possible. Next time you're in a convenience store, take a look at the candy aisle and notice how many forms of Reese's candies there are. I counted 18 one time, all a variation of the old chocolate and peanut butter standby. This marketing strategy is everywhere. If you don't like what a company offers, it will figure out how to offer an alternative that will lure you into spending your money.

What does this have to do with happiness? It creates the impression that the individual reigns. My tastes and preferences are unique and must be met. If they're not, then I'll go elsewhere. Companies excel at determining your wants and meeting them, all in the name of creating a dopamine surge that convinces you that you're happy.

What works in a capitalist economy is plainly disastrous as a theological presupposition. While we've established that God is interested in our happiness, it's not on our terms. God knows what makes us happy. He also knows that the distorted marketing attempts to accumulate more and more of those things only plays to our self-centeredness. One of the greatest contemporary ironies is that the largest supplier of merchandise in the history of the world excels only in selling us things that thieves break in and steal and moth and rust destroy. We can't get no satisfaction, or at least any real and lasting satisfaction, from anything that Amazon brings to our doorstep. Only God can do this. And if we achieve a certain level of spiritual insight, we realize we really want nothing less.

Happiness that comes from a new sweater or new set of golf clubs is fine as far as it goes, but the sooner we reach a certain spiritual clarity that stops equating the latest gadget for the higher forms of happiness, the *beatitudo*, the better we'll be. The constant search for the next temporary pleasure, whether from a drug or from a package, creates its own unquenchable unhappiness. An effective theology of suffering helps us to stop the chase and become comfortable in sitting for a time in our own unease. We become happier by accepting a degree of unhappiness.

Carl Jung called this irony "holding the tension of the opposites." In the Bible, we find this represented in the numerous examples of suffering that ironically lead the sufferer closer to God. The clearest example, of course, is the cross where Jesus' humility and death were transformed into our salvation. Therefore, we accept the good haps and the bad haps as part of life, we don't substitute the lower forms of happiness for the ultimate, and we wait patiently as the ebbs and flows of life wash over us and around us. That is reasonable happiness.

You Find What You Look For

The themes of light and dark, or seeing and blindness, dominate the whole narrative of Scripture from the very first page. A list of examples would be so lengthy as to be unnecessary. It is a theme that is explicit or assumed in every verse of the Bible. The biblical writers, prophets, apostles, and the Messiah Himself took the issue of good and evil very seriously. This dichotomy goes to the heart of every aspect of reality and our existence. We are witnesses to and participants in a titanic, spiritual struggle that is as old as The Garden.

Any scriptural reference to discerning the times (Jesus in Mt. 16:3) or having the "eyes of your heart enlightened" (Paul in Eph. 1:18) refers to the fundamental reordering and re-creation of the way we view the world. Our ultimate discernment focuses on the saving work of God through Jesus Christ. All of history is summarized in three broad chapters: The Creation, The Breaking, and The Recreation. God created everything, and it was good. The first couple "broke" the good, created order, and each of us inherited that subsequently flawed spiritual gene. But from that very first crack, God began to mend. The cross was His ultimate healing. Jesus is The Point of everything. Through Him we can look forward to the re-creation of the new heavens and a new earth.

This insight allows us to argue from greater to lesser. We see mini-battles on a daily, even moment by moment, basis. It's happening all around us, all of the time. It manifests in our reactions to minor scrapes of the universal struggle, as in responding with anger to a child's interruption, or embracing fear over trust during a time of uncertainty and challenge. It can also mean the moments of joy when that same child gives us a new piece of refrigerator art or the feeling of peace when we let in that driver in front of us.

When Jesus, in the Sermon on the Mount, spoke of having the eye as the lamp of the body, He was referring to this pull and tug of light and darkness. He then added that we are to have a "sound eye" (Mt. 6:22). The word in Greek literally means *single*. Jesus wants us to have a single eye. It's a reference to focus. What will we focus on?

Drive on the busy streets of any of our cities and you likely will find bountiful evidence that "no one knows how to drive." I've heard that line from people when I lived in New Orleans with its crush of traffic, and in bucolic Murray, Kentucky where sitting through two light cycles is a major disruption. We've all been there, from mildly impatient mutterings to a pounding of the steering wheel, spittle flying tantrum.

Yet in the same situation we might take the moment to enjoy a meaningful podcast or call a friend (hands-free of course). I've had both responses, if it makes you feel any better. An aside here, I've been told I use driving illustrations quite a bit. Guilty as charged, but only because it is a great revealer of the inner spiritual condition. Sitting behind a wheel is fraught with spiritual hazard. Now you know why the Pope always has a driver.

What will I focus on during my next drive? There are going to be good haps and bad haps. How will I use my single eye? What will I focus on daily, even moment by moment? There will be bad haps and good haps. How will I use my single eye?

You find what you look for in life. Look for evidence that things are bad, and the evening news will give you plenty of ammunition. Look for beauty, truth, and goodness and you'll find that God has woven those through creation.

That's the fundamental key to being reasonably happy. The good and the bad are unavoidable facts of life, yet we have a God-given choice to acknowledge the bad while choosing instead to focus on the good. That enables a consistent, reasonable happiness.

What's more, you not only find what you look for in life, to a considerable degree you *become* what you look for in life. Both good and evil have a remarkable transformative energy that affects whatever they touch. Look too long at the darkness and the darkness works its way so deeply into your soul that you see all of life through the shadows, and you'll not even be aware of it. Fortunately, light works the same way. Consistently seeking the light creates a constant exposure to it, for we are simply never bereft of light. It's simply a matter of choosing to see that light and stop staring at the darkness.

When the Choice is Harder

I was adopted at birth by two genuinely wonderful people. Bill Ellis was a good man who combined faith, humor, and strength in an inspiring way. Dottie Ellis was a delightful lady who earned the nickname "Sunshine" at her workplace. Our home was filled with lots of love and laughter, and a few shadows.

As I mentioned before, when I was four years old, Dad contracted multiple sclerosis. He was a flight instructor for the Air Force. One of my favorite pictures is of Dad in his high-altitude gear. He was strong and heroic. Within a very short time, though, he was grounded and never taught again. The family moved from his last assignment at Fort Rucker back to the Ellis homestead in Lexington, Kentucky. Dad became, in his own words, a house husband. Mom, whose most cherished dream was to be a stay-at-home mom, went to work at a savings and loan as a teller.

Dad was 40 at the time of that tumultuous upheaval. In many ways, he was entering the prime of his life and career. Everything changed dramatically from that point forward. I don't want to paint a bleak picture, for my parents would not want that. Between spells of exhausting weakness and substantial paralysis, Dad was able to walk falteringly and even drive the car until I left home. He maintained his humor and his faith.

In later years, of course, the disease, as well as several other health problems, caught up with him. He entered a nursing home. I was living in another state and monitored things as well as I could, and I knew this was not a temporary move. During this latest transition, I told Mom that I'd never heard Dad complain about his health or situation. Ever. I asked her if he ever had. She said that one time, when he was first diagnosed, he wept. Then she added, "You adjust and move on, Terry. That's all we can ever do. Adjust and move on."

I've long marveled over my parents' view of life and faith. I've seen enough trauma in life to know that adjustments for some people are harder than others. And I've often wondered how my parents' attitude provided a kind of launching pad for me. I had a very healthy environment. Am I genetically predisposed to this outlook as well? Truly, God only knows.

This I do know, when I walked through the darkest period of my life I'd begun to look only at the shadows, and those shadows nearly overtook me. My return to the Light was the result of God's marvelous and mysterious providential forces. God wove together His will with my choices. The dual agency was at work. I know with equal conviction that only when I began to choose again to look at the light did my life turn around, and then only with God's help.

For some people, the choices are much harder than for others, but we must never concede to any darkness the power to completely quell our ability to choose the Light. Reasonable happiness is possible for anyone because God has so ordered His broken creation. The Prayer provides a spiritual framework to guide our choices.

A Far Deeper Reality

While the Greek word for happiness is not in the New Testament, we do find another word to describe God's ultimate goal for us. That word is "joy." Again, for those who view God as grim, this comes as something of a shock.

Jesus clearly taught that He came to give joy and wanted to complete our joy (John 15:11). He will allow nothing to steal our joy (John 16:22). Joy is the second fruit of the Spirit (Gal. 5:22). Paul wrote that we are to rejoice in the Lord in all situations (Phil. 4:4). Peter grounded our experience of joy in our knowledge of Jesus and the certainty of our eternity with Him (1 Pet. 1:8-9). References to joy are sprinkled throughout the Bible. It's obviously important.

"Joy" in Greek is derived from the same root word as "grace." That means joy is not something we can manufacture. It's something we receive from God. It's grounded in His character. Joy, therefore, is His gift to us. That's remarkably good news because it means joy is unconnected to the haps of life.

I've often heard about the 50/10/40 principle for happiness. It goes like this: happiness is 50% genetic, 10% circumstances, and 40% our internal mindset. This "rule" has much to commend it and is reflected in some of what I've already written. We do have genetic predisposition to a certain outlook on life. Some of us may struggle more with endogenous depression, and that would certainly hamper our ability to be happy. We do have to deal with the 10% of real circumstances. These are the haps of life. No doubt, a challenging day can make happiness harder to feel. Finally, many people have not taken time to develop coping skills that help them think about the world in a different way and find those things which create happiness. They've never accepted responsibility for their own happiness and are always waiting on external circumstances to change to make them happy.

What's left out of the equation, however, is a transcendent reality that is beyond time and circumstances, that is, God. Psychologists, mainly Dr. Sonja Lyubomirsky in her book *The How of Happiness*, developed the 50/10/40 rule and can be forgiven for not doing a deep dive into the metaphysics, but that's really the thrust of The Prayer. We need help to be happy. Providentially, we have a God who provides joy.

Happiness and joy are separated by degrees on a continuum. Happiness is more along the lines of Aquinas's *felicitas*. Joy is the ultimate *beatitudo*, the heavenly bliss. Again, happiness is not bad or too light to consider, but we must realize that all the things that bring us pleasure in this life are simply somewhat flawed echoes of a far deeper reality. Joy, the confidence in God's presence and care, gets us much closer to *beatitudo*, but we don't need to sacrifice reasonable happiness in the pursuit of ultimate joy. Let's just recognize their legitimate uses and limits. There is something that calls to us in every expression of beauty, every sublime moment, every instance of divine awareness.

That deeper reality is heaven, the place where we will no longer be looking through the glass darkly. We'll know as we have been known. In the presence of God, we'll know the supreme happiness of the second phrase of this part of The Prayer.

Contrary to popular belief in some corners, a firm conviction about heaven does not mean a disconnection with earth. My pastor growing up, Brother Pierce, would speak loftily about the glories of heaven that await us, but then he would warn, "Don't be so heavenly minded that you're no earthly good."

But let's do be somewhat heavenly minded, or maybe better, spiritually minded. We need a higher perspective. We need divine help. Exercise, wealth, fame, pleasure are temporary solutions to an eternal problem. To return to Chesterton's idea, we're trying to get to the South Seas in paddle boats.

The Prayer provides a sturdy vessel, and the navigation tools make good on its promise. The theological ideas present in each phrase are extraordinarily profound. It will take some time and careful thought to master enough of them to begin your journey, but it's not too hard. And you don't have to be a mystic to get there. You do need consistency. Just keep praying The Prayer and remember God longs to bring you to your longed-for destination: reasonable happiness in this life and supreme happiness forever in the next.

Toward reasonable happiness:

- We all want happiness but we're very poor at knowing what it is and how to get it. Many people have forgotten what happiness is.
- We tend to embrace unhealthy substitutes for God in our pursuit of happiness. This inevitably results in greater unhappiness.
- God wants us to be happy and has designed a way for us to find happiness in and through Him.
- Though we are endowed with an ability to be happy we're also wired neurologically for fear. Fear often exaggerates the challenges we face and overwhelms our ability to find happiness.
- Life is hard. It's always a mixture of what we want and what we get. We must find a strategy that enables us to be reasonably happy when life is challenging.
- We cannot link happiness to the events in our lives. If we do, then the events become the determiners of our happiness. That leads inevitably to unhappiness.

We find what you look for in life. If we look only for the pain, we'll find it everywhere. Pain and frustration will be all we see. But we can also, with God's help, look for grace God has woven into life.

CHAPTER THREE

GRANT ME SERENITY TO ACCEPT THE THINGS I CANNOT CHANGE

"I have learned, in whatever state I am, to be content."
Philippians 4:11

"We must make ourselves indifferent to all created things."
St. Ignatius

Leslie and I have owned schnauzers for nearly 35 years, one or two at a time. One of the two we presently enjoy is Blair, whose twin passions in life are to be loving and to eradicate every other species that comes into her backyard. She watches out the back door and the windows with constant vigilance. When an offending squirrel walks across the top of the fence or has the audacity to hop through our yard, Blair loudly insists on going out. With total concentration and commitment, she thunders after the interloper until it deftly leaps onto the nearest tree and scampers away to safety.

Blair has been doing this for ten years. Even now as I tap out these words, I can see her down the hallway lying on top of the bed in the guest bedroom, steadily watching out the window for the next offender. But for all of her decade-long unbroken dedication, her record is unblemished by success. She's never caught a squirrel. Or a bird. When she was very young, my daughter says she caught a chipmunk. Other than that, and a very occasional lizard, she's had no success. A total failure.

But here's the thing about Blair that separates her in her failure and frustration from me and my failure and frustration: Not once has she ever come back in the house after yet another miss, laid on the couch, and wondered to herself, "Can there be more to life than my fruitless pursuit of squirrels?"

From all appearances, Blair projects the life and affect of a totally satisfied dog. Feed her in the morning, let her out a few times during the day, pat her and play with her, and this dog seems to innately realize she has it made. She's totally accepted the parameters of her life and does not whine or complain.

I'm not the first dog owner to wish he was more like his dog.

Of course, our ability to reflect on life is what separates from every other species. We strive for meaning. We want life to "make sense." This takes many forms and often revolves around handling challenge. When faced with something unpleasant or something we want to change, we'll figure out a way to make the change. Unlike Blair, if I want to get rid of the squirrels, I strategize, find suitable traps, and watch videos of how to catch squirrels. I can change things around me, and I want to change things around me because I'm convinced that life should be pleasant and successful, and I can make it so.

When faced with a challenge, most of us are going to react in this way. Whether the particular "bad hap" is something relatively mild or bordering on catastrophic, our natural and first impulse is to change the circumstances in and around us. Sometimes that means making adjustments, such as steering out of the way of an imminent accident. If the offense is from a person, you may talk to that person, a discussion that may take the form of rebuke, advice, or, in the case of a child, sending her to her room. You might actually try to simply escape the situation or person. Running, or withdrawing, is a natural and sometimes useful survival instinct.

In all of these responses, we've tried to exercise a measure of control. That's natural, normal, and usually neutral. Some people are actually quite adept at it and take pride in their ability to change the circumstances and/or people around them. The challenge, of course, is that circumstances often have a way of morphing beyond control and people hate to be controlled, especially those who've established their own healthy identities.

No doubt you've run up against disagreeable circumstances you cannot change, and hopefully you're aware enough to realize that you must not try to control another person. You might be the sort who has had that latter revelation thrust upon you, or sadly you may be still trying to arrange everyone around you to suit yourself. That never works for long, and with both circumstances and people, you will eventually come up against an unalterable and inveterate problem. What choice, then, is left to you? Can we control or change all the variables in our lives?

The Invictus Distortion

The eldest of six children, William Henley embraced from an early age the Victorian challenge of always keeping a stiff upper lip. At age 12, he contracted tuberculosis in the bones of his lower left leg, an extremely painful condition causing frequent abscesses that needed to be regularly drained. The year was 1861, so anesthesia was not an option. On those occasions, William's younger brother Joseph recalled that William would "hop about the room, laughing loudly and playing with zest to pretend he was beyond the reach of pain." [McDowell, Margaret B. British Poets, 1880-1914, Vol. 19. Detroit, Michigan: Gale research Co. p. 202]

Doctors eventually had to amputate the leg below the knee. That seemed only add to Henley's resolve. He finished school, endured the loss of his father at age 19, then worked as a journalist for eight years. He developed the same problem in his right leg, and the condition frequently interrupted both his schooling and work. Henley strenuously objected to a recommended second amputation. He sought a second opinion and underwent multiple surgeries with long hospital stays over a period of three years.

During the last year of his hospitalization, he penned the famous biographical poem "Invictus." Each of the four quatrains begins with a description of the bleakness, pain, and challenge of life which Henley met with an "unconquerable soul," or a head that is "bloody but unbowed," or completely "unafraid." Most famously he ended with "I am the master of my fate; I am the captain of my soul."

Henley's personal force and appearance inspired Robert Louis Stevenson to model the peg-legged Long John Silver after him in *Treasure Island*, a physically incomplete man ruling and menacing men who were whole. Henley's personal life matched his words. His poem inspires, and the sentiments and qualities of character he embodied are essential to any success in life.

However, most of us suffer from the "Invictus" distortion; that is, we aim its power *outside* of us. Personally, *"my unconquerable soul"* is just not powerful enough to illuminate the "black night" that covered me. I could not conquer addiction. It conquered me. Thoroughly.

I've "winced" and "cried aloud" through many "fell clutches of circumstance." My head has been both "bloodied and bowed." Life is very adept at crippling everyone. Even Henley, for all his inherent strength, was not able to vanquish his diseases. An accident led to the recurrence of his tuberculosis, and he died at age 53.

And who can seriously claim to be *unafraid* in all of life's "bludgeonings?" I literally questioned in my 40s whether I had ever truly been afraid. Only after the repeated blows from the perfect storm of various traumas in my 50s did I realize how fear shot through my life. I'd wager that if you scratch the surface of any life, you'll find a swirling variety of dark fears. I wonder if Henley recognized the dread feeling of fear as he watched his young daughter, Margaret, battle illness throughout her brief life and die at age 11?

Clearly, NO ONE is master of their own fate at every turn. No exceptions. We all run into situations that absolutely beat us up and take us down. The only real surprise is that we are so surprised when it happens. We walk through much of life with a series of unbroken successes, as Lincoln put it, and that creates the illusion that we conquer and control *every* situation. That is the Invictus Distortion. Boldly walk away from this poem thinking of yourself as the master and captain over all things and fate will snicker.

Henley is not wholly wrong. I'm not for a moment calling into question his apparently genuine, deep, and lifelong ability to maintain an inspiring courage and humor in the face of extreme challenge. It's just that all of us have to come to grips with our limitations. We don't win all the time. From reports of those who knew him, Henley appears to have been reasonably happy even though his life was marked by extreme and consistent challenge. But how? And how can we reasonably find a similar strength?

The *direction* of the poem is important. The true power of "Invictus" lies not in our ability to control people and things around us. That is the source of some of the greatest horrors in human history and more personal disappointments than grains of sand on the seashore. Fate doesn't care about our courage. For that reason, the poem points inward, not outward.

It's the remarkable power of the human mind, infused by the presence of God, that can absolutely transform our outlook on life. Staying close to the true Master of Fate and putting God in rightful charge of our souls is the beginning point of the reasonably happy life. Real strength begins with a frank admission of genuine weakness. This polarity of strength coming from weakness is one of the clearest and most overlooked themes of Scripture. You have to fall before you can rise.

The Illusion of Control Is Not Entirely an Illusion

The failure to face reality squarely is surely one of our most common neuroses. As I discussed earlier, our species actually has a remarkable ability to control situations. Most things around us run very smoothly, and when there is a problem, we can call a repairman or a helpline, or watch a YouTube video. It really is a great time to be alive.

The ability to control and manage successfully so many areas of our lives, however, creates the illusion that we can control *every* area of our lives. So, we're genuinely stunned when we run up against something that we can't fix, or the doctor has no prescription for, or God seems silent or impotent in the face of.

We may be the first generation in history to suffer the illusion to this degree. Solomon in the mysterious book of Ecclesiastes discovered that even with all his wealth, power, and wisdom, life was still a dreary disappointment. We're still trying to learn this lesson. In fact, I'm not really sure there are any new lessons to learn. For all of our cleverness, our most fundamental task is to learn the same lessons that everyone else has had to learn throughout history.

One of those lessons is that life is a sine curve. We have good times, and we have bad times, over and over. Remember the Byrds's "Turn, Turn, Turn?" They lifted the lyrics right out of Ecclesiastes. "A time to be born, a time to die; a time to plant, a time to reap; a time to kill, a time to heal." The point is that these times are common to everyone. Further, as we love to remind ourselves that bad times will pass, we also need to admit the same is true of good times. And we're very uncomfortable with that. In spite of all our power we simply cannot maintain only good times (haps).

Financial advisors talk about the "regression to mean." A talented money manager, a hot stock, or mutual fund may perform well above the average return for a period of time. Inevitably, however, the performance will come back down to the average, or to the mean. Why? No one can manage all the variables. The belief that someone will prove to be the exception, the genuine and permanent "golden boy," created opportunities for conmen to foment the 2008 financial crisis. That disaster did not come about because of a failure of tested and proven investment strategies. It happened because a large number of people thought they were smarter than everyone who came before them. But no one can predict perfectly the wild political events that surge through our society regularly, or the development of some new technology that renders an earlier generation obsolete, or a pandemic!

As I write this, our nation is in the middle of the COVID-19 crisis. No one had this on their agenda, and right now the outcome is murky. Of course, we'll survive the pandemic. Humanity has been doing that since there's been humanity. But what will be the cost in human lives? To the economy? How will life change in some permanent ways after this? It's a giant social experiment in shattering the illusion of control.

We don't need a pandemic to teach us this lesson. Life provides plenty of opportunities to learn it. Parenting, in my experience, has probably been the biggest reality check. Bring a child home from the hospital, and you immediately realize you're not fully in charge as that little 8 lb. 10 oz. bundle of "joy" disturbs every routine you cherished as an individual and couple. On down the road, I've had a constant stream of parents across the decades come to me bewildered that the same kid who was once a clinging shadow now barely acknowledges mom. And the dad who is highly adept at running a business battles ulcers because his management techniques don't work in the home.

Again, the illusion of control is not entirely an illusion. I'd argue that we're highly adept as an advanced society in controlling a lot of variables and making adjustments when things go badly. Recently a derecho (from the Spanish word for "straight") blew through the upper Midwest. Hurricane force winds severely damaged huge swathes of crops. As bad as it was, the impact will probably be in the form of higher prices for some commodities. No one is suggesting that a large portion of the American population is now subject to starvation.

This situation is completely different from our ancestors whose very existence could be threatened by a swarm of locusts. Or a drought. Or a saber-tooth tiger. Or a common infection. Realistically, none of these formerly common threats is on the radar of the average American today. Why? Because incrementally those same ancestors across many generations controlled more and more of their environment.

Every now and then, though, something in one of those categories of threats breaks through to remind us that our control is not complete. No, we don't have to contend with large wildlife any longer. The animal threats to us now come at the micro level. COVID-19 is a virus, the most numerous biological entity on the planet. Weather events do change lives and take lives. Accidents and diseases change our lives when we're the victim or when we love a victim. Think of how often life shifts permanently after a phone call to inform you of a diagnosis, an accident, or some other mishap.

We want control, and when we don't have it, we have to make some very fundamental decisions, and sometimes those results are truly disastrous. In the book *Alcoholics Anonymous*, Bill

Wilson describes the self-centered alcoholic as one who tries to set up the whole show and eventually becomes indignant and self-pitying when everyone (and life) doesn't play their part as assigned (pp. 60-61). The alcoholic often responds to the shattering of control by drinking, which can be a form of control or a complete relinquishing of hope. Responding badly to a profound shift in reality is not limited to alcoholics.

No one, I think, handles the shattering of the illusion of control seamlessly. Wrestling with reality inevitably produces some level of disappointment, fear, anger, resentment, self-pity, etc. What do we do when we realize that in spite of our purest desires and loftiest ideals, life often does not cooperate?

God, Grant Me

The first three words of The Prayer offer a radically different approach to life and our place in it. "God, grant me." Faced with an uncooperative reality, we have the option of taking our concerns and complaints to God.

The Prayer is popular and a part of the general cultural conscience largely because of Alcoholics Anonymous. The Prayer, in its three-line form, came to the attention of the Bill Wilson and the AA staff in New York in 1941. The Prayer had a very definite appeal to AA members because the second of the 12 Steps teaches members to believe that a power greater than themselves can restore them to sanity. For people who have genuinely wrestled with life and have come out of that experience completely broken, the idea that God can restore them is a genuine lifeline. What a contrast this is to the self-directed life that brings people trouble!

Self-directed living has been around since people have been living, but it has gained a certain traction today chiefly through the influence of several strains of philosophy. Friedrich

Nietzsche (d. 1900) was frankly a brilliant and complicated man. His best-known one-liner is "God is dead." These are the words of the madman in his "Parable of the Madman" who bursts into a marketplace of unbelievers saying "I seek God!" When he is laughed at and derided by those who don't believe in God, he responds "God is dead. God remains dead. And we have killed him."

Nietzsche did not believe in God. So, how does a person face the challenges of life? Nietzsche proposed "the will to power" which in many ways sounds akin to Henley's "Invictus." It's the idea that man takes complete responsibility for facing a blind and uncaring existence. The popularity of the current idea that we create our own meaning and happiness apart from God is an echo of this powerful and pervasive philosophy.

Jean Paul Sartre (d. 1980) bears mentioning here also. He's probably the most influential philosopher of the 20th century, best known for his development of existentialism. Central to his thought is the idea that being precedes essence. This is a fancy way of saying the individual decides and determines his or her life without regard to metaphysical ideas like God. Self-assertion is the way. Sartre did not believe he could be truly free if God existed, so he rejected God as an obsolete and infantile idea.

Young people, especially since 9/11, have increasingly embraced these ideas, though they're not likely to know where they came from. Suffice it here to say that the idea that we can and even should get through life without God is a powerful and prevalent idea. In the face of challenge, you must rely on your individual strength and will to survive.

This brief foray into the roots of atheism provides us a contrast with the Christian understanding of God, His presence, and His willingness to be involved in our lives. Instead of a blind, pitiless existence, Jesus taught that we are all beloved sons and daughters of God. Rather than being alone in a vast but cold universe, we have a God who cares for us and is involved in our lives.

Jesus' entire mission underscored these truths. Incarnation (literally "in flesh") is the theological word that describes the historical event when God, who is spirit, was born into our world. Ironically, many atheists profess to admire the moral teachings of Jesus but reject His claim that "if you have seen me you have seen the Father" (John 14:9). They discard as myth God's ultimate effort to reveal Himself. However, for those who accept Jesus' claim, some remarkable opportunities unfold. We discover a God who listens and responds because He loves us.

Prayer will always have a mysterious quality to it, but that doesn't mean it can't also be simple and accessible. The greatest endorsement of prayer for us is the fact that Jesus prayed and often withdrew by Himself to do so. If God the Son while He was on earth needed God the Father to listen and grant Him strength, insights, solutions, etc., then we certainly could benefit from the practice as well.

To that end, Jesus was very interested in teaching us to pray. He taught His disciples a prayer that we recite to this day, The Lord's Prayer or Model Prayer (Matt. 6:9-13). He was also quite insistent on the fact that "God grants." As noted in the previous chapter, God gives good gifts to us when we ask (Matt. 7:11). Finally, and perhaps most importantly, Jesus understood that we would struggle with prayer. To help us, He told two parables that specifically address our doubts: The Parable of the Persistent Widow (Luke 18:1-8) and the Parable of the Friend at Midnight (Luke 11:5-8). Both make the same point, but let's take a closer look at the Parable of the Persistent Widow.

One of the most misunderstood and misapplied teachings of Jesus is the Parable of the Persistent Widow. Luke is very clear about the reason Jesus told this parable: He wanted us to pray always and not lose heart (Luke 18:1). What follows is the story of a powerless widow who had been defrauded in some way. She approached the uncaring judge and was rebuffed. But she kept coming until finally the unrighteous official relented and pronounced a judgment in her favor, not because he finally saw the rightness of her claim, but because she kept pestering him.

Now here is what we normally do with this parable: we allegorize it. The woman becomes any of us who has a request of God. The judge is God who acts like an unresponsive official in a poorly run government office. You can leave a message, but no one is likely to call you back. The application of the parable, when understood this way, is that we must keep praying and praying and praying to get God's attention and receive what we want.

I have heard this parable preached and taught in this way many times. I have heard the exhortation that we should knock down the doors of heaven with our prayers. Applied in this way, God sounds rather reluctant, and prayer simply becomes a way of wearing Him down. Everyone has prayed for something they've not received, and misunderstanding this parable can lead to either giving up because it's too much trouble to get God's attention, or to the idea we must wear Him down in order to do so.

Is this what Jesus meant to teach? Of course not. It's not a true encouragement to pray if we are taught to keep asking and asking with the conviction that sooner or later we are going to provoke God into giving us what we want. It makes us sound like the kid in the grocery store checkout line who incessantly whines for candy until the frazzled parent eventually gives in. That interpretation creates infantile Christians who will forever pray for their own selfish ends. This theological train wreck of an interpretation also makes God a means to our ends. It reduces Him to a cosmic Santa Claus with little or no backbone.

This parable is meant to *contrast* God and the unrighteous judge, *not compare* them. The point of the parable, the point that we often miss, is that God is completely *unlike* the judge. He is a loving Father who personally knows and genuinely cares about us. A loving Father listens to His children enthusiastically. He does not need to be coerced by repetitious prayers in the belief that only in that way will you get His attention. We already have His attention.

Our Father in heaven loves and listens to us. Our prayers go directly from our lips to His ear. Add to this Paul's insight that the Spirit intercedes for us (Rom. 8:26). Interestingly, Paul first admitted that none of us really knows how to pray as we should. In my personal struggles with prayer, I find it greatly comforting that the man who authored nearly half of the New Testament books also struggled. But he kept praying because he believed in some mysterious way that we don't need to comprehend that God grants our requests as they align with His will and purpose for us.

Many years ago now, I remember reading about AT&T setting up a booth on one of the busy sidewalks in New York City and inviting people to sit down and say anything they wanted. Their message then would be relayed by satellite into space. They offered no guarantee anyone would hear it, of course, but it was an intriguing promotion. Is anyone out there listening? Does anyone care? Can anyone help?

The Christian faith answers each of those three questions with a powerful "yes," and on the direct authority of Jesus. We don't need to will ourselves to power. We have Someone who will be that power for us. That's the essence of the Good News. Frankly, existence can sometimes appear blind and pitiless. But the first words of The Prayer mean we're not meant to face that struggle alone.

Shattered Lives

We don't have to sit down in a booth and have our message beamed out into space. A heart composed to reach out to God is all that is required. Bent knees, bowed head, and closed eyes are optional and often useful. The idea is actually the same, however. You're about to whisper something you trust God will hear. What will you ask for? The Prayer's first petition is for the most necessary quality of life: serenity.

One of my favorite illustrations over my years of preaching was to take a common dinner plate that represented our lives. I would wrap it in a towel, then take a rubber mallet and smash it. The effect was quite dramatic, guaranteed to waken even the drowsiest balcony person. I really enjoyed it.

Unfolding the towel revealed all the shattered pieces, and I would make the analogy to our lives. Most people have a sense, at least during some chapters of life, of their brokenness. It comes in many forms. They may feel fearful and anxious. Others feel that they don't quite fit in. I've heard many people say they felt they just never got the "How Life Works" instruction booklet that everyone else seems to have. The atmosphere of anger so prevalent today is merely an outward symptom of an underlying brokenness. Broken relationships, destructive habits of action and thought, addiction, etc. are more examples of the shrapnel of our inner conflicts.

Both the Hebrew and Greek words for peace mean wholeness. Peace is not simply an absence of conflict. It's the sense that we fit together individually and in the world. Our lives, in peace, are not broken. Though life attempts to shatter us repeatedly, we can find a peace that keeps us together and whole.

In this unitive experience we find meaning, and that applies even when the hard blows strike. In fact, it applies especially when the hard blows strike or it's simply of no use at all. Peace enables us to integrate every experience in life into a meaningful whole. Nothing is left out. Nothing. Peace can transform even the most dreaded circumstances into an occasion for growth, even though the occasion, and the memories of it, might be painful.

Once we accept this, we discover that real peace is not just the pleasant arrangement of circumstances. It goes far beyond that. Jesus, significantly on the night before He died, said, "Peace I leave with you, my peace I give to you. Not a peace as the world gives, but My peace" (John 14:27). There it is. So clear. There are two kinds of peace. The world's peace comes when things go our way. I have no problem with this peace at all. God, grant me more of it! It's a peace that comes when the sine curve is at its highest.

But the real peace we seek is the one we need when the rubber mallet strikes. Our shattered lives are full of sharp edges, and sometimes we cut ourselves and others with those edges. We feel out of control, because we genuinely are. No amount of money, physical security, health, power, or intellect can provide what we really seek. We're looking for peace from our first genuine experience with this out-of-control world. We need something that we cannot give or produce ourselves. It has to come from a Power greater than ourselves. Emphatically, Jesus offers *His* peace to heal our shatteredness.

When we pray "God, grant me the serenity" we are praying for His peace to infuse our lives and put the pieces back together. We're like the child who builds a tower with blocks and when everything tumbles in, we turn to our Parent with tears and questions. God smiles and says, "Let Me help you with that."

The first part of the very first phrase of The Prayer takes us to the heart of our most basic challenge. We are not in control, and our frustration at this has probably been intense and possibly destructive. God offers a gift of serenity. It is a gift of calm and quiet and relief. We're not in charge, and that's okay. We weren't created to be in charge in the first place. This great relief comes from God when we learn to embrace one of the most misunderstood, illogical, even offensive spiritual concepts imaginable.

The Power of Acceptance

Most people start wrestling with the day from the moment they wake. The alarm interrupts their sleep, often a fitful sleep for restless individuals, and they begin acrimonious negotiations by punching the snooze button a few times. The following rounds may be with surly children, or an unsatisfactory wardrobe, snarled traffic, dissatisfied coworkers, an unreasonably demanding boss. The late rounds take place back at home with an inattentive spouse, the return of surly children, nothing on TV, etc. Sprinkle in a tough medical diagnosis, or a lawsuit, or an in-law or two and you have an agenda that leaves no room for happiness. Life is a wrestling match.

But it doesn't have to be.

What if you simply refused to wrestle? No, you can't rid your life of every disagreeable element. Control would be trying to eliminate the alarm, the coworkers, the boss, and the children(!). That's not an option. In fact, the attempt to control is simply a way of externalizing the real source of the problem.

Every life, all of life, has rough edges. Remember the sine curve illustration? The sine curve is not simply a macro image of life that happens over periods of months and years. It's micro as well. Each day has its ups and downs. Even every hour. As described in an earlier chapter, we're "wired" to focus on the perceived threats, and that's what we wrestle with every day.

The point here, however, is not merely to start focusing on the ups. Acceptance is merely the frank admission that life, at its easiest, comes with loathsome alarms, surly children, and snarled traffic. Life is a mixture of what we want and what we get. It *always* is.

The "celebrity deceit" is the idea that good looking, wealthy, popular people *must* be happy. In fact, we think that anyone who has about 10% more than we do is certainly much happier than we are. But that's simply not true. Wealthy people have the very same levels of discontent, though the specific areas may vary. Again, that's Solomon's point in Ecclesiastes, but we forget.
So, if every day, even every hour is affected by the inescapable sine curve, then what do we do? We stop wrestling. Acceptance is the absence of unwise reactions. It's a position of observation without the attendant drama of complaint and discord.

Acceptance is a shift of focus. The multiple low sides of each day's sine curves always clamor for attention. We expend a tremendous amount of energy either directly engaging with the sources of that clamor in the form of arguing and criticizing, or mentally and emotionally ruminating about them, which is actually much more common.

Acceptance is a position of spiritual and emotional neutrality. We can decide not to engage in a negative and useless manner with all the low sides of the sine curves. We can simply accept the situations and people as they are, without thinking that our calling is to change them.

My first church staff position was as a summer youth director in Bluff Creek, Louisiana. Having been raised in the city, I was fascinated by this genuinely rural lifestyle. The boys in my youth group delighted in showing this uninitiated city slicker how to hunt squirrels and racoons. Leslie and I had been married only a couple of weeks when we arrived, and we embraced this delightful new experience.

I remember driving down one particular gravel road for the first time. Another car was a couple of hundred yards ahead, kicking up a plume of red, south Louisiana dust. As it passed a home on the right, I saw a wild-eyed dog lying by the mailbox at the side of the road with this crazy concentration on the approaching car. As the car passed, it tore off down the side of the road, barking and snarling for all it was worth until it reached the property line. Then it raced back to the mailbox and resumed its crazy-eyed stakeout. When I passed it did the same thing.

I admired the dog's restraint in staying on his own property, but I learned that was what that dog did all day. Every day. It just waited until a car came by so that it could bark and snarl and run. It never prevented a car from coming. It never changed the course of a car. I doubt the drivers even were aware of that disturbed, crazy-eyed dog.

I've come to realize how much like that dog I can be. An event, a person, or a memory can come under my scrutiny and before I realize it, I'm going the equivalent of barking, snarling, and running around. What's especially interesting to me is that, particularly when it comes to a memory, that person or event is not even aware of how agitated I've become. Can there be a more useless expenditure of my spiritual and emotional energy?

Acceptance means I don't chase every car. Life gets a lot easier when I just watch the sine curves go up and down. I don't even have to engage the sine curves that stop and try to get me to fight. Most wonderfully, in the quiet that has replaced all that former commotion, I've made a sacred space for God to speak and act. In the moments, good and bad, I discover that I'm never alone. God accompanies me through each, and His peace becomes my peace. I need serenity to accept, but acceptance also leads to serenity.

We have plenty of space in later chapters to deal with the objections you're mentally raising right now. Let me simply summarize here that acceptance doesn't mean approval, agreement, or resignation. I don't ever have to approve of any degree of pain or injustice or inconvenience I encounter. I absolutely don't have to agree with someone who unfairly or inaccurately criticizes me or who holds a different opinion from me, and I don't just give up in the face of challenge.

Acceptance is a choice to shift focus from the problem to the solution. Too often we simply marinate in the circumstances that we cannot change. We complain and criticize and wail, and the circumstances don't care. Acceptance means that we've already acknowledged the downside of the sine curve, but we want now to engage in changing something we are in control of, and that is our reaction to the sine curves.

The Rhythm of Reversal

The Bible is a remarkably honest book. It's certainly not sanitized. The stories of the men and women who would become our greatest saints include painful chapters of failure and suffering as well as some of the darkest sins imaginable. Paul, the author of nearly half the books of the New Testament, had the opportunity to control his own narrative, and he chose to be completely honest and authentic about the sine curves of his life. He describes one of the most revealing episodes of his life in 2 Corinthians 12.

The letter of 2 Corinthians is a literary wrestling match. Paul was not happy with the church at Corinth. Many members had turned on him. Some said he wasn't much of a preacher. Any preacher takes that very personally. They said he wasn't much of a leader. They disagreed with some of his teaching. They distorted many of the practices of the early church. Some members even said he didn't look very impressive. That's *very* personal.

The real source of the problem was the "super-spiritualists" in the church who felt they'd outgrown Paul. They ranked their gifts as superior. That set up an ugly division in the church, and not just with Paul. When I hear people today talk about wanting to get back to the pure ways of the first-century church I wonder if they've ever read their Bibles.

In chapters 11 and 12, Paul decided to take on his opponents on their turf. In many ways, it's a silly section of Scripture. Paul even admits that he's sounding "like a mad man" but he's going to compare resumés with the super-spiritualists. Of course, he wins. He was a Pharisee, so he certainly knew the very jots and tittles of scripture. He'd been on many mission trips and faithfully encountered all manner of danger. He'd established churches. He even wrote that he'd been caught up into the third heaven! He could check a lot more boxes than any of those superficial Corinthians.

His greatest insight in this section, however, was that they were all using the wrong scorecard. Strength, accomplishments, ecstatic experiences were not the real measure of spiritual accomplishment. How one handles weakness is true gauge of real and deep spirituality, and for Paul that lesson came in the form of a thorn.

We don't know what the thorn was. Some speculate it was failing eyesight. Others wonder if it was the daily stress of dealing with various churches. I tend to think it was a bad back. After all he walked everywhere, and if he was laid up, he couldn't carry on the mission.

What is truly interesting about this episode was Paul's initial response and what he learned from it. He did what any of us would do. He prayed for the thorn to be removed. It was a good and understandable prayer. The great apostle to the Gentiles had something that interfered with his ability to be the great apostle to the Gentiles. As a man of obviously great faith, he confidently asked God to remove it, and he trusted that it would be so.

But it wasn't. The thorn remained even though Paul prayed three times for its removal. Why would he share an episode of apparent failure? Especially when he was involved in a tussle with people who loved to point out their supposed superiority?

God provided the answer. "My grace is sufficient for you, for My power is made perfect in weakness" (2 Cor. 12:9). Paul assessed that removing the thorn was in his best interest. He sought strength and freedom from any constraint as the true metric of success. In other words, he wanted control and an uninterrupted series of good haps. Not only did Paul not understand the grading scale, he didn't even grasp the deeper spiritual ground rules of how to keep score.

This episode is one of several powerful illustrations of a basic principle we find throughout the scripture. It's the rhythm of reversal. We judge a situation hopeless or at least unpleasant, and God turns it into an occasion for profound spiritual growth and insight. The principle behind the "first shall be last the last first" teaching sprinkled through the gospels.

The list is extensive: God's selecting David to be the next king because He doesn't look on the outward (and small) appearance but on the inner spiritual potential. God's calling Amos, a rural nobody, to prophesy to the elites of Jerusalem. Mary Magdalene becoming a disciple. The woman at the well having a one-on-one with the Messiah. Twelve ordinary and powerless men becoming the founding members of the church. The widow honored for her little contribution. Ultimately, the transformation of the darkness of Good Friday into the brilliant light of Easter Sunday.

Every shattered feeling we experience is but an echo of the earliest and first Breaking. The absolute glory of our lives today, however, is that the first line in God's job description is reversing the brokenness by transforming it. The bad that seeks to undo us changes into the good that helps us grow. Power is not the answer to the problem of brokenness. Grace is. And grace is the most powerful force God wields. It is love in action.

I'm sure this was a hard lesson for Paul to learn. God doesn't remove all thorns. Acceptance is not easy, especially at first. We see its effects on down the road in Paul's story. In his letter to the Philippians, he wrote, "I have learned to be content in whatever state I'm in...I have learned the secret of facing plenty and hunger, abundance and want." Contentment is another word for acceptance. Does it really work? Paul wrote Philippians while he was in jail. He could do nothing about the conditions of his cell, or the unfairness of the charges, or his future. He had no control over the sine curves. He chose to accept the grace available to him and in that grace, he found strength.

The great irony of the first phrase of The Prayer is that by accepting our lack of control we find strength. Admitting weakness is never a failure in Christian spirituality. It is, in fact, the way to open the door to God's entry into our lives. What life presents to harm us, God uses to strengthen us.

Don't Try This Alone

Paul's contentment in that jail cell was not self-generated. It was not his own mastery of his fate, even in deciding to be content. Never for a moment did he consider himself master of his fate, nor captain of his soul. In the verse following his claim to be content in all circumstances he wrote, "I can do all things through Him who strengthens me."

The overarching theme of all of Paul's writing is found in two words: in Christ. He truly believed in the remarkable spiritual union of the believer and the Lord. This should not surprise us.

Jesus Himself prayed to the Father that His followers would "be one, as I am in You, and You are in Me, that they may be in us" (John 17:21). Paul believed that through faith he was united with Christ. He also reversed the language to say that Christ was in us.

Jeremiah prophesied this theological shift about 600 years before Paul's experience of it. Through the prophet God foretold of a new covenant that would be different from the old covenant inscribed on stone. God would put His law within His people. Each person would know the Lord personally, not relying solely on someone else to instruct them. God would write this new law upon their hearts, and everyone from the least to the greatest would know God personally (see Jer. 31:31-34).

For Paul, this fundamental insight meant a major change in focus. As a Pharisee, he studied the law and committed it to memory. To characterize the Pharisees as always wearing the black hats in the Bible is unfair. They were trying to work God's law into every area and every moment of their lives. Some, like Nicodemus, maintained an openness to new ways God would work.

Paul was not like Nicodemus. He claimed that he was blameless in regard to the law, unsurpassed in his zeal and scruples. These were not idle boasts. The Pharisees were exceedingly capable of reining in all manner of behaviors. Paul genuinely excelled at being a Pharisee. All that religion did for him, however, was make him very critical and judgmental. Recall that his distorted pursuit of the law led him to persecute Christians.

All of his passionate focus on the law ironically turned his attention inward, but in a self-centered manner. He relied on his own strength to fulfill the law, and in his success, pride took over. He was attempting to be the captain of his soul, and again, he was rather good at it. His religion, however, had a self-imposed limit of which he wasn't aware. Everything was up to him. It took a blinding encounter with the Lord on the road to Damascus to change his perspective. He came to believe in Christ who could do for him what he could not do for himself. Paul's righteousness was a self-righteousness. In Christ, he found grace to become what he really wanted: to be accepted by God.

Then, eventually, came the final shift. As Paul's sight cleared, he realized that he was "in Christ" and that Christ was in him. If we only externalize God, then we risk laboring under a tremendous burden of unworthiness, for we're trying to live up to the Other. When we recognize that the Other loves us so much that He dwells within us, then something truly remarkable happens. We find the joy of God's love and grace. External circumstances no longer whip us from the polarities of happy and unhappy. Our lives are grounded, not in the sine curve of life, but in an unchanging, loving, and gracious God.

Theologians speak of God in two categories. First, God is transcendent. That is, God is different from us. He is completely holy, completely loving, and completely gracious. He is all-powerful (omnipotent) and all-knowing (omniscient) and always present (omnipresent.) In other words, God is many, many things that we are not. Most people are aware of God's transcendence. They know He is different from us. Unfortunately, that is where most people stop, with an externalized God that doesn't relate to them and to whom they cannot relate.

The second category is just as important. We speak of God as personal. That is, God is very much like us in some very important ways. He loves. He rejoices. Most importantly, He relates. The scripture aims more and more at this target as we move through the books. This personal nature of God is Paul's fundamental insight, and we find it sprinkled throughout his letters with the words "in Christ" and "Christ in you."

Paul's insight provides a powerful way for us to view the presence of God in our lives. In the face of a loss of control, we are uniformly tempted to try to get God on our side to change the unpleasant circumstances. The temptation here is to manipulate God and treat Him like a genie in a bottle. While there's certainly nothing fundamentally wrong with bringing to God all of our concerns and requests, we must balance this potentially highly self-centered praying with a more exalted view of God.

God is not one thing in the universe. He's not properly thought of as even being the biggest thing in the universe. He's not one example of "being." God is both exterior to all of existence and constantly present in all of His creation. He's the sheer act of being itself.

When Moses first met God, he asked a natural question arising out of the mythology of Egypt with which he'd been raised. "Who are you?" he asked. When he would go to the people, they would naturally want to know who this God is who sent him. What is he to say? God's answer is impossibly deep and mysterious. The Hebrew can be rendered in a number of ways, but "I am that I am" is about as good as we can get. God's name is a form of the Hebrew verb "to be." It connotes existence, pure existence. God is not part of the existence. He is the matrix of existence.

So, when we attempt to deal with life, we try to determine what role God plays in the sine curves. That's always the entry point. How can God help me? But to really understand our involvement with God, we must move beyond this and try to grasp that God is life itself.

Jesus' prayer in John 17 is an extension of God's encounter with Moses at the burning bush. Jesus made a staggering request in His prayer, that we may be one with Him as He is one with the Father. Jesus did not pray that the Father would solve our problems in life, but that our lives would be profoundly connected with His life.

When we begin to grasp even a little bit of this truth, we can stop evaluating the events in our lives as either good or bad. God is in all. Nothing can separate us from His love and presence. We accept the thorn or enjoy the rose with equal trust in God.

When I was going through a difficult time of decision in my life a few years ago, I felt a rising fear. The decision I felt God leading me to would mean some dramatic changes in my life and some attendant uncertainty. One day, I was speaking with my good friend Bill about my struggles. He was quiet for a moment then said, "Terry, God's got this."

God's got this. Those three words cut through my fear. They reminded me that whatever "this" is, is in God's being and will for me. I can trust God with every "this," with the good haps and the bad haps.

Though God's answer to Moses was profoundly theological and deep, it was also very simple and personal. Basically, God told Moses that he wouldn't face this upcoming challenge alone. "I am that I am" is another way of saying "I've got this."

Accepting Reasonable Happiness

Shattering the illusion of control can be very unsettling. It's more accurate to say that we come to realize that complete control has been shattered all along. Our desperate attempts to prevent the hammer blows of real life and then try to put the pieces back together is actually the source of our unhappiness. Hammers fall, and lives break. Every day.

Yet there is also a remarkable relief in finally accepting that life is often out of order and there is little to nothing we can do about it. This is one of the chief truths that will make you free. The illusion absolutely needs to be shattered because we won't allow God to put the pieces back together until we admit our brokenness and the brokenness of the world. One of the most basic and powerful prayers is to affirm that God is in charge of our lives and this world. It's a clear example of the way the spiritual world works. We surrender in order to win.

I did not come to this understanding easily, and I certainly don't claim to have implemented it completely. I do remember what it was like to feel the weight of the world and to feel that I was responsible for carrying it.

Being a minister has never been harder, and it's been going in this direction for some time. Our culture used to be much more Christian. I'll leave it to others to debate whether the faith was deep and genuine and really helpful, but without question we've seen a trend over the last four-plus decades of less and less church participation. What used to be a commonly spoken religious language and set of expectations is rapidly being left behind by an increasingly secular world. Youth sports leagues in former times would never schedule practices on Wednesday evenings in the south so as to not interfere with church programs. Today "travel teams" expect team members and families to travel every weekend during the season and afterward.

The result of our increasing secularization is a marked decline in church attendance. About 25 years ago, an older minster told me they were running an attendance campaign in their church revolving around the number two. They posted it everywhere throughout the campus. The message? "Give your church two hours each week: Worship and Sunday School." This was a Baptist church where committed members used to invest four to six hours each week in church activities.

The reasons for this are many, and surveying the trends and causes behind them is not the purpose of this book. I reflect on it here because I acutely remember a very heavy burden of responsibility for battling that trend. Sisyphus often came to mind, rolling his stone up the hill only to watch it roll down again. I felt like Rev. Sisyphus but too often unsuccessfully dodging the boulder as it rolled back downhill. As pastors today deal with the restrictions on worship and other gatherings, they are wondering how many people will come back and how they will be able to fund the programming and personnel costs of leading a church. That boulder is getting bigger.

The picture I've just painted of myself when I was a pastor might be construed as one of dedication and tireless commitment to a challenging calling. I've come to see it as a personal example of a crippling pride. Deeply ingrained somehow in me was the notion that I was responsible for every metric of the church. If something didn't go well, I felt responsible. If someone wasn't happy, I took it personally and mentally rehearsed how I should have responded differently.

Even when the metrics were good, the pride was still there. Frankly, I seldom felt any sense of accomplishment when things were good. It was more like relief. Still, who is the focus in this scenario? It's not God. It's me. Yes, there are some people who will make it all about you and either blame or praise depending on the performance. I listened way too much to those people and began to rely more on my gifts than the Giver.

The thought "I could have done more, and I could have done better" replayed in my head on a never-ending loop. More and better is a grace-less strategy that besets almost everyone, and it inevitably leads to disappointment, fear, anger, resentment, and self-pity. God never made me push a boulder uphill. I chose that, and it rendered me spiritually vulnerable. One Man gave His life for the church. God never asked me to be the second.

Early in my recovery, I learned that I needed to resign. "I resign" was literally my prayer and commitment. I resigned not from the pastorate. That wouldn't happen for a couple of years after treatment. I resigned from being in charge of my life and this world. I resigned from begin over-responsible for everyone else and from the control implicit in that prideful approach. I resigned from listening to what everyone else said about me and decided their opinion was not my concern. I resigned from concocting expectations of everyone and everything around me.

My morning prayers include the line "Help me remember throughout this day that You, not I, are in charge of my life and this world." I've learned a great deal about life and faith through my addiction and recovery that I didn't hear from a professor or read in a theology book. I learned acceptance. That has freed me to genuinely enjoy the good haps in my life and have a much healthier theology of suffering to handle the bad haps.

St. Ignatius taught his followers to be "indifferent." That sounds terribly off-putting, but if you know anything about St. Ignatius and The Society of Jesus he founded, you know that that they are very active in serving people. Discerning God's activity and responding to His prompting is the core of Ignatian spirituality. Indifference refers to fully accepting all circumstances and trusting that God is at work in them all, the good haps and the bad haps. The focus always is on God's character, providence, and power, not on your own abilities, performance, and poll numbers.

Understood in this way, acceptance is not resignation. It's trusting that God truly is at work in all circumstances. It's a powerful commitment to believing in God's providence. We accept with equal trust and hopefulness the good and bad circumstances, knowing that God is active at far deeper levels than the surface events themselves.

Many writers have suggested that attachment is the equivalent of addiction. Not everyone who reads this book or says The Prayer is addicted, but we are all attached to things that are simply not in our spiritual best interest. We cling to the attachments, believing that the object of the attachment will bring us serenity. The object may be wealth, pleasure, fame, or power. These are the four substitutes for God. Any attachment other than God will inevitably disappoint, and we'll find ourselves fighting with the world, trying to arrange it to suit our interests.

Reasonable happiness is detachment. It means putting down our fists and opening our hands. God won't put anything in a closed fist. Fists don't hold anything but fear, anger, resentment, and self-pity. Fists tightly close around these emotional and spiritual poisons. By contrast, open hands are ready to receive. When we open our hands, a personal, loving, and ever-present God gives us grace. In fact, you'll find that grace is what you really needed all along.

Grace truly is sufficient, as God taught Paul with his thorn. Always. When the hammer strikes, we turn to God first, not to our own feeble efforts to master of our fates, change people around us, or manipulate God. In His grace, God grants us the serenity to accept, and enables us to accept serenity.

Reasonable happiness, therefore, begins with the most unexpected irony. Acceptance is control.

Toward reasonable happiness:

- The fact that we can control a great deal of life creates the illusion that we can control all of life.
- No one is master of their own fate. We are limited.
- We can fight these limits, rail against them, complain about them, but at some point we have to accept limits if we are to be reasonably happy.

- God wants to help us in our limits, and He has made it very clear that He wants to hear our prayers for help.
- Acceptance in prayer enables us to enter "the rhythm of reversal" where the very thing that threatened to break us becomes the occasion for God's grace to strengthen us.
- Life is like a sine curve. It has ups and downs. Serenity is the straight line that runs through the sine curves. We don't struggle always to reach the high points of joy or try to bring up the low points of trouble. In serenity, we're connected to an unchanging God of love.

We can become "indifferent" to events in our lives, instead of being controlled by them, and let God lead us. We then find that acceptance is the most powerful means of control.

CHAPTER FOUR

COURAGE TO CHANGE THE THINGS I CAN

"Prove me O Lord and try me; test my heart and my mind."
Psalm 26:2

"Everyone thinks of changing the world, but no one thinks of changing himself."
Leo Tolstoy

The first phrase of The Prayer provides a huge relief, as we realize that we're not in charge of all the events and people in our lives. Personally, this was a great revelation for me. As a pastor, I had an exaggerated sense of responsibility for nearly everything. I see it now for what it was, an expression of pride. How delusional do you have to be to think that it's all up to you? That over-responsibility created a great deal of anxiety, for if someone wasn't happy with me or some aspect of the church (and someone is ALWAYS unhappy) then a significant part of me felt that I could or should do better. That's plainly ridiculous, but I could not see it when I was in the middle of it. It created in me a very spiritual vulnerability and was one of the pains I was trying to numb by drinking.

Learning about the need for and the depths of acceptance changed my perspective immediately. I humbly resigned as captain of my world and shifted that responsibility back to God. He is in control (more on that later). I felt as if I had been Atlas, carrying the weight of the world on my shoulders. I shrugged. The world fell away, and I didn't have to pick it up again. Like many of the greatest insights in life, this is a battle that doesn't stay won. I have to fight that tendency to take charge on a daily basis.

However, as we now move from the first phrase of The Prayer, we may have a mistaken impression that acceptance means giving up. It may sound like a call to retreat, to disengage, to give up. If God is in charge, then I'm just going to float along. The misperception of the first phrase is that we give up striving, seeking, and knocking.

"Am I just supposed to join a convent?" That's one of the objections I've heard. Those new to the prayer derisively talk of withdrawing from the world as the strategy of cloistered nuns and isolated hermits. When encountering this, I always offer a defense for the cloistered nuns, for we have no idea how much their prayers impact the world. But the question is a good one. What do we DO now if we have decided to simply accept the unchangeable things?

The second phrase of The Prayer is a powerful call to real and meaningful engagement. We don't have to be Atlas ever again. But the courage to change reminds us that reasonable happiness cannot be an isolated happiness.

A Word from the Author

No, not the author of this book. You're getting my words in pages and pages. I want to introduce the author of The Prayer, Reinhold Niebuhr (1892-1971). Niebuhr penned the first three lines of the prayer in 1934, though upon later reflection, he stated that he was influenced by earlier ideas and phrases that became the early version of The Prayer. It's undergone numerous edits over the decades and has appeared in numerous forms. The origins of the long version of The Prayer are even more obscure and elusive. Suffice it to say that The Prayer has been crowd sourced.

We do know a great deal about the man who is chiefly credited with the version as we have it most commonly today. Niebuhr was one of the most influential Christian ministers of the 20th century. Educated at Yale Divinity School, Niebuhr became a leading voice in the social justice movement of the time. He could be a very harsh critic of industrialism, capitalism, the church, ministers, and even socialism. Touring Europe after WW I led him to embrace pacifism, but the rise of Nazism led him back to a reluctant support of war when absolutely necessary. He did not view the war in Vietnam as necessary and marched in opposition to it.

The bent of his politics aside, this was a man of action. He believed in the power of the Gospel to change the hearts of people and the tides of society. He dedicated his life to change. Nothing about this man suggests that he meekly gave up in the face of injustices. He was called to be an agent of change, and he embraced that calling.

So how does this square with the call to acceptance? The second phrase of The Prayer articulates not just the necessary balance to acceptance but forces us to consider the target of change. While challenging public policies and social institutions requires courage and commitment, it is secondary to the more difficult challenge of looking in the mirror to change what we see there. That change requires even greater courage.

The Aim of the Change

One of our most natural impulses is to change our environment. This drive for security and comfort took us step by step from caves to houses with air-conditioning, hot tubs, and blow driers.

We're very adaptable and highly adept at altering our environment. Our success in controlling and changing every*thing* inevitably morphs into every*one*, and that is pure disaster.

My mother loved the movie *My Fair Lady*, and I remember as a child watching it and listening to the album. We'd sing the songs together. I actually liked Henry Higgins. Of course, Rex Harrison made that easy. He was such a contented and convincing bachelor, and when he sang/spoke "Let a Woman in Your Life" I would join in with gusto as he warned of the dangers of ever letting a woman in your life. "She'll redecorate your home from the cellar to the dome, and then go on to the enthralling job of overhauling you."

Higgins was not going to be controlled by any woman and tended to look askance at the entire gender. It's blatantly sexist, of course, and I suppose something of a wonder I grew up with a healthy view of woman. Only later did I realize that George Bernard Shaw, the author of *Pygmalion*, the play on which *My Fair Lady* is based, really delighted in portraying Higgins's complete lack of self-awareness. The good professor would trumpet his opposition to a woman trying to change him while at the same time trying to win a bet that he could take a "squashed cabbage leaf of a guttersnipe" and through language and etiquette lessons pass her off as nobility at an embassy ball. It's genuinely charming hypocrisy.

And it highlights one of our greatest blind spots. A healthy individual will and should resist at every turn attempts to be controlled. "You're not the boss of me!" is not just a childish exclamation. It's a lifelong creed for many of us. We don't want anyone trying to control or change us. At the same time, however, we will try to control and change the people around us, and usually the ones who are closest to us.

The reason, of course, is clear when you stop and think about it honestly. People carry around within them a certain dissatisfaction with themselves. They don't like where life has taken them, and at some very deep levels they recognize a certain personal responsibility for the path they're on. Sometimes this dissatisfaction can be as innocuous as disappointment over not being able to lose 10 pounds, speak a second language, or play the piano. Few of us can claim to be completely satisfied with who we are and what we're doing.

At its worst, this low-level dissatisfaction inflates to full-blown self-loathing. This is a common and somewhat surprising feature in addicts and alcoholics. Though they appear very defiant and full of denial about their problem and its effect on people around them, in the quiet moments of clarity they realize what they've become and how they're hurting other people. That realization, ironically and tragically, leads back to more dependence on a drug. The solution to this common problem lies in a healthy view of God, but that is a subject for another chapter.

The point here is that looking in the mirror is so very difficult that we tend to turn our attention outward. It's far easier to complain about other people and situations than go through the very difficult process of self-understanding and change. Critiquing someone else is much more comfortable than performing a personal inventory to try to understand who we are and why we act the way we do. Plus, the outward aim gives us a delicious sense of superiority.

Few people realize that Jesus employed humor in His teaching. One of the most memorable examples is in the Sermon on the Mount where He asked, "Why do you see the speck that is in your brother's eye but ignore the log that is in your own?" (Matt. 7:3). He said that with a smile, I'm guessing. Any audience will remember that visual image. People with little or no devotion to Jesus' teaching will quote the speck/log teaching.

Jesus was warning against our universal tendency to judge. Again, even secular people will condemn judging, though they, frankly like most Christians, don't understand the actual meaning of the teaching. Jesus certainly wasn't saying that we should not distinguish between good and bad. Only a few verses later, He spoke of a way that leads to life and a way that leads to destruction (Mt. 7:13-14). Right and wrong are real moral categories, not just cultural constructions.

The judging that Jesus condemned here is our tendency to be censorious. That is, we love to point out the wrongs of others and the unfairness of society without mercy. Ironically, we do this without a shred of the self-awareness that puts us in the same need of grace no matter how much or how little we've failed.

We've all known the sting of being censored. People who are severely critical grate on us with their faultfinding and carping. C. S. Lewis, as he often does, put it best in *Mere Christianity* where he wrote, "The sins of the flesh are bad, but they are the least bad of all sins. All the worst pleasures are purely spiritual: the pleasure of putting other people in the wrong, of bossing and patronizing and spoiling sport, and back-biting; the pleasures of power, of hatred. . . A cold self-righteous prig who goes regularly to church may be far nearer to hell than a prostitute. But, of course, it is better to be neither." (p. 95)

"Of course, it's better to be neither." I just love that, for it highlights the need to make moral distinctions while at the same time highlighting how much easier it is for me to be a blind self-righteous prig who points out the failings of the prostitute. This is the source of so much of the negative energy around any religion that is long on law and short on grace. It's the aim of the little boy's prayer, "God, please make all the bad people good, and all the good people nice."

Looking outward keeps us from looking inward. The sense of superiority we gain from it is false through and through. Like a drug that promises to take away our pain, the outward focus leaves a huge hangover we're constantly trying to ignore. It's called unhappiness. The only way to address it is to change the target of our high-powered analysis. We can never control another person, and we're inevitably frustrated by the effort. We have to turn to a more difficult task. We have to look within.

The Hula Hoop Principle

I haven't tried to hula hoop for years. I'm not sure I still can manage it successfully. Though I lack the practice, I am clear on the theory. It's a one-person show. I've never seen two people inside a hula hoop.

"Changing the things we can" draws on the hula hoop principle. You only focus on what's inside the hula hoop. God doesn't call you to change the world before He calls you to change within. Again, because that internal change is enormously more difficult, we turn the focus outward. At some point, however, we have to realize, to paraphrase Pogo, the enemy is us.

An aside here, God doesn't ever ask you to change the world. Ever. He invites you to become part of what He's doing in the world. This distinction is very important. To take on the mantle of changing the world personally is to invite the hard fall that comes after pride. We run ahead of God, always an exhausting and dangerous place to be. I speak from personal experience.

God offers Himself as the Chief Diagnostician in this effort to look more deeply into the mirror. He helps us discern ourselves, to look within and see what shadows need to be illuminated. The psalmist shows us the way: "Search me, O God, and know my heart. Try me and know my thoughts. And see if there be any wicked way in me, and lead me in the way everlasting" (Psalm 139:23-24). This is a courageous prayer. You're inviting God to come into the deepest parts of your heart and mind and take a look around. Don't pray it lightly.

This holy scrutiny is an often-overlooked work of the Holy Spirit. Jesus described the Spirit as the Comforter or Counselor who resides within us. The Spirit reminds us of the teaching of Jesus and provides the assurance of God's very presence within us (see John 14). These are powerfully comforting truths.

But Jesus also described the Comforter as the Spirit of truth (John 14:17). That too is comforting until we realize the lies we often live, the little ones and big ones. These are the self-perceptions we all have that convince us that we've done everything right and the other person has wronged us. It's the outward focus that prevents us from seeing our role in our ruptured relationships. Truth is a direct challenge to lies, and we all live in certain lies about ourselves.

On the same evening as the previous teaching, Jesus later added that the Holy Spirit will come and convince the world of "sin, and righteousness, and judgment." The Greek word for "convince" is *elegko,* a rather difficult word to precisely translate. It has the meaning of rebuke, convict, admonish, and to point out a fault. It can even be used to indicate shame. This sounds very uncomfortable. In our hands, this word is deadly, for we inevitably end up condemning with only the aim of condemnation. In God's hands, the word means that He helps us see where we can invite His grace more deeply into our souls.

We've all felt God's impact in this role in our consciences. The Spirit whispers to us words of comfort and words of warning. When we are right and selfless and helpful, we feel a soul-deep satisfaction. When we are wrong, self-centered, and hurtful, we initially feel something is incongruent. God created our souls to resonate with Him, and when we are off track, *something* feels wrong. Interestingly, if we continue with the wrong long enough it ceases to feel wrong. Then we become genuinely dangerous creatures.

Along these same lines, Paul wrote in Philippians that we are to have "the mind of Christ" (Phil 2:5). It's the same idea with a different person of the Trinity. We can think more and more like Christ. Again, the idea of resonance applies. Our thoughts become one with Christ. We see God, ourselves, others, and the world through the mind and eyes of Christ.

If this remarkable reality is to be ours, then obviously things have to change within us. We have to allow God to rid us of our shadows. When we begin this process of discovery, we might not even be aware of our shadows. That's why it's so uncomfortable to even consider the possibility that they exist. But we'll never see the light until we get rid of the darkness.

Wrongs, Defects of Character, and Shortcomings

One of my earliest, foggy impressions of entering treatment for alcoholism is that they certainly talked a lot about what was wrong with me, and not just the alcoholism. Counselors and fellow patients challenged me to see what was wrong *in* me. Repeatedly. Anyone familiar with the 12 Steps is bound to take notice of the emphasis on wrongs, defects of character, and shortcomings. We're supposed to identify them and ask God to take them away.

Like most everyone in early recovery, this emphasis on what's wrong inside seemed to me misguided. I drank too much. That's the problem. So how do I stop drinking so much? The answer through the program that has saved millions is, "you have to look deeply inside and figure out the reasons you drank so much." They wanted to talk about my vices. I wanted to highlight my virtues.

It took a little while, but I soon realized that my virtues were not the reason I was drinking myself to death. My vices gave rise to the spiritual vacuum that my alcoholism filled. Only by identifying those underlying spiritual vulnerabilities would I be able to turn from alcohol and back to God.

This process of brutal self-analysis and completely honest ownership of every aspect of life is not limited to people in recovery from addiction. Everyone is in recovery, because everyone has underlying spiritual vulnerabilities that lead to overt wrongs, defects of character, and shortcomings. Everyone. Until we learn to control, with God's essential help, the inner sinful inclinations, we'll not become the children of God we were created to be.

A word about the word "sin." It's off-putting to many people and should make everyone at least a bit uncomfortable because it hits close to home. Many people today treat it as obsolete and regressive, a trend that began in the 20th century and is treated with finality by many people today who believe it to be an impediment to their lives. Can the word "sin" be used as a club to threaten, intimidate, and condemn other people? Of course! And water can be used to drown, but we don't ever think about getting rid of water.

Interestingly, even as psychology exiled the word, some of the leading voices in that field argued for understanding and retaining it. Karl Menninger famously authored *Whatever Became of Sin?* and was essentially trying to revive that old religious word to describe the problems we face. Personal guilt and sin are too often glossed over in our rush to blame social or genetic factors. He wrote, "There is sin…which cannot be buried under verbal artifacts such as disease, delinquency, or deviancy. There is immorality. There is unethical behavior. There is wrongdoing." His concern in 1973 was that the sense of personal moral responsibility was faint and growing fainter. He predicted that if people would confront sin in their lives, the result would be less depression, not more.

Hobart Mower served as president of the American Psychological Association in 1954. In 1960 he wrote, "For several decades we psychologists looked upon the whole matter of sin and moral accountability as a great incubus and acclaimed our liberation from it as epoch making. But at length we have discovered that to be free in this sense, that is, to have the excuse of being sick rather than sinful, is to court the danger of also becoming lost... In becoming amoral, ethically neutral and free, we have cut the very roots of our being, lost our deepest sense of selfhood and identity, and with neurotics, themselves, we find ourselves asking: Who am I, what is my deepest destiny, what does living mean?" ("Sin, the Lesser of Two Evils," American Psychologist, 15 (1960): 301-304).

Sin, without question, is one of the chief and most overlooked reasons for our unhappiness, let alone our spiritual peril. We can't be reasonably happy if we're spiritually handicapped by these obstacles. Sin at its base is not the overt action but the underlying bent. Our common mistake is to look solely at the overt action, and absent that assume that we're in great shape. Yet we remain unhappy and wonder why.

In the Sermon on the Mount, Jesus addressed this very tendency. He would name an overt sin and then dig underneath it to reveal its source. For example, most of us, I hope, could say "I've never murdered" and mentally check off that commandment as fulfilled. But Jesus took us deeper to the levels of hatred, anger, and resentment where we all struggle (Matt. 5:21-22). He was trying to alert us to the fact that we can avoid the overt and ignore the covert.

The greatest spiritual men and women have been trying to tell us this consistently for thousands of years, but we seem to have to rediscover it personally in every age. The overt sins are sometimes gross and obvious and reel down the middle of the street shouting obscenities. Those are easy to identify and condemn, and we do enjoy condemning for it shifts the focus away from us. The sins that lie quietly in a heap on the sidewalk are more numerous, though and cause more damage.

Some years ago, I wrote an article about the frequent virtue and vice lists scattered throughout the New Testament. The most famous of these would be the works of the flesh and the fruit of the Spirit (Gal. 5:19-23). I researched Greek moral philosophers that pre-date the writing of the New Testament. I found it fascinating that they too had those kinds of lists, and much more extensive actually than the New Testament. What I found even more interesting is that the virtue lists, while longer than those found in the New Testament, paled in comparison to the lists of vices that sometimes filled pages of the Greek writers' works.

The writers of the New Testament, following the lead of Jesus, did a better job of getting at the root of the problem. They employ a dozen or more Greek words that can be translated as "sin," but we read as trespasses, wickedness, depravity, ungodliness, etc. These are the inner tendencies that lead to the visible transgression.

The point is that anyone who gives careful consideration to the matter realizes that we have a spiritual problem that manifests itself in a myriad of overt and covert vices. We exert a great amount of energy, hopefully, in avoiding the overt actions. That's good and necessary. But if we stop there, we're clipping the branches and leaving the root. Also, for the purposes of this book, it is the roots that give rise to a great deal of unhappiness.

Why devote so much space to sin? The writers of Scripture clearly are very much interested in the inner spiritual state of a person, and not merely the outward conformity to a law or standard. Additionally, the word "sin" is not a bad word. It's merely a truth to which we must pay close attention. Ignoring sins, or if you prefer wrongs, defects of character, and shortcomings, imperils our ability to see and hear God. And if we can't see and hear God, then we have no chance of being reasonably happy. Just like my discovery in treatment for alcoholism, it's not your virtues that cause you problems. You have to look within and find the fault-lines of the inner life.

Looking with Grace

THE greatest misperception about looking within to discover the wrongs, defects of character, and shortcomings is that we're going to feel terrible about ourselves if we do. This common misunderstanding feeds into the idea of God as perennially aggrieved and unhappy with us. Who would want to draw near to that kind of God? That would only leave us feeling condemned and ashamed. In fact, if you're not going to go about this in the right way then I'm not sure it's wise to go about it at all.

Grace is the key. Grace is God's love in action. It is the fundamental predisposition of God to accept, forgive, and recreate each one of us. Grace is God's nature, and it truly is amazing. I wrote this particular section on Good Friday after having spent an early devotion reading the Old Testament prophecies and the New Testament accounts of Jesus' trial and death. What stands out in these readings more than anything is that Jesus did this because He loved us. He was willing to do anything possible to open up the way for us to return to our Creator and allow our Creator to recreate us.

The root word for "grace" in Greek is the same root from which we get the word "gift," and that highlights its source. God is the giver of grace. We don't manufacture it. In fact, we don't have to DO anything or that would negate the power of grace and turn it upside down. All we have to do is receive it by turning to God with our honest need for it and engage in the practices that open our souls to it.

It helps, of course, to have a healthy view of God, which unfortunately is difficult to do with all of the bad theological noise out there. We love to project our prejudices on God. We view Him as harsh and condemning, not because He is, but because we are. We unknowingly make an idol out of our worst fears and hatreds and then reject it without ever encountering the true God of grace.

Charles Cooley, a renowned sociologist in the early 20th century, came up with The Looking Glass Theory, which suggests that we gain our sense of self from the perceptions of those around us. If our parents are loving and approving of us, then we have a much better chance of developing a healthy view of ourselves. Conversely, if the significant people in our lives are condemning and disapproving, then it's very difficult for us to feel a sense of personal worth and acceptance.

I've found this theory to be especially useful in our thinking about God. If you view God as harsh and condemning, then you are going to feel disappointed in yourself. Again, if that's your god, then you are going to have a very hard time looking within because you're already sure of what you're going to find. It's bad, and you have no way of addressing the problems you uncover.

If, however, you accept God's radical acceptance of you, then you can draw near Him without fear. You have a way to handle the worst that is in you, and that is to put it in God's merciful and gracious hands. I truly wish you could read the following words as if God speaks them directly to you: "Do not be afraid, for I have redeemed you. I have called you by name. You are mine" (Isaiah 43:1). Here is the Great Discovery: God does speak them directly to you. With the God of grace, redemption precedes righteousness. We don't have to be good enough to come to God. We just have to come.

I'm convinced one reason people retain an image of a god of war and thunder is because that's a god that easy to stay away from, and if you stay away from that god, you never have to change anything. If God is truly on our side, however, then we can go to Him without fear. Perhaps we'll have some discomfort. Change is usually uncomfortable. That's where the courage phrase of The Prayer comes in. We turn from our fears and come before a God who is always ready to welcome us home. With His help we have a remarkable opportunity to embrace the changes we need to make.

Perspective: The Fundamental Change

Hopefully, we've now established two firm foundations that can lead us to reasonable happiness. First, that we must learn the deeply spiritual discipline of acceptance. There's a real limit to what we can change and most of us need to rein in our limits. Second, there are some things we're expected to change, but not on our own or in our own strength. The first phrase of The Prayer, "God grant me," applies here also. We ask God's help and rely on His guidance and strength to make changes within our hula hoop.

The most important change is perspective. Perspective is the lens through which we see the world, ourselves, and other people. We all carry with us some preconceptions and prior decisions that determine how we see the world. We have to be willing to take a look at everything about those lenses to see what we need to hold onto and what we need to let go of.

St. Paul had to go through this change of perspective. Recall that he was a Pharisee, and actually a very accomplished Pharisee. He had studied the law under Gamaliel, one of the great rabbinic names in Jewish history. His track record as an enforcer is well known. He was a fan of neither Christians nor Gentiles. Yet he became the Apostle to the Gentiles. How?

He writes of his transformation in 2 Corinthians 5, "From now on, therefore, we regard no one from a human point of view (literally a flesh point of view). Though we once regarded Christ that way, we regard Him thus no longer." At the height of his Phariseeism, Paul regarded Jesus as nothing more than a charlatan who deservingly died a humiliating death on a cross. We have no hard evidence of this, but I have to believe that prior to his encounter with Jesus on the Road to Damascus, Paul must have been giving Jesus a second look. God is not in the habit of kicking down doors. Perhaps when Paul cracked open the door of his mind and heart, the Light flooded in, blinded him and then freed him. He certainly was changed forever.

Our change in perspective may be less dramatic but no less impactful. If we can conceive of ourselves as beloved sons and daughters of an engaged and powerful God, then we can become aware of God's presence and providence. Before this change, we wrestled with the world, trying to control and then growing angry or despairing when people and things don't cooperate with our plans and wishes. With a new perspective, we see that God truly is in control and our greatest need is to trust Him. This change enables us to choose a wise, trusting, and helpful response to all the unalterable events in our lives.

Without a change in perspective, we have no chance for happiness, for we're at the mercy of every change in the wind. A screaming world combined with our disjointed and overwrought emotional responses creates a jumbled background of noise that prevents us from seeing, hearing, and relying on God. Perspective enables us to see what we overlooked, to listen to what we should be hearing, and to feel what we should be feeling.

Perspective is the fundamental spiritual change that enables all the other changes we can make. It must be intentional, and it must be reclaimed and nurtured every day through prayer and stillness before God. It is a huge soul-shift that turns all of our spiritual attention to God and enables everything else.

So, what are the other changes we can make? There are as many changes as there are virtues. I'm going to list and briefly look at three: forgiveness, gratitude, and trust. Each one constitutes a subject for an entire book, and I don't claim the list is either exhaustive or necessarily agreed upon by a group of clergy members or spiritual writers. The list does represent my personal struggles and my observations of others over a lengthy career as a pastor. They also represent some of the most common struggles people face in early recovery from addiction, which simply magnifies the challenges common to all people.

Whatever you think of my list, I hope you'll agree that it's a very good place to start, for it address the three times of life: past, present, and future. I'll address each one in more detail later in this book, but for now I'll provide a few brief comments on each. I want to note in particular how we resist each one, how our resistance correlates directly to our need for it, and how perspective helps us grow in each of these graces.

Forgiveness

Forgiveness focuses on the chains that have bound us to something in the past. Whether we realize it or not, we tend to drag with us a lot of hurt, resentment, hatred, guilt, and shame. You may prefer to think of these as burdens we carry. That's a useful image because one of the Greek words in the New Testament for forgiveness literally means to "lay aside" or "bear away" as in letting go of or removing a burden. Instead of carrying these caustic spiritual emotions around with you, lay them aside. That's a much lighter way to walk, and dramatically increases the potential for reasonable happiness.

We can think of the need for forgiveness as vertical and horizontal. Vertical refers to our need for forgiveness from God. Having touched on this briefly already, I won't spend a great deal of time on it. Suffice it to say that grace means we are forgiven, A-Z. Nothing is beyond God's earnest desire to forgive us of every wrong we've ever committed. The cross stands as a powerful reminder of how far God was willing to go to secure our forgiveness.

The horizontal dimension of forgiveness refers to our need to be forgiving of the people around us, past and present. Generally, people are much more open to the idea that they are forgiven by God than the idea that they need to be forgiving of people. That's why Jesus connected both the vertical and horizontal in the Lord's Prayer. We ask God to forgive us (vertical) as we forgive others (horizontal).

The two axes of forgiveness also provide a clue as to how we resist each one. Vertically, we may think our past is to some degree unforgiveable which inevitably produces a fear of God and a desire to avoid Him at all costs. So, we resist forgiveness by simply removing it is a possibility.

Horizontally, we consider some sins against us as unforgiveable. We hold grudges, and we hold grudges with great gusto. A friend once confessed that he "liked the taste of resentments." In a perverse way, they do feel good for they make us feel superior, and they distract us from the changes we can make in ourselves, which is the point. The false ego, the one that is unredeemed and hopelessly self-centered, always loves the taste of resentment.

Our new perspective helps us both vertically and horizontally. Vertically, we have to change our thinking about God. If we retain the idea of a god of war and thunder, then we're liable to forever feel unforgiven. Who wants to get near a storm?

But if we simply accept as true the fact that Jesus secured forgiveness for us all on the cross, then we have the opportunity to let go of the guilt and let God bear it away. A great misconception about forgiveness is that God withholds it until we either ask in the right way or do enough to earn it. The truth is forgiveness is a settled question. It's a known value in the equation. The variable is our willingness to accept it.

We are not better judges of ourselves than God. Ironically, many people who struggle with forgiveness tend to think of God as harsh when in fact it is they themselves who withhold grace by tightly clinging to a dark past. God can bear away only what we're willing to release. He's already paid the price or opened the door, or any other image you want to use.

In some Christian traditions, when you receive the bread and the cup to the minister or priest will say "the body of Christ for you" and "the blood of Christ for you." These are reminders of what Jesus promised at the Last Supper and what He accomplished on the cross. The most moral among us and the most immoral among us stand in need of this grace, and God offers forgiveness to all who come. This is why we call grace amazing. It doesn't make sense, and it doesn't need to for anyone to trust in its effectiveness.

Addiction wrecks so many lives because it is so very graceless. In active addiction, we deeply hurt ourselves and the people around us. In early recovery, the awful dawning realization of this produces a load of self-loathing. Many people feel a guilt they're sure will never go away. I've had the opportunity to help some change their perspective on God. What a blessing it is to watch them realize that God forgives them. They still have a great deal of work to do to make amends to people they've hurt and establish a new life, but receiving this grace from God makes all things possible.

Having received forgiveness, we turn to the more difficult horizontal task of forgiving. Our new perspective of God's grace should help, but an honest survey of your personal resentments will reveal how reluctant you've been to share the grace you've been given. We are great defenders of our resentments, not realizing how hypocritical we are to accept from God what we are unwilling to share with others.

Jesus told a parable about the unforgiving servant who was forgiven a huge debt by his master only to press charges against a fellow servant who owed him a relative pittance (Matt. 18:23-35). The story is clear, and the meaning is obvious. But at the end of the day, we prefer to go to bed with our resentments intact.

I was leading a Bible study at a church in Mississippi one time and the topic of forgiveness came up. I handled it pretty much in the same way I've outlined in these previous few paragraphs. During a break, a man came up to me and told me about his daughter who had been murdered some years before. He explained that two men had been convicted of her murder and were serving life sentences. Tears welled up in his eyes as he said, "I've forgiven those two men." The tears told me that his forgiveness was both genuine and difficult, and forgiveness is always both.

I struggle with resentments, and I think I'm not alone here. The mention, or even the thought, of a name from an increasingly distant past can awaken in me incredibly strong and negative spiritual emotions. I can still think with a stunning freshness of what I should have said or should have done. I've prayed over these repeatedly, and it helps.

Not long ago, I was struggling in prayer with some of those resentments again. I found myself rehearsing the grievance, and I realized with a fresh insight that I was the only person on the planet struggling with this right now. No one else really cares, and no one else could do anything about it. Then the words came to mind, prompted I'm sure by God, "You can just forgive them." I knew that, but for some reason it just made sense in a new way. So, I said the words about each name I was struggling with at the time. In succeeding days, whenever a dark memory surfaced, I said the words, and my happiness increased.

I let go of some chains that day and in the days afterward. I laid aside some burdens. Now without question some of these battles just don't stay won, so I have to repeat the words again. That's all right. I'm not God, and sometimes I'm just a slow learner.

And some of these battles are harder to fight than others. Some people have been hurt in unspeakable ways. No one should rush in with "you need to forgive!" Deep hurts take time to heal.

The Greek language has a second word for forgiveness, and it may help for the tragically wounded. The word is *charizomai*, and it comes from the Greek word for grace. God "graces" us when He forgives us. We "grace" others when we forgive them.

To grace someone means to unconditionally bestow a favor. This idea is especially useful when the offender is not willing to confess or interested in being forgiven. Because grace is so thoroughly divine, we need God's help in offering it. So, with God you just give grace. You become a conduit of God's grace. Let it flow through you. Your offender may still bear their own guilt, but through grace you can let go of your end of the chain. You're a little freer from your past. That too will increase your happiness.

Gratitude

Of the three graces I'm reviewing here, gratitude is the easiest change to make and offers the most immediate returns. If you're having a bad day, begin to think of gratitude. Inevitably, that will shift your focus from whoever or whatever is bothering you to who or whatever is blessing you. Gratitude has turned around so many days for me, and I've watched its impact on others. As accessible, useful, and powerful as gratitude is, it's amazing how much we resist it.

A young woman called me one time and began rehearsing a familiar litany of complaints. There literally was nothing new in her situation. Every account she related was simply the latest grievance of a well-established pattern of relationships and way of looking at her life and her world.

I interrupted her and said, "What are you thankful for right now?" She was silent for a moment and then stammered "What?" I repeated the question, then added "I want you to tell me 10 things you're thankful for right now." I was very insistent, probably because I was a little tired of hearing some new facet of the same old complaints.

She started, and I don't recall exactly what she said. Something about her children, her health, etc. She laughed a bit about one or two of the items on her list, enjoying recalling the event or person that brought her a good memory. I do remember precisely though that we got to number five and that was it. She'd had enough and wanted to return to her litany of complaints.

To some degree, she couldn't help it because complaint had become such a habit in her life. She didn't realize that she still had the potential to change but needed courage to do it. She wasn't ready, at least not enough to make the entire shift. I don't know if she ever did.

We're generally more comfortable with complaint and criticism and seldom realize how deeply they've become entrenched in our lives. It takes a sustained commitment to suppress and hopefully eliminate them from our minds. Ironically, the complaining that gives us a perverse pleasure also eliminates the potential for reasonable happiness.

Each of the three graces has a polar opposite. The polar opposite of forgiveness is resentment. The polar opposite of gratitude is self-pity. No one wants to be accused of having self-pity. It sounds, well, pitiful. It is, and we don't realize how pitiful we sound when we make complaint and criticism a habit.

The key to understanding the danger of self-pity is in the first word: self. When we complain and criticize, we focus on ourselves. We may object that the focus is on our complaint, but in reality the focus truly is on our response to the object of our complaint. We're unhappy when we complain. We're hurt, or outraged, or disgusted when we complain. Those are real emotions with genuine impact, but the problem is with our focus and perspective.

We complain about a boss, a spouse, finances, politics, etc. and can do literally *nothing* to change any of them. In chronic complaining, all we've done is demonstrate our ongoing victimization and unwillingness to change. Again, most of us don't even realize how self-centered and unproductive complaining is.

I've long enjoyed the story of Catherine Marshall's personal struggle with self-pity and criticism. It illustrates beautifully how we all struggle with the courage to change.

She had developed a long-standing habit of being critical of others, but after reading Romans 14:13, "So don't criticize each other," she became aware of the Lord nudging her not to be critical for one day. She became aware of what she needed to change.

Her initial response to the challenge was very predictable. She tried to rationalize her criticisms as a God-given gift of analyzing and evaluating, but she soon had to admit to the hard edge of most of her evaluations. Our ego will defend every wrong, defect of character, and shortcoming that we have. We fear that if we don't have them, then we'll in a sense disappear or become irrelevant. We see at this point her "self" trying to reassert itself. But she decided to give the experiment a solid effort.

Lunch with her husband and friends was normal except for the unusual silence of one person, Catherine. She had not committed to silence, only to not be critical. She was surprised, however, how often her usual conversation was critical and judgmental. She was silent only because she couldn't contribute to the conversation without judging.

"It was midafternoon that something wonderful began to happen. The floodgate of ideas began to open and creative thoughts flowed through her in a way she hadn't experienced in a very long time. By day's end she marveled at all that had transpired simply because she refused to entertain a critical attitude. A letter to encourage a friend, insight into praying for a college student, seeking her child's forgiveness, all filtered through her freely because there were no negative thoughts to stop them. With God's help through the gift of self-control she was able to resist the temptation she had succumbed to for years. Her one-day experiment became a lifetime habit. [*Stories for the Heart*, p. 73]

Gratitude is awareness. It connects God's direct action with our present experience. In self-pity, we complain because we can't control. In gratitude, we recognize Who is really in control and become grateful for the countless ways God has worked grace into our lives.

Do you see the shift? Self-pity attempts to get people to agree with us, to be impressed with our critiques, or most often to feel sorry for us in our plight. Self-pity ascribes an unalterable power to something external to you. Gratitude shifts the focus away from self to God. In another one of those spiritual reversals, what we think initially will undo us (i.e. letting go of our chronicle of complaint) actually recreates us.

Combatting complaint through gratitude immediately returns a dividend of reasonable happiness. Of course, not everything is going well in our lives. In fact, there are times when the world seems to be bucking and shifting under our feet, as in a shelter-in-place order during a pandemic. But God never leaves us without many, many more things to be grateful for. Finding those things is just a matter of perspective, and that change leads to reasonable happiness.

Trust

I like to conduct informal surveys, and one that I've repeatedly used over the years is to ask an audience if they struggle more with the past or the future. Probably 75% say they struggle more with the future. This may be because people are generally more forgiving of themselves and less likely to dwell on past mistakes and guilt. I'd like to think they've embraced forgiveness, which as I mentioned above, focuses on dealing with the past. The future, however, is for many people a truly terrifying unknown.

I'm sure that's why an entire line of The Prayer focuses on the need for trust (Trusting You to make all things right). We're an anxious people. Fear is a fundamental response, and nothing is more fearful than an unknown future. Trust, therefore, is an essential response and one of the most important things we can change.

None of the changes we can make are easy. That's why we ask God for the courage to change the things we can. Of the four changes that I've noted in this chapter, however, trusting God is the most challenging. A change of perspective means looking at people and events around you with a different set of eyes. Forgiveness means dealing with a painful personal past or a painful person in the present. Gratitude means looking mostly at the present to note the ways in which God is taking care of you. Notice that each one of these deals with things that have already happened or things that are happening.

Trust focuses on something that has not taken place. We don't know what is going to happen, and we excel at envisioning the worst. This pervasive human tendency is to some degree a survival skill. I've had more than one person tell me they have to envision the worst so they can plan for it. I'm not quite at that level, but I struggle with anxiety. I worry. It's much better than it used to be, but only because I've recognized three important errors in my worried thinking and try each day to change. I'm not alone in these three errors.

First, we ignore the fact that the worst almost NEVER occurs. The old saying is that "99% of the things you worry about never happen." I think that's an underestimate by a large margin. We worry about so many things, yet somehow make it through each day for seventy, eighty or more years. The fact is, we devote a tremendous amount of energy to running from paper tigers.

Second, while fear may be a fundamental and primal response, maturity means reining in unwise and destructive primal drives and instincts. Only the most base and depraved person would suggest that promiscuity is normal because it's a primal instinct to have sex. We rein in the primal drive because God has shown us how best to use this instinct. Yet how easily we allow anxiety to become a constant and even defended companion.

Third, worry is the most common way we edge God out. Worry, at its base, is self-focused, for we assume that we have to change things for a more pleasant future. We believe at some level we're in charge of our lives and our world. We're saying we don't trust God to take care of us.

Let's take a very common example: money. Money is a great indicator of spiritual values and practices. Money is not bad. The Scripture says the love of money is (1 Tim. 6:10). Money is simply powerful. We can use its power, or energy, for good or ill.

Because of its power, we tend to think of money as the chief way we can control our lives. Few of us think we have enough money, and we're convinced that if we had even a little bit more money, then we'd be happy. In other words, we could either pay our bills or buy something we've always wanted or, more commonly, simply not worry about money at all.

Sociologists tell us that we do need a certain level of income to take care of basic living expenses, and it's a fairly low and attainable number. Beyond that, they note absolutely no correlation between higher incomes and more happiness.

That's because most people live at about 105% or more of their income, and it doesn't matter what the income is. Anyone can understand the concepts of needs and wants, but we are constantly expanding our wants and shifting them over to needs (a function of highly effective marketing). So, we convince ourselves that we *need* far more then we really do. Combine this with the fact that we can access far too much credit and we have a recipe for disaster that we read about in every article about per capita debt, student loans, bloated mortgages, and personal savings. It's an alarming spiritual problem. We're chasing happiness with money and losing the race. The result is a tremendous amount of unhappiness, the root of which is a skewed view of money.

What is our solution? Get more money! But unless we change the 105% (or more) rule then it doesn't matter how much we make.

Here's the choice I propose: You can either have more money OR you can have complete peace of mind about money. Which would you take?

Nearly everyone would take the money because they believe that would give them peace of mind. But it doesn't, or at least not for long. Tolerance is a common concept in drug addiction. It's the idea that you constantly have to have more of the drug in order to get the same high. The fact is, eventually no amount of the drug actually gives you a high. People end up taking more and more of the drug simply to feel some degree of normalcy. The same is true of money. If we don't make the internal spiritual changes that drive our craving for money, no amount is going to bring us happiness.

Genuine trust needs to be 100%. If you come up against a situation where you struggle with trust, that means that everything up to that point has been theory, or perhaps practice. Every challenge, even with money, is a challenge to trust God to take care of you. Anything short of full trust is an effort to control, and control is the antimatter to trust. Complete trust cannot coexist with any degree of control.

Fortunately, grace operates in this arena as well, for none of us trusts completely. We must not, however, use the excuse that we're not perfect as a reason not to embrace progress. God will use the anxiety you feel in any area of life as a call to trust Him more deeply. Thankfully, He always works with whatever we can bring to Him.

The internal shift and commitment to finally and completely trust God is a huge thing that we can change. The challenge to trust God with your finances is simply one of the clearest and most evident ways to see how deeply we actually do trust God. Relationships, particularly with family members and even more so especially with children, is another. Serenity in any area of life is in the direct proportion to the degree we let go and trust God more.

Courage to Change

I occasionally hear people criticize The Prayer for its apparent impassivity. Serenity, because it's connected to acceptance, sounds apathetic. Especially in our culture where we encourage strength, taking on the world, and even changing the world, The Prayer sounds remarkably naïve and obsolete.

I think anything of deep and abiding spirituality must be seen as out of step with our acquisitive culture. The fact that The Prayer sounds strange and dissonant means it has something eternal to offer. Our culture, for all its bluster and bravado, is actually rife with fear and anger. The effort to change things around us is a futile attempt to live in our own strength.

Until we gain control of our own choices and then make the fundamental choice to walk with God in every detail of life, we're going to be unhappy but unaware of the reason why. Jesus said if we are to follow Him, we must deny ourselves and take up our crosses. The denial of self is simply the courage to change our inner direction. We are called to be salt, and light in the world. These are genuine agents of change. But if we try to dash ahead of God we will fall.

I'm very sure that is one of the keys to my personal spiritual vacuum that I tried to fill with alcohol. Even though I was, in a sense, contractually obligated to be spiritual and reliant upon God, I had become over-responsible. I was like Elijah who, after defeating the prophets of Baal, ran ahead of God and became exhausted and downcast. I needed to make some changes within, and The Prayer showed the way.

Perspective. Forgiveness. Gratitude. Trust. These powerful graces provide a completely different way of viewing the world and our own reflection in the mirror. They are extraordinarily hard to cultivate. That's why this phrase of The Prayer begins with courage. These are the battles that don't stay won, but it's time to have the courage to start fighting again.

Toward reasonable happiness:

- The Serenity Prayer is NOT a call to give up trying. We are still to ask, seek, and knock.
- Instead of focusing on trying to control and change people and events around us, we are to focus on what God wants to change in us.
- Our reluctance to look within is the result of self-loathing. We fear to confront the worst in us. Instead, we focus on the faults of the world and those around us.
- The Bible uses the word sin to describe the wrongs, defects of character, and shortcomings we all have. Our problems at their root are spiritual in nature and can only be addressed by God.
- Grace is God's love in action. It is a gift that we receive by drawing close to Him.
- Perspective is the most important internal change we can make. If view ourselves as beloved sons or daughters of God then we have the spiritual temperament that enables us to draw close to Him.

Our willingness to forgive others, our decision to be grateful to God, and our commitment to trust in God are three powerful changes we can make. These are soul-shaping changes.

CHAPTER FIVE

WISDOM TO KNOW THE DIFFERENCE

"If you lack wisdom, ask God, who gives to all men generously and without reproaching, and wisdom will be given to him."
James 1:5

"The pessimist complains about the world; the optimist expects it to change; the realist adjusts the sails."
William Arthur Ward

This third line draws to a conclusion The Prayer as it is most often prayed. In many ways it is the most difficult of the first three lines. We may struggle to implement acceptance, but at least we can grasp the concept. Changing the things we can works more into our wheelhouse of wanting to take action and change, even though we have to make some huge soul-shifts in understanding the changes for which we're actually responsible.

Knowing the difference is the ongoing challenge. It is the practice of the theories in the first two lines. The Prayer has an immediate appeal, but when we turn our eyes from heaven to look back on our spouses, children, jobs, finances, health, pandemics, etc., how do we draw the lines? Frustration with implementation is the most common reason people give up on The Prayer in particular or even prayer in general.

No genuine spirituality comes easily, and in our Keurig-culture of individual tastes and quick results, we're not willing to wait around for something to work quietly and slowly. Unfortunately, that means a new spiritual insight or practice works for about two months before people want to move on. Hopes are high that the COVID crisis, especially with the enforced Sabbath it has created, will have lasting benefits spiritually. I genuinely hope so, but the past does not engender confidence. I was a pastor during 9/11, and what we hoped would be a lasting spiritual revival turned out to be a two-week bump in attendance.

The Prayer is not just a door of discovery. It is a path that must be walked with patience and perseverance. If you're struggling with imperfect decisions about what you must accept and what you can change, then simply keep walking with the rest of us limping saints. We all struggle.

Remember, the choice is not between despair and ecstasy. We're not built for enduring ecstasy. The pursuit of that kind of perfectionism is the enemy of our goal. The real choice is between chronic disappointment and reasonable happiness. The latter is very attainable if we cultivate some basic spiritual virtues and disciplines, and for that we need wisdom.

Can't Do Anything About Somali Pirates

Leo Honeycutt was a newsman for the bulk of his early career, though our friendship began in his second career as an author. Both professions require a deep and abiding curiosity about people, events, and the world in general. Leo has a naturally thoughtful mien, as if he's always looking for a story that he can research and understand.

Back in the days before cable television overwhelmed us with choices and watered down much of the content, Leo hosted a very successful and highly acclaimed local morning show. 4 a.m. mornings were the norm for some 15 years before he left that high profile career in his mid-40's. He exchanged the energy and lights of that particular form of media for long hours of eye-blurring research in library stacks and staring at micro-fiche readers.

I asked him recently what led him to make the change. His answer was thought-provoking and revealing but knowing him now, it did not surprise me. In the frenzy to attract ratings, his editors wanted him to highlight the dark side of society, and if the story wasn't dark enough, to dramatize it. They encouraged the staff to skewer politicians, paint the rich as greedy opportunists, those kinds of things.

He got to the point that he simply couldn't maintain his journalistic integrity in that kind of environment. In our conversation, he summed up his feelings at the time in this way, "I was not going to report on the 10% that was bad and represent it as 90% of real life." He added, "I felt the Lord leading me to do something where I wasn't making people feel discouraged."

That impressive spiritual decision took place long before I met him, but it also set up a later comment that caught my attention. I was teaching a class in church along the lines of worry and our need to focus on God. Though it wasn't the specific topic, I essentially was trying to make the point of the first few lines of The Serenity Prayer about not overreacting to every event and to choose our responses. With that ever-present thoughtful and inquisitive look, he offered that he'd come to an important insight during the period when piracy was a regular problem along some of the most vital shipping lanes in the world. The nightly stories aggravated him until "I realized I couldn't do anything about Somali pirates."

In a variety of ways, most people allow Somali pirates, or their like, to hijack their serenity. Genuinely review what has upset you in the last few days and you're likely to discover that you can't change a single one of the things that gave rise to your agitation. The fact is, you've been conditioned to forfeit your right to reasonable happiness. Reclaiming the right and power to make different decisions requires wisdom.

Two Boxes

Before nearly everything was digitized, our desks regularly had an inbox and an outbox. Most young people probably never thought about the fact that the email "inbox" is so named because we Neanderthals literally had physical boxes, cubbyholes, or trays often actually labeled "inbox" and "outbox" on our desk to hold papers. The former was usually piled high with items that needed attention. The latter despairingly less so.

The Prayer awakens us to the existence of two boxes in our lives. One is labeled "Can't Change." The other is labeled "Can Change." For much of our lives, everything in the "Can Change" box is externalized, and it's piled high. We want to change the people or events around us. People resist our well-intentioned but self-centered efforts, which makes us even more disappointed. As for events, we probably can't change them either, so we just chew on them and complain incessantly about them. We never think about shifting the contents of the boxes.

When it comes to Somali pirates, my friend made a conscious decision to shift those rascals from the "Can Change" to the "Can't Change" box. He couldn't do anything about them. Complaining was pointless, for they weren't listening. He decided to set them aside, leave them alone, and move on.

This very practical decision rests on a fundamental theological foundation. When we have a "Can Change" box piled high with items beyond our control, we're basically trying to usurp God's role. For all the noise and confusion and variability of life, our central mission is very straightforward. We're supposed to trust God in all circumstances. "Thy will be done" sums up our assignment. "My will be done" sums up our distorted practice.

We end up praying The Serenity Prayer in Reverse. "God grant me serenity as I wrestle with everything and everyone around me. Courage to keep fighting with everything even though it's fruitless, and the ignorance to resist looking in the mirror for the real problem."

Our struggle to properly distribute items into the two boxes is as old as Eden, and this part of The Prayer takes us to the heart of one of the most profound theological mysteries.

God created a perfect world for the first couple. The word "Eden" means a pleasant place, and it certainly must have been wonderful. God designed the first couple to be "one flesh" (Gen. 2:24), a reflection of God's perfect unity among the Trinity. Unity describes everything about those early days of Creation. It was, as God said, very good (Gen. 1:31). Then the shattering began.

It all started over one tree, the tree of the knowledge of good and evil. God allowed for the first couple to eat of everything in the garden, except that one tree. Theologians have long speculated about that one prohibition. Could God have said "don't eat the avocados" and reached the same point of decision? The Scripture is quite specific, however. It was that particular tree. Why?

A brief review of our present shatteredness reveals important clues. We think we know right and wrong. We want, in fact demand, the right to make our own decisions. When resisting some law or command, we might retort "But it's not what *I* want to do." We've taken over the knowledge of good and evil, consistently get it wrong and wonder why we feel so out of control and unhappy.

That's why the serpent chose this particular gambit. Notice the subtle distortions in his question: "Did God say you shall not eat of *any* tree?" Of course, that's not what God said, and Eve rightly points out that it's only one tree that was prohibited. So, the serpent challenged God's character. "He's lying to you, Eve. You won't die, and He just doesn't want you to be like Him."

When Adam and Eve listened to the serpent and took the fruit, they switched everything in the two boxes. They wanted to be like God instead of trusting God. They sought to control and change. In the end, God respected their choice, but the whole human race was destined from that point to endure the consequences.

The choice in Eden is played out in every individual life that's ever been. Our first parents, it seems, bequeathed to us a basic stubbornness to want to change and control instead of accept and trust. C.S. Lewis observed, "There are only two kinds of people in the end: those who say to God, 'Thy will be done,' and those to whom God says in the end, 'Thy will be done.'"

Until we get the basic divine order right in our lives, we'll forever be banging our heads against the wall and then complaining about the headache. The reasonably happy life means embracing some initially very uncomfortable concepts like commandments, obedience, laws, and duty. We treat all of these as if God is trying to limit and frustrate us when, in fact, He's merely trying to save us. He alone "knows good and evil." One of the great ironies of life is that what initially looks like bondage results in freedom, and vice versa. It's another one of those great reversals God sprinkles throughout the Scripture and our lives.

Rightly directing our trust toward God and away from us initially helps us realize that there are two boxes. As the writer of Proverbs put it, "trust in the Lord with all your heart and lean not on your own understanding" (Prov. 3:5-6). Now we can begin to shift the contents and that requires much more than knowledge could ever supply. We need wisdom, not knowledge.

Wisdom in the Information Age

When Neil Armstrong stepped on the moon, I was 11 years old. I'd been fascinated by the stars from my earliest memories, and when we began launching our own chariots of fire, I was hooked. I built a model of the Command Capsule and the Lunar Lander. I watched the grainy black and white first footfalls on the moon and I looked up into the night sky at our closest celestial cousin and thought, "the population right now on the moon is two." I loved it.

Looking back on those days, it's a true wonder we made it off the surface of the earth. I read occasionally that something like my iPhone has many, many times the computing power that those early astronauts had on board their entire spaceship. Look at the old pictures and videos of those days, and you see ashtrays filled with ashes and butts on the control panels for moonshots, and a lit cigarette hanging from the mouth of an engineer who may at the same time be calculating oxygen levels in the Command Module.

Today, we have nearly immediate access to an unimaginable amount of information. Do we know more than those early engineers with their slide rules and nicotine-stained fingers? Very likely. Again, I'm writing this in the midst of the COVID-19 quarantine. When I check out Facebook, I see that suddenly half of my friends are experts on epidemiology just because they clicked on an article ten minutes earlier.

Lost in this sea of knowledge, however, is any regard for wisdom. The ancients pursued wisdom. We pursue Wikipedia. With all of our knowledge, can anyone seriously suggest that we're better off in truly important matters of the soul? Our access to knowledge deepens the illusion of control, and it substitutes for wisdom to such a degree that we forget the word.

It's another lesson from Eden. Our first parents chose the tree of the knowledge of good and evil. Notice it was the tree of knowledge. There's absolutely nothing wrong with knowledge. I'm a curious sort. I like to learn. I like information. But Adam and Eve showed us the initial mistake that we keep repeating. We seek knowledge not realizing that knowledge will never save (then or now) if we don't have wisdom to direct it.

Defining wisdom is actually quite fun. Wisdom and knowledge are not antithetical, but they're not exactly complementary either. Frankly, you can have wisdom without knowledge and make it through life very nicely. But try having knowledge without wisdom and, well, you get a big slice of our contemporary culture.

Think of knowledge as raw material. Wisdom is understanding how to put it together in the most satisfying ways. I've been in many villages in the Amazon Valley where people live very happily and safely in homes made of poles and thatch. Do I have a safer and more comfortable home because of studs and brick? Of course. I simply have more raw materials at my disposal. In both cases, it's the wisdom that enables both the villager and the city dweller to keep the rain off their heads.

Wisdom is how life works. The ancients pursued wisdom because they recognized its priority in life. They hardly eschewed knowledge. The same culture that produced Socrates with his search for wisdom produced Aristarchus who beat Copernicus to the truth that the earth is not the center of the universe by about 1,700 years. Our wise ancestors simply realized the primacy of wisdom. Today, we've gotten them reversed to the point that you hardly ever hear about wisdom. It's all knowledge. No wonder we've forgotten how life works.

Surely, we can trace much of the rush and noise of our present culture to this unfortunate reversal. No one could possibly argue that we're a happier people today. All of our counseling and medications haven't put a dent in the overall rates of depression, though it's enormously difficult to measure such things, and especially across ages. We're unhappy to such a degree that I'm not sure we even recognize our own unhappiness. Could the answer be as simple as we've completely forgotten about the need for wisdom?

If wisdom is how life works, then our major pursuit should be determining what is most important in life and giving priority to those things. A cursory review of our typical day shows how infrequently we do this. The things that agitate us or completely throw us off the rails are often not matters that are central to a well-lived life. A flat tire or a snide remark ruins our day, and we may never get around to being thankful for God's lavish gifts to us, to the whole of humanity, and all of creation.

Social media is a good proving ground. I've truly lost track of the number of times someone's post has fired me up. I've even carried my computer to Leslie to show the offensive story or comment or whatever. I thunder, "He's done it again! Look at this!" Without realizing it, I've just forfeited a significant portion of my serenity to something that is absolutely not central to my well-being.

Jesus devoted quite a few lines in the Sermon on the Mount to priorities. Treasure in heaven, a sound eye, serving only one master, seek first the kingdom are the clearest examples. In those sections, He also spoke about anxiety. Neglecting the former produces the latter. All anxiety is a loss of focus on God that can be corrected by the recovery of wisdom, that is, determining what is most important and giving priority to those things.

Taking an intentional and extended break from social media and using that time to sit silently before God is surely a wiser way to live. When I'm disturbed, my first reaction is to focus on what disturbed me and then I might wrestle with it and try to change it. That's an overt commitment to knowledge and power as the way to get though life. That approach *never* brings enduring happiness. Quietly trusting God, focusing on what the disturbance means about what I need to change in *me*, that is the path of wisdom and the way to reasonable happiness.

Bears and Mosquitoes

The previous section focused on what might be called general wisdom. Again, being able to arrange and keep and live by priorities is essential. Reasonable happiness is impossible apart from proper priorities.

The Prayer calls for a specific wisdom. When presented with an event, or a hap, how do we respond to it? Is it something we cannot change? In all likelihood the answer to that is yes, for as I hope to have established already, we grossly overestimate what we can change in the events (or haps) and people around us. If we cannot change the event, then can we change something internal to us? There is the real power.

Take the fairly easy example of the offensive Facebook post of the previous section. A substantial part of me wants to engage the offender. I literally will rehearse a response, sometimes writing it out and editing it so it will have the most impact. I'm not engaging in a conversation. I'm trying to change someone else with the power of my words.

An alternative was suggested by my wife. "Why don't you just unfollow him?" I stood gobsmacked before my wife. My visceral response is that that would leave the offender unchallenged and unchanged. As I continue my edits prior to posting, however, the wisdom of my wife's words begins to sink in. If I post this, the offender is highly unlikely to see the light, or more specifically my light. In fact, my semi-hostile response will likely elicit a semi-hostile and defensive response from the offender. Which of course, demands another round from me.

It's all remarkably silly when I step back and take a look at it. With a single click I can remove the post and set my sights elsewhere. Of course, if I keep to this better nature, I won't post that "I'm unfollowing you!!!"

Is this something I can change? Or is it something that I can't change and need to just accept? Remembering that acceptance doesn't necessarily mean agreement or approval. I can choose to accept and unfollow. With serenity intact, I can move on to the next challenge, and every day brings numerous challenges of trying to determine the difference.

One of the great obstacles to determining the difference is that you will always be challenged by someone to keep getting worked up about something. We're very good at recruiting people to our various causes and more than a little perturbed when they fail to share our agitation.

This COVID-19 crisis came during an election year, which is just what we needed to help settle the jittery national consciousness. I've seen families split because of differing political views. This has been happening since we've had democracy for sure, but I'd wager an amount of money that matters to me that it's more fractious today. So, we'll see aggressive recruiting on both sides, that is, attempts to change. And when the change is refused or ignored, we'll be labeled as either fascist or communist in the current jargon. It's a very binary view of life and very common in many, many areas.

The fact of the matter is we're being conditioned to react in these binary ways. Remember my friend Leo Honeycutt's words earlier in this chapter. "I was not going to report on the 10% that was bad and represent it as 90% of real life." He added, "I felt the Lord leading me to do something where I wasn't making people feel discouraged." I'm not going to begin bashing the media here, which is another binary response. It's the media's nature, by and large, to dramatize and vilify, but only because it is *our* nature. This is highly important.

The general media, and social media is merely a reflection, a state of mind, or nearly a living entity. It would not project itself in this manner unless it was appealing to something very fundamental in the human psyche. We're conditioned to fear, so we market apocalypse. That will get people to pay attention. We all stop to watch a train wreck.

Without realizing it, we've hamstrung our ability to determine the difference between what we can control and can't control; what we must accept and what we should keep wrestling with. We externalize control and change because it's far easier to carp about politicians, big business, big pharma, the media, etc. than it is to turn all of that high-powered and flawless critique inward to the things that we really can change.

The wisdom to tell the difference means determining whether an event needs to be accepted for what it is, or whether we can redemptively and graciously engage in change. So, there is certainly a legitimate call for political engagement, improvement of a community, counseling a struggling person, or even appropriately confronting someone who repeatedly offends or harms you.

Most of life, however, doesn't consist of these larger causes. These are the bears in life. They're real and have to be dealt with occasionally. The mosquitoes of life are the real blood suckers, and we have enough of those buzzing around us on any given day to drain us. Jesus didn't say a word about how to overthrow a totalitarian and murderously oppressive regime. Instead, He talked about turning the other cheek, going the extra mile, and being anxious for nothing. Why? Because those simple sacrifices bring us the real peace and happiness we're seeking. Reasonable happiness is always an inside job.

It's not that hard to tell the difference between a bear and a mosquito. We've just lost the awareness that there really is a difference. By and large, ignore the bears. Pay attention to the mosquitoes. You'll discover reasonable happiness when learn to swat them away with the various graces God lavishes upon you, and thankfully He provides a few tools develop the skills.

The Power of Pause

When confronted with a bear or a mosquito of a problem, our response is usually swift. We react. The problem is the reaction is often cloaked in fear, or, its first cousin, anger. I'm not alone when I say that when I am either fearful or angry, I don't think well or pray well. Quick reactions mean I will spend a great deal of my time running or flailing around. Either way, I'll end up exhausted and unhappy.

I earlier touched on some of the inner workings of our brain and mentioned a little structure called the amygdala. This rather primitive area of our brain is highly sensitive to threats, perceived or real. Introduce a fear stimulus like a snake, for example, and the amygdala immediately initializes a cascade of responses that include the release of adrenaline which enables you to jump out of the way quickly.

The amygdala will induce the same response to a rubber snake. If, in a moment of shear lunacy, I decide to toss a rubber snake on my wife's lap as she's reading quietly in her chair, she will scream, thrash, jump out of the chair, and probably initiate divorce proceedings. Now, my wife knows with every fiber of her conscious being that I would never, ever do something as stupid as bring a live snake into our den and toss it on her. We tease and have our fun, but she *knows* that I would never be that clueless.

Her knowledge and certainty of my relative stability in this area is a product of her cerebral cortex, an area of higher thinking, processing, and function. Interestingly, this area is slower in its processing than the amygdala. The reason is clear, your brain is designed for survival. It's much more important that you immediately get out of the way of any potential danger than it is to reflect on whether the danger is real or not. Leslie's amygdala has her jump just in case her husband really has lost his mind. Once she's safe, she can figure out at leisure whether or not the snake was real.

Because the amygdala "thinks" much faster than the cortex, we are more likely to respond with fear or anger to stress-inducing stimuli. This applies to bears and mosquitoes. Even though our response to each should be proportional and measured, we tend to react to both in exactly the same way. That produces a great deal of our unhappiness.

In the real world, we don't have so many bears, but we react quickly to the mosquitoes of any inconvenience or stress. The reaction is wholly out of proportion to the threat or even the discomfort. Think back to the last argument you had with your spouse, and if you can even remember what the subject was, you will probably admit that your reaction was out of proportion to the offense. A key to reasonable happiness, in fact, is *choosing* a response that is appropriate to the event.

That's where the power of the pause comes in. This spiritual discipline is a very intentional brake to the fear/anger-based reactions we become accustomed to. It shifts the neurological driving force for a response from the amygdala to the cortex. That naturally lowers the amount of anxiety we feel and creates the potential to be reasonably happy.

Psalm 46:10 counsels us to "be still and know that I am God." Be still. How strange that sounds to our busy ears! One interesting benefit from the enforced Sabbath our society underwent as part of the COVID-19 crisis was that people found the opportunity to slow down, and they liked it. For a while, some of the noise of our culture quieted down and people enjoyed the stillness.

Surely this is why God instituted a Sabbath in the first place. We need a day of rest. After days of figuratively tilling our fields, working the land, hunting, and gathering, we need to pause. The benefit is certainly physical, but the real benefit is spiritual. It's amazing what you can hear if slow down long enough to listen.

The battle between busyness and stillness is not a modern phenomenon, though it does seem more intense. The story of Jesus coming to the home of Mary and Martha is one of the most memorable examples of this pull and tug.

Mary, Martha, and their brother Lazarus are better known for the story of Lazarus' death and resuscitation by Jesus. It's a powerful story. Equally meaningful, however, is the time Jesus apparently made his first visit to their home in Bethany (Luke 10:38-42). Lazarus may have already become a disciple, for the gospel of John tell us that Jesus deeply loved him. Because Bethany was only two miles east of Jerusalem, it's natural to assume that Jesus often stayed there when visiting the Jewish capital.

Imagine that first visit. Mary and Martha may not have even met Jesus yet, but they'd learned from Lazarus of His miracles and powerful teaching. They heard the whispered hopes that Jesus must be the Messiah.

We have no contemporary analogy for what this must have meant to the two sisters. The Messiah was coming for a visit! The Messiah. Martha, no doubt with Mary's help, set about preparing food and making all the arrangements any of us would make for the arrival of a famous person in our homes. When Jesus arrived, Martha continued seeing to all of the details.

Mary, however, enthralled by the Teacher, sat at His feet and listened and watched.

In a scene that is without question humorous, a flustered Martha bustles into the midst of that tender scene and orders the Messiah to tell Mary to help her serve. Let that sink in. Most sisters have some measure of tension about how things should happen. One doesn't make her bed right or put the dishes away. The other one is always trying to boss and correct. Seldom, however, does one sister try to throw the other one under the bus in such an epic and stupendous fashion.

After the fit of temper, the room was still. Mary was mortified. Martha was expecting divine intervention. Everyone held their breath. Then Jesus with a smile relieved all the tension. Martha, He said, was anxious and troubled about many things. Remember what area of the brain is most active when we're anxious, fearful, or angry? Martha was in full limbic mode. But Mary was still, taking advantage of a divine pause to listen and learn from the Son of God Himself. I truly believe Martha understood how she'd allowed busyness to come between her and a divine moment.

God Himself rested, and the Jewish people regard the Sabbath (the word means "to cease") as one of God's greatest gifts to us. It's not an imposition. It's an opportunity. We can cease, pause, and listen for God. We need this pause more than one day a week. It's intended to be a spiritual practice that we engage throughout the day, any time we're agitated or fearful. We pause.

The pause is a holy space, a few moments, where we sincerely and intentionally ask God how we should respond to a situation. Think of the breath you draw when you're challenged in some way. The next words formed from that breath can be hurtful words of anger, or quiet words of prayer that seek God's wisdom. You're giving God in those moments the opportunity literally to shift your response from the primal reactive parts of your brain to the more thoughtful and reasonable parts. This is the way He's designed you. He's available to give you wisdom to know the difference between the things you should accept and the things you can change. You'll find that wisdom in the pause.

The Power of Patience

If wisdom is the most neglected virtue in today's world, patience is a close second. We've become so accustomed to instant gratification that we don't even realize how it has crept into our lives and edged out the need for patience. I remember jokes about how microwave ovens and instant coffee were speeding up our fast-paced society. Today we can order any product online and have it arrive in two days or less.

It's genuinely fruitless to complain about our fast-paced society. It's a fact of life now. We're not going to go back to slower days when we grew our own food and rode buggies over dirt roads. It is worth noting again that for all of our wizardry in creating easily obtainable products, we're not a happier or more contented people by any measure. Ironically, access only seems to create more discontent, for we're more aware than ever of what we can't or don't have.

The seeker of reasonable happiness must be very intentional in developing patience in the midst of a culture that encourages impatience. We cannot possibly tell the difference between acceptance and change when we're constantly presented with the illusion that we can change anything with a few clicks of a mouse.

The Scripture teaches us two very important things about God. First, He is always working. Second, He's in no hurry. We can kick and complain about that all we wish, but it's not going to change the fact that God has an established pattern of saying "I'll help you in My time and in My way."

For this reason, the Psalms in particular have a great deal to say about waiting on the Lord. "Wait for the Lord; be strong, and let your heart take courage; yea, wait for the Lord" is a good example (Ps. 27:14). Notice that waiting (or patience), therefore, comes with strength and courage. Waiting on God, trusting God, is not a weak position. It takes strength and courage, because we have to fight the egocentric predicament that is constantly telling us to change things to suit ourselves and to do so quickly.

God appears sometimes to move at a glacial pace. Through the prophet Isaiah, He promised the Messiah. How long, O Lord? About 700 years was the answer.

When we resist the wisdom to know the difference, we try to force things. We might even pray about the irksome situation, but then when it (or he/she) doesn't change, we assume that God is leaving it up to us. We charge ahead, barreling through life and then wondering why the situation has just gotten worse and we're tired and frustrated.

The most familiar and comforting "waiting verse" in the Bible is probably Isaiah 40:31. "They who wait for the Lord will renew their strength, they shall mount up with wings like eagles, they shall run and not be weary, they shall walk and not faint." Who would not be encouraged by this verse? We feel tired and run down, beaten up by the world, criticized and condemned by people around us, and God speaks to us through the prophet that we will regain our strength, fly like eagles, and walk and run without getting weary. Anyone would want that!

But we don't want the waiting. That's the qualifier of the flying, running, and walking. When things or people don't change, we start flapping and running about, wondering why we're so tired and nothing external to us is really different.

We're generally very practical. We like to figure out how things work, and when something's not working the way we want it to, we're going to try to fix it. I used two *Reader's Digest* how-to books to plumb and wire an addition to one of our former homes. I had no experience in plumbing or electrical work. I'm quite proud that I was able to do this and regularly try to work it into casual conversations. This can-do spirit produces a lot of improvement in our lives in many, many ways.

But not in the deeply spiritual ways. For real spiritual change, for peace and reasonable happiness, we can't forge ahead with a can-do attitude, the focus of which is our own ability and strength of will. We have to wait on God and be patient. When we feel the need to get practical, we need to shift to getting spiritual.

The New Testament gives us two words for patience. When Paul listed patience as one of the fruits of the Spirit (Gal. 5:22), he used the word *makrothumia,* which means a patience with people. God, give us more of that! Especially when we feel the urge to change the people around us. That's God's work. He'll use us only when He's made it abundantly clear that He wants to use us and then when He provides the opportunity.

As important as patience with people is, the second word, *hupomone*, may be even more important. It refers to a patience with situations. James wrote that trying times both call for and produce this kind of patience, or, as the word is often translated, endurance or steadfastness (James 1:2-3). When faced with a trial, we're tempted to complain, question God, and even fling away from faith. We don't want to wait. We're not willing to let God work.

Again, God is always at work. In countless ways, through countless people around you, God is weaving together your future. John Piper famously said, "God is always doing 10,000 things in your life, and you may be aware of three of them."

Waiting on the Lord is the safe and wisest choice. We may not be able to figure out how to make a situation better. We may not be able to figure out if we should challenge someone to change. Almost always, however, we can determine how to not make a situation worse. Running ahead of God always make it worse. The wisdom to know the difference requires patiently waiting on the Lord. We remain steadfast. We endure. We wait.

Thought-Direction

"Reverent agnosticism" is a term I ran across many years ago, but I don't recall where I first saw it. Elton Trueblood or J. B. Philipps are good guesses. Though many people use the term today, whoever coined it was wasn't referring to non-believers. He was referring to some matters of faith that simply aren't crystal clear. The word "agnostic" literally means "not knowing." It's not a bad concept at all. People of great faith don't have all the answers. The ones who will admit that have humility.

Socrates is famous for understanding the limits of his knowledge. For him, humility was the beginning of wisdom. Humility opened him up to the great mysteries of life and the world.

Solomon had the same idea in the book of Proverbs. In one of the more puzzling verses in his collection he wrote, "The beginning of wisdom is this: Get wisdom" (Prov. 4:7). You can't get much more basic and straightforward than that. He didn't say go to school and earn degrees or take an online course. His answer leaves us kind of standing there wondering what we're supposed to do next. Perhaps that's the point. Getting wisdom is not engaging in a lot of activity. It's the result of a relationship with God in which we begin by realizing we're not Him.

The starting point for wisdom is both the realization you don't have it and the earnest desire to acquire it. Proverbs repeatedly warns of those who are wise in their own eyes. In other words, you need humility.

In discerning which box we need to place all the events and people in our lives, we need humility, for humility keeps us from relying on our own resources and clinging to our old and useless preconceptions. Think of humility as a change of "thought direction." Without humility, we always look to ourselves, not realizing how self-limiting that is. We'll make the same mistakes repeatedly, which get us into the same conflicts with people around us. We always assume that it's the other guy's fault. We end up exhausted, spiritually vulnerable, and completely unaware of where we are or how we got there.

Humility changes our "thought direction" from self-centeredness to God-centeredness. We're then willing to admit we really don't handle things well on our own. We're also willing to change our minds about a person or situation. It's amazing to me to watch a person stubbornly cling to an old way of thinking even though that way of thinking simply creates agitation. However, I did the very same thing in my active alcoholism. I never realized until treatment and some time in recovery how self-centered I'd become in my thinking. It's a daily battle to change my "thought-direction." Thankfully, it's not a battle I have to fight alone.

We have the remarkable potential in Christ to think like God. In a soaring passage, Paul wrote that we are to have the "mind of Christ" in us (Phil. 2:5). This is truly remarkable, for it means that we can think like Jesus, or more to the point have the thoughts of Jesus flow through us. This is the ultimate change in perspective. We begin to look on all the world the way Jesus does.

Both before and after this particular verse, Paul mentioned humility. In humility (2:5) we count others better than ourselves (how counter-cultural is that?) Then Jesus humbled himself (2:8) as He went to the cross. This passage is full of wonderful images. Jesus did not grasp divinity but took on the form of a servant. He emptied Himself. The implications are huge. Jesus became exactly like us so we could become exactly like Him. The key is humility.

Turning our thought-direction to God when we run up against problems will have one of two results. We'll find strength to endure the problem we can't change. Or, and this is truly miraculous, the problem that has twisted us up so badly will simply dissipate. Either way, we end up being reasonably happy.

A Well-Meaning Bull in God's China Shop

My daughter, Lauren, has a wonderful gift for words. In discussing generally what we can and can't change, and what we should or shouldn't change, she thoughtfully remarked, "I sometimes feel like a well-meaning bull in God's china shop." That image is forever seared in my mind.

She's right, and I say that lovingly. When she embraces a direction, she will move in that direction inexorably. Historically, she swats away alternative opinions as mere distractions from her chosen course. It's not an unusual constellation of qualities in the young, particularly in the young who have achieved highly and have a post-graduate degree or two. I recognize thoroughly her tendencies, for she came by them honestly.

God does have a certain way He's arranged the world and life. He knows how it will best work. He's set up a very fine china shop for us to browse and enjoy. Yet all of us have some degree of that damnable tendency to rearrange things to suit ourselves. It never works, but we always seem to think that next time it will. All we do is leave a broken mess behind us.

Thomas Aquinas wrote of four substitutes for God: power, wealth, pleasure, and honor. The first three are easily identifiable. That fourth word means something more along the lines of fame or reputation. We want to be recognized and acclaimed. To any degree that we pursue those four apart from a fundamental, initial, and enduring submission to God's will means that we will break a lot of china.

God knows the vacuum in our hearts. He also knows the fallen tendency we have to try to fill that void with one of Aquinas's big four. With power, I try to manipulate and change. With wealth, I try to control the environment around me and ensure that I will have no challenges I can't buy my way out of. In pleasure, I try to insulate myself from unwanted feelings and substitute feeling good for being good. With fame, I shift my inner sense of well-being to people and things that are external to me. With all of them, I'm expressing dissatisfaction with the way God has arranged his shop. I'm convinced that I have a better way, and I'm going to thunder ahead, hooves pounding and horns crashing.

I bring up my daughter here because she and my son represent for me one of the greatest challenges I've faced trying to implement "the wisdom to know the difference." What are the non-negotiables as parents? When do you allow some leeway? When do you draw a line? And being the father now of a man and a woman, grown children, it presents a whole new set of challenges. Do you offer unsolicited advice? Or is that control?

As a pastor, I truly lost count of the number of times parents would present these kinds of issues to me, especially when a child, young or old, was going through a tough time. Grandparents, many of whom have become increasingly responsible for raising their grandchildren, also suffer through times of estrangement, unsure of their role in both the causes of the strain or their role in repairing the breach. They can be absolutely forlorn as they describe the child who used to cling to them now being an adolescent or adult who hasn't spoken to them for months or even years. Do they accept something that can't be changed? Or do they need courage to walk carefully into that china shop?

While every situation has unique details, I've found the wisest course is to pray and wait. Pray an honest prayer of uncertainty as a parent or grandparent, confessing to God your confusion and pain. Then simply give that child or grandchild over to God. Let Him have it. Then wait and watch. I've witnessed countless situations where over a period of months or even years, the hot fires of hostility cool, and the relationship is restored. When you can't discern precisely something you can do to make a difficult situation better, that is usually God's answer to not do anything to make it worse. And "the worse" is usually something along the lines of charging into the middle of the shop. People who regularly grab the bull by the horns to solve a thorny problem often get trampled by a very angry bull. Let God work in every situation. Give Him time and watch the results.

Two exceptions come to mind to the pray and wait approach. If you've clearly wronged someone, or if they think you've clearly wronged them, then go to them, apologize and ask, "how can I help make this right or better?" You do this without any expectation they will respond in turn by admitting their wrong and offering amends. You clean up your side of the street, as we say. Anything beyond that will appear to be an indictment and prosecution.

This is a very sacred act. It's conducted in compete humility and trust. The only desire is to control what you can control (your culpability and willingness to address the situation) and to be of loving service to another person. You're not even asking for forgiveness. You've offered grace, and you're placing in their hands the complete and total opportunity to return grace. Whether they do or not is simply not your concern.

A second clear example of the need to take action, and how this may be done most helpfully, is when a loved one, adult child or otherwise, is struggling with an addiction. My main vocation now is being a professional interventionist. When families or organizations want to approach a struggling individual, they ask me to train them and lead the meeting where we try to persuade the addicted person to accept help.

These are enormously difficult challenges for families. When someone calls me, they're almost always somewhat uncertain if anything needs to be done and completely uncertain if anything can be done. They're also very afraid of "making things worse."

About 80% of the family members I work with are very certain that "he won't go to treatment." When I ask why, the answer is usually along the lines of "I've talked to him several times. He just gets angry." One-on-one, you always lose with an alcoholic or addict. An addict excels at keeping you off balance. We know how to shift the conversation, either by pushing your buttons or simply denying there is any problem. "They won't go" is based on experience.

What the alcoholic or addict has never faced, however, is a room full of loved ones who are there to calmly express love, concern, and offer a reasonable plan for addressing the problems. One-on-one, they win. One on twelve, and they almost *always* go to treatment. The number is 90% or better. Why? What makes the difference?

The family has led with love and there is no anger or disappointment expressed in the intervention. More than that, the intervention is a deeply spiritual encounter. Prayer is a strong feature of our preparation, and I usually begin the meeting by asking the person of concern if I can lead a brief prayer. I've never been refused. I ask God to bring His peace into the room and help us listen. This not a ploy or a placebo. It's an actual invitation for God to manifest His presence among us. The family has acted uniformly with wisdom and grace. Real change is then possible.

Life is complicated and often difficult. With love as the reigning theme, we're much more likely to get it right and not barrel through life wondering why we've left behind so many hurt feelings and damaged relationships, and trying to figure out where all our cuts came from. Waiting on the Lord and following, not sprinting ahead, brings the reasonable happiness we seek.

Wisdom in Action

Mom first started showing signs of dementia when I was a pastor in Murray, Kentucky. Her condition rapidly declined until I had to move her from her beloved Lexington to an assisted living facility in Murray. Dad's multiple sclerosis and other health problems made his condition must worse, and he already lived in a nursing home in Lexington. Because of the rushed nature of the move, I was not able to obtain a room for him in any nursing home in Murray. He would have to stay behind in Lexington for one to three months waiting for a place to open up.

Telling him this, leaving him there, and taking his wife away was one of the most difficult things I've ever done. Mom had lived in an apartment and Dad in the nursing home, but this move would mean they would be in different cities. Mom had lost much of her ability to process and was not really fully aware of what was going on. Dad understood, and it hurt him deeply. It's the only time I saw him cry.

Several weeks after the move, I received a call from a nursing home. They had a space, but it was only a temporary room, small and unadorned. But it was available. I went to see the room, and my heart sank. It was concrete block, institutional monochrome, windowless, dimensions maybe nine feet by 10 feet. I agreed to take it because I knew Dad would prefer almost anything to being separated from Mom.

He was excited when I spoke to him on the phone. I told him of the spartan arrangements and that it would be temporary until a regular room for him opened up. They couldn't promise how long it would take. Nothing muted his enthusiasm.

I made the four-hour drive to Lexington, bringing with me the youth director at our church in case I needed any help along the way. We loaded all of Dad's belongings into the trunk along with his wheelchair and returned to Murray.

I was apprehensive when we arrived at the nursing home. What if he didn't like it? He would never let on, of course, but I hated the thought of his being disappointed. Life had been particularly hard for him the previous five or so years. He had endured numerous falls, the MS was worse, and the wheelchair had become a permanent part of his life. Surgery to remove a brain tumor had left him weaker. He also endured prostate cancer and glaucoma. I wanted him to at least have a nice place to live.

Wheeling him down the hallway of the nursing home, I anxiously explained again that the room was very sparse, but that eventually there would be a larger one available. I brought him to the doorway. Standing behind him, I looked into the meager room containing an unmade metal frame bed with support bar running over it. My heart sank a little more when I thought that I could have at least brought in some pictures or something to warm it up. I began again, "Dad, it's a small room, but . . ." He raised his hand, interrupted me and said, "But it's nice. I'm sure glad to be here."

My dad had accepted his physical lot in life. He could do nothing about the myriad problems that beset him. That's the first line of The Prayer. He'd put all of his energy into adjusting his attitude to his station in life. That took the courage of the second line of The Prayer. As a man of faith, he seemed to continually filter all the "haps" of his life through the mind that Christ had developed in him. I'm sure that gave him the wisdom to express gratitude for a small, cinderblock, nursing home room. He gave me an enduring image of a reasonably happy man.

The wisdom to know the difference is not a destination. None of us ever graduates with a terminal degree in wisdom. We can cultivate certain spiritual attitudes and practices that make it much more likely that when the time of real testing comes, we neither fall back on fearful resignation nor trust in our own strength to pull us through. We wait faithfully on God and watch the results with reasonable happiness.

Toward reasonable happiness:

- Wisdom is knowing how life works.
- We need wisdom to discern the difference between what we can change and what we cannot change.
- We live in the "information age." Knowledge is voluminous and accessible. But knowledge without wisdom can be superficial and even dangerous.
- The big problems in life are usually few, but the small problems can pose a greater threat our happiness. People often endure the "bear problems" much better than the "mosquito problems."
- Fear reactions (and the resultant anger) are primary and very fast. They get in the way of wisdom.

- We need to cultivate the "power of pause" in order to choose an appropriate response to a difficult situation. This requires the cultivation of patience and humility.

If we try and grab the horns of every charging bull in our lives, we'll end up exhausted and trampled. Cultivate prayer and patience as a default response.

CHAPTER SIX

LIVING ONE DAY AT A TIME, ENJOYING ONE MOMENT AT A TIME

"Behold! The kingdom of God is within you!"
Luke 17:21

"Somebody should tell us, right at the start of our lives, that we are dying. Then we might live life to the limit, every minute of every day. Do it I say! Whatever you want to do, do it now! There are only so many tomorrows."
Pope Paul VI

One of my favorite plays is *Our Town* by Thornton Wilder. In the first two acts, we watch George and Emily grow up, fall in love, and get married. At the beginning of the third act, we learn Emily has died giving birth to her second child.

She goes to her "grave," which on the set is simply a chair, sitting next to others who've passed on before her. She's not stricken with grief or fear. She's more reflective than anything. She greets the other people who are quietly sitting there in their "graves," each one waiting for the "earth part of them to burn away" before they go on to eternity. Being new to this experience, she's still reflecting on the life she just left. As she thinks about all she missed in life, she begins to desperately want to live one day over again. Just one day, and this time to get it right. She's granted her wish to relive her 12th birthday.

She returns to that day, knowing all she knows now and wanting to squeeze everything she can out of every minute. Her parents greet her and prepare for her birthday, baking a cake and bringing home presents. Emily is being celebrated as any 12-year-old would on her birthday. But something is missing. It's all too superficial. She wants her parents to slow down, really talk and listen. The day is not about the presents and the cake. Life is too precious and it's all going too fast. She desperately wants more.

Disappointed, she cuts short her one-day visit. She has painfully learned a lesson that we're missing the point of life, and it's too late for her to try to get it right. As she trudges back to her grave, she asks the narrator of the play a very poignant question, "Do any human beings ever realize life while they live it? Every, every moment?" The narrator replies thoughtfully, "No. Saints and poets maybe. They do some."

We deal with time continually. We live in it. We try to use it wisely, even trying to "save" it. We're late, seldom early, and gauge ourselves accordingly. We run out of it and want more of it, so we try to stretch it. We waste it and lose it. Though it's difficult to define precisely, we have a rather large vocabulary to describe what we do with time.

For all of our interest in it and devotion to it, time certainly remains the source of a great deal of our problems. The past drags us down. The future scares us to death. The present gets lost in the shuffle. Mentally, we're everywhere except where we need to be, and the spiritual cost of our scattered minds is enormous.

Up to this point in The Prayer, we've asked God for three things: serenity, courage, and wisdom. We can count on God to deliver. He really does love to hear the voices of His children, and frankly, I don't believe there is any such thing as unanswered prayer. God is responsive. Always. He wants to give us serenity, courage, and wisdom. That much is settled.

The Prayer now shifts, however, from what we receive from God to some very specific things we must do to open up ourselves to His gifts. And the very first commitment on our part has to do with time. We can't receive all God has for us, much less realize life every, every moment until we learn how to use time wisely.

However, this phrase of The Prayer doesn't have anything to do with budgeting time or making lists. It's a call for a spiritual attitude in which we become aware of the rhythms of grace God weaves into our days. Those "grace-waves" enable us to live one day at a time and enjoy one moment at a time. That's a key to being reasonably happy.

Enjoying God

One of my favorite *Far Side* cartoons depicts God at His computer watching an unsuspecting man walk under a piano that is being let down from an upper story of a building. God's hand hovers over the keyboard, His index finger pointing downward, about to hit the button labeled "Smite." That sums up the way many, many people think about God.

For any of us who regularly talk to others about God, a common experience is to hear someone say, "I don't believe in God." My initial impulse is to challenge and prove, but that's not the best approach by a long shot. Instead, I just reply, "Tell me about the god you don't believe in." I let them talk. I listen. Always, in my experience, I can respond "I don't believe in that god either."

In his classic devotional book, *Your God Is Too Small*, J. B. Philipps had the same observation. He devotes a great deal of the book to the inadequate images of God people regularly carry around with them. "Resident Policeman," "Parental Hangover," and "Perennial Grievance" are three of the destructive "gods" that people believe in. These overbearing gods arrest, punish, and generally menace because we are always breaking laws and generally not living up to expectations.

I wrote earlier of the advantage I had being raised in a loving and faithful home. I literally grew up with the image of God who chose me and loved me. That was easy because I'd been adopted by good parents who had chosen and loved me. Never forget, you get your first theology from your parents.

Over the years, I've realized more and more deeply how exceptional my experience was and how it continues to have an impact over 50 years later. Especially having worked more closely for a while now with genuinely hurting people, I've seen that when it comes to how they think about God, feelings of fear, anger, disappointment, and even disgust are not uncommon. Very often they have tragically traumatic childhood experiences that skew their view of God.

I hurt for these hurting folks because God has essentially no limits on how He's shown us that He loves every person who has ever walked the earth. You cannot honestly read the Scripture, and I mean the whole of Scripture, and not come away with any other accurate impression. Of course, I've had many people throw up to me the stories of God's punishing people in the Old Testament as if that is normative. Leaving alone for the moment that any story alone can give a distorted picture and that they can cite those stories without any larger context, they are certainly ignoring the clear and broad progression of the biblical revelation.

A young man one time challenged me with "What about Sodom and Gomorrah?" This kind of question is not unusual, and it's not a bad one, except that people who ask it are not likely to stick around for the answer. My point here is not to offer interpretations of difficult passages, but to point out that literally no skeptic has ever challenged me with anything like "What about God loving me so much that He gave His only Son, and that if I believe in Him, I can have eternal life?"

Parts of the Bible obviously are difficult to understand. The whole direction of the Bible, however, is very clear. No one should focus on one unusual brush stroke but miss the beauty of the painting. The message of the Bible is the gospel, and that word means "good news."

People are surprised and relieved, if they take it to heart, to find out that God is really very fond of them. This in spite of the fact that many of our Christian creeds and catechisms reflect the scripture and point out this fact. The Westminster Shorter Catechism, written in 1646, consists of 107 questions about every theological issue. The very first question concerns the basic purpose of every human being. The answer is "Man's chief end is to glorify God and to enjoy Him forever." Glorifying God simply means to reflect His values in our lives. The real kicker is that we're also to enjoy God.

Enjoy God. Again, many people fear God or are angry with Him or dismissive of Him. They're not enjoying Him, or the even idea of Him. Yet here, in a very significant document that guides a great swathe of Christianity, we're told to enjoy God.

In case you think this is isolated or unusual in the church's teaching, look at the Church that started it all. The Catechism of the Roman Catholic Church includes lines like these: "At every time and every place, God draws close to man." "Only in God will we find the truth and happiness we strive for." "God has created man through love, and through love continues to hold him in existence." "The ultimate end of the whole divine economy is the entry of God's creatures into the perfect unity of the Blessed Trinity." Truth, love, happiness, unity. These are not the words of an angry resident policeman. They are the words of a God we can enjoy.

Why do we struggle here? We tend to carry around in us the residue of guilt. We *feel* guilty and inadequate. Where does this come from? Listen carefully and objectively to your own inner voice and you'll discover that very commonly it's telling you that you're really not measuring up to your boss, to your coworker, your spouse, to God, and most hurtful of all, to yourself. This is such a common experience that I'm never surprised when people talk about their lack of self-confidence and self-love.

What we miss here is the easy transference of our own critical voice to God. Interestingly, one of the names for the devil is "Satan," which means accuser. When you have an accusing voice rattling around in your head, you can absolutely be sure that it doesn't come from God. He does not deal in doubt, shame, blame, and guilt. I think it's universally true that we're reluctant to let go of the very things that God long ago forgave. We're listening to the wrong voice, and if we listen to it long enough, it becomes our own.

We can't hope to live one day at a time and enjoy one moment at a time as long as the divine image is distorted or absent. It's hard to have a good day with a dark presence hovering over us. With God on our side, however, we can discern Him in every moment.

This assurance of a good and loving God who is actively involved in our lives is expressed in the Bible as joy. In an earlier chapter, I suggested a difference between happiness and joy. Here is where we need to make the distinction clearly. Happiness is bound by time, as the very word indicates a connection to an agreeable event.

Joy is far deeper. It's not connected to events. Rather it's a reflection of God's character, which is why we can enjoy Him. The word for joy in Greek comes from the same root as the word for grace, and that is a very important clue to its meaning. Joy is an expression of God's grace and presence in our lives, both of which are limitless and immutable. Joy is a gift, therefore, the second fruit of the Spirit (Gal. 5:22).

With joy as a basic reality, we can turn to the rest of reality with hopefulness and a lightness of heart. We know to Whom we belong and that creates a laughter of the soul. We're secure, and in this joyful security we begin to see all the threads of grace God weaves into the world.

Joy, and the subsequent enjoyment of God, is so clearly an absolute birthright of a follower of Christ that it's truly amazing that so many miss it. Yet they do. The result is chronic complaint and dissatisfaction that precludes the possibility of reasonable happiness.

Lessons from a Bad Example

Mr. Dale (not his real name) was a member of one my churches. He was one of the pillars, for better or worse, having contributed a great deal to the life of that congregation over the years, and possessing in the winter of his life a somewhat exaggerated sense of his own importance and sway.

Mr. Dale was simply one of those fellows God seems to sprinkle in every church. To say he was negative is simply to state the truth, although he might say he was realistic. We could always count on Mr. Dale to throw a bit of cold water on any good idea.

A friend of mine at the time told about a trip he made with Mr. Dale. Mr. Dale was driving, and they were heading home from a trip to a nearby city. Mr. Dale, my friend said, was deeply involved in surveying the various problems of the world. His tone was typically dire. He was nothing if not predictable, and predictably his authoritative critique seamlessly moved from one topic to another as he bemoaned numerous facets of life.

So enthralled was he by his flow of negative observations that he passed up the exit they were to take to get them home. My friend, realizing the imminent error, tried to alert Mr. Dale but couldn't squeeze in a word of warning. Finally, as they were a few miles beyond the exit, he finally interjected, "Mr. Dale, where are we going?" Mr. Dale, completely oblivious, replied with great fervor, "We're going down! That's where we're going! We're going down!"

I've touched on this before, but it bears repeating. The world is absolutely full of aggravation, and some of it's serious enough to constitute genuine, deep, and ongoing suffering. A chirpy optimism that fails to acknowledge this reality is shallow, naïve, and potentially even dangerous. The world can be hard and unforgiving. That is reality, but only a part of reality. It's equally shallow, naïve, and dangerous to ignore the grace that God lavishes on us each day, but that approach simply doesn't have the native appeal of complaint.

For some reason, the complainer and critic has assumed a perceived higher intellectual status, as if their ability to carp and doubt somehow reflects a greater insight unavailable to the rest of us simpletons. It's pure nonsense, of course, but perhaps it gives some people a way to feel superior. This certainly explains a great deal of the negativity in politics. Whichever party does not hold power appears to be contractually obligated to advance the notion that we are on the precipice of destruction. This currency does have real value in shifting political fortunes, but it hardly constitutes the truth.

Back to Mr. Dale for a moment. I was his pastor for a number of years, and generally, we got along well enough. I tried not to overreact to his capacity to pass out wet blankets whenever I offered an idea or program, and the success of the church appeared to mute some of his dark assessments.

One time, however, I challenged him about his attitude. I don't recall the issue or event, but I said something to him along the lines that his negative attitude was an obstacle and not at all helpful. The exchange was not hostile. As the pastor, I felt I needed to address an issue with Mr. Dale as one of the leaders in the church.

He surprised me a week or so later when he brought a manila folder to me in my office. He told me that he'd given some thought to what I'd said and went on to explain that in that folder he'd kept newspaper clippings and other items from across the years of various things that annoyed him. It was, and this is my observation, his own personal outrage reservoir. He told me he was going to throw it away, for he realized that it made him think negatively.

I was completely floored, and grateful, and happy for him. Frankly, I was probably happy for me, for it meant that neither I nor the church would have to endure his pervasive evaluations. He meant what he said. I have no doubt about that. And I don't doubt that he threw away the folder as he said he would. However, sadly his old habit didn't die and reasserted itself soon after.

Jesus said some stubborn demons can only be exorcised through "much prayer and fasting." For a one-time commitment to become a lifelong habit takes a great deal of daily discipline. At the very least, from Mr. Dale's story we can take away a word of warning not to let some demons make their home in our thoughts. They tend to cling tenaciously and mute the sound of God's comfort and hope.

The Telescope of Discontent

The telescope is a wondrous invention. The most famous telescope, The Hubble, opened up the heavens to us. We saw unimagined wonders. One of the most famous Hubble pictures was the result of the deep field instrument "staring" at a single spot in relatively empty part of the sky. That spot is about the size of a grain of sand held at arm's length. The resulting composite picture is stunning. There are over 3,000 objects in this "empty part of the sky." Each one is a galaxy, and each galaxy contains hundreds of millions and perhaps billions of stars.

Each one of us possesses a telescope of discontent. We use it to focus on a relatively small part of our lives where our complaints and discomforts reside. Those pains and inconveniences are there, no doubt, and sometimes there are many of them. But if we only look through the telescope of our discontent, we end up with the impression that discontent and discomfort are all we have. What's more, we really, really want other people to come and look through our telescope.

I'm not being dismissive of genuine suffering that is real, deep, and possibly permanent in many lives. In no way am I suggesting such a person has no reason to complain. In fact, I'm saying the exact opposite, and it applies to every one of us. We all have reasons to complain. That's reality.

But it's not all of reality. We'll take a much closer look at this topic in the next chapter on finding peace through hardships, but suffice it to say here that our most inspiring stories come from the crucible of suffering. What the scripture has to say about this truth is quite spectacular and life-altering. Here, however, let's simply note that whether your suffering is the size of a grain of sand or takes up a huge swathe of your sky, there are other places to look.

What makes the telescope of discontent even more pernicious is our tendency to point it at others. If I'm looking through my telescope at what I perceive to be your problems, then I don't have to look at mine. In another example of the humor of Jesus, we recall His teaching about the log and speck. We're to imagine a man with a log in his eye pointing out the speck in someone else's eye. The crowd, hearing that for the first time would not have missed the humor, and Jesus might have even said it with a smile. The deeper point of the story is not only that we who have logs in our eyes shouldn't point out specks. That invites the speck people to open up on the log people. Jesus simply doesn't want us to be turning our telescopes on one another. "Be merciful" sums up a great deal of Jesus' teaching on how to get along with other people. Mercy enables us to navigate even the trickiest relationships.

The inward focus can be equally destructive, and what's worse is that we're usually unaware of the tendency. The acid of complaint eats away at our souls and renders us incapable of gratitude. The burden of resentments weighs us down and then we only complain about people who are either no longer in our lives or who could become blessings if we dropped the weight. The poison of anger only makes us sick. And the storm of pain causes us to shrink in on ourselves so that we can't see anything else clearly.

I didn't even mention fear in the previous paragraph, but if you scratch the surface of just about anyone's life, fear pours out. I had a friend tell me one time that he'd been seeing a counselor for a while and discovered he had "a lot of fears." I remember thinking at the time, "what do you have to be fearful of?" I literally could not relate, until my serious bout with alcoholism forced me to look honestly at the fears that shrouded my mind. What I did not realize is that my simmering anger was a symptom. I learned in treatment that "if you want to see how fearful I am, watch how angry I get."

All of these negative spiritual emotions create a kind of gravity that draws our eyes away from God. It's no surprise that when we look at anything long enough, we'll start to think it's the only thing to see. Living one day at a time can simply devolve into the expectation that life is going to be relentlessly difficult day after day. Enjoying one moment at a time is a cruel jest.

Becoming aware of the telescope of discontent is the first step in realizing the sky is a lot bigger than we thought. We all have it. Some of us have used it so long and so often that we're going to be reluctant to release it, unknowingly forfeiting the opportunity for reasonable happiness. The good news is that it's never too late to let go. The challenge is remembering that you probably will have to keep turning it loose.

The Rhythms of Grace

I greatly enjoy my annual silent retreat at the Manresa Retreat Center run by the Jesuits. For four days, we learn the spiritual exercises of St. Ignatius. The only time we speak is during prayers or if we have an individual session with one of the Fathers. Other than that, silence. I think it's so wonderful because it's so unusual. A sign in the dining hall sums up well the intent of each retreat: "Silent and Listen have the same letters." It's a terrific reminder of a basic Ignatian principle: we grow spiritually by first watching and listening, and only then responding.

St. Ignatius encouraged followers to engage in a pattern of attentiveness and responsiveness. Attentiveness means paying attention to the ways God is at work around you. The Ignatians are also big on the notion that God gives us all things for our enjoyment. All creation points back to God who lavishes His gifts on everyone. Our challenge is to notice. In fact, one of the most basic descriptions of genuine spirituality is awareness. Once we're aware, we respond by entering into God's mind and work. Thus, we first become recipients of His gifts, then instruments of His grace and peace.

Attentiveness means we're not asking God to create something new. We want to notice what He's already created and what He's in the process of creating. For His part, I believe God is simply wanting us to open our eyes and ears to see and hear all His graces surrounding us.

Years ago, Dr. Glaze, one of my favorite seminary professors, had us focus on John 1:16. John, the writer of the Gospel, spent three years with Jesus watching the miracles and hearing His words. Of that time, he wrote, "From His fulness we have we all received, grace upon grace." Dr. Glaze said it was like John thought of grace as waves on the shore of the sea, wave after wave constantly washing over anyone who followed Jesus.

That image of grace like waves stayed with me and gave rise to my idea of "gracewaves." They are constant, as Dr. Glaze suggested. We can extend the metaphor if we move into the realm of physics. Right now, as you read these words, an untold number of electromagnetic waves are passing through the room in which you're seated. Some of them actually pass through you. You can become aware of some of them simply be keeping your eyes open and seeing the spectrum of visible light. Other waves, however, require different detectors. Your cell phone picks up one kind of wave. Radio waves are slightly different. Very special detectors alert you to everything from gamma rays to the delightfully named ELFs (Extremely Low Frequency waves).

Think of faith as a receptor that enables you to detect the gracewaves around you. You can set aside the telescope of discontent and genuinely move through the world with wonder, seeing all the evidences of God's love and grace that He's tucked within every day and every moment. You'll genuinely be amazed by how much is there that you simply overlooked. Don't be harsh with yourself for missing out. We all do. It's been happening to God's children for centuries.

Hagar was a serving girl to Sarah, Abraham's wife. Her story is a bit convoluted but, in keeping with traditions as they were over 3,500 years ago in a very different world, Sarah "gave" Hagar to her husband. Sarah was in a rush to fulfill God's promise to make a great nation from Abraham. Because she was barren, Sarah thought of another plan. Hagar bore a son to Abraham. His name was Ishmael, and he became the father of the Arab race.

Eventually, Sarah conceived and gave birth to Isaac. So now there were two sons, from two women, trying to fulfill one promise. In the inevitable jealousy that followed, Sarah drove away Hagar and her child. In the harsh wilderness near Beersheba, Hagar ran out of water, laid her child under a bush so that he might die in the shade, and moved off a small distance so she too might die.

The Bible tells us God heard the cries of the child and sent an angel to assure Hagar of her survival, and then we come to the verse which reads, "God opened her eyes, and she saw a well of water" (Gen. 21:19).

Look carefully at the verse again. Do you get the impression that God miraculously created a spring there in the wilderness? No. The wording suggests that God simply made her aware of the well that was always there. Her grief, fear, hopelessness, etc. had blinded her to God's presence, providence, and provision. Hagar filled her waterskins and saved her son's life. God made of him a great nation.

The Scripture often presents faith in terms of seeing. Light and dark are related common themes. Jesus' healings of the blind have a metaphorical meaning. Paul wrote about our need for insight and that the "eyes of our hearts" may be enlightened so that we can see all that God has for us. Hearing is another metaphor for faith. The wisdom literature in the Bible, mainly Proverbs and James, encourage readers to listen to the words of wisdom. Jesus ended the parable of the sower with the enigmatic words, "He who has ears, let him hear" (Matt. 13:9).

With both senses, the meaning is clear. We spend a great deal of our lives blind and deaf to the grace of God. And God spends a great deal of His time trying to help us see and hear that we may become more deeply aware of His presence and plan.

The World Shouts, God Whispers

In speaking to groups about the challenge of seeing and listening for grace, I sometimes will play a "city sounds" track while I'm talking. It's full of the noise of honking, engines revving, other traffic sounds, sirens, someone shouting, etc. I keep speaking about the need to listen for God, all the while turning up the volume of the noise. Quickly, of course, the cacophony drowns out my words. It's very irritating, but I hope effectively shows that the world shouts and drowns out everything else.

By contrast, God has chosen, by and large, subtlety. Of course, He can thunder from Mt. Sinai, and blow through a room like a rushing, mighty wind at Pentecost, but a great deal of the Good News is much quieter and more personal.

Elijah's story of his encounter with the prophets of Baal is one of the most memorable examples of this truth. He had just called down fire from heaven to consume an offering in front of hundreds of those frenetic, defeated, and exhausted prophets. It was a spectacular victory for Elijah punctuated by a slaughter of the losers. Those were coarse days. In his energetic revelry, Elijah ran from Mt. Carmel to Jezreel, about 17 miles, only to find that Jezebel, the wicked queen and Baal sympathizer, didn't take the defeat graciously. She vowed to kill Elijah.

He ran for his life and by all reasonable appearances entered a period of depression. He wanted to die and thought he was the only one who believed in God. He even sounds a little disappointed in God, reminding Him of how faithful he had been.

God commanded Elijah to come out of his cave and watch as a rock-breaking wind blew through the valley below, then an 8.0 earthquake rattle the land, and then a firestorm raged over the devastation. Each one was a powerful demonstration, yet God was in none of them.

When God finally did really show up, it was in a still, small voice. The Hebrew is a little uncertain here. I heard a Jesuit Father say it meant "a light, silent sound." A silent sound, I like that.

Isn't it interesting in the story that the stunning victory for Elijah was not sustaining? In fact, it led to exhaustion and disillusionment. Couldn't Elijah have rallied himself, remembered how God showed up at Mt. Carmel, and stood up to Jezebel? Perhaps. Or perhaps we're to understand that we're not meant to live at those high rpms. God rarely shouts. When he wants to speak to us, He usually whispers a light, silent sound.

The world shouts. Our egos scream. God whispers. If we can't find a way to settle things down around us, and more importantly, within us, then we're not going to hear the light, silent sounds of God. Jesus often withdrew to a "lonely place" for prayer. He needed the quiet to hear the whispers. The Son of God needed quiet places to hear His Father. How can we possibly think we need any less? What's more, once things settle down in our minds, it's amazing how things, even people, tend to settle down around us. We simply don't realize how much our personal noise contributes to the noise. We need the stillness of being with God alone to hear His still, small voice and to receive His peace.

The Christian community is often guilty, I think, of highlighting the loud at the expense of the quiet. The most memorable testimonies from my early years were those of people or preachers who told stories of rather loud encounters with God. I remember thinking myself a bit inadequate for having had a relatively normal and sedate childhood. If I'd been a member of a biker gang, my conversion story as a nine-year-old would have been much more impressive. Alas, I just felt led to walk down the aisle one Sunday morning and publicly profess my love for Jesus. Simple as that.

The way we read the Bible skews our perception of the usual ways God interacts with us. We can read page after page of God's miracles, not realizing that between the miracles were days, weeks, even centuries. What were people doing in the meantime? They were recalling God's wondrous deeds and drawing assurance from those stories that God was real, still at work, and can be trusted to take care of them.

I'm not closing the door on the big miracles. God can do whatever He desires and in whatever form He wishes. We can certainly agree, however, that the so-called big miracles are not normative. Actually, when you think about it, it's hard to get much bigger than coming to earth as a man, giving Your life for all humanity, and rising from the dead. We now, all of us, live in the meantime. We can look back on God's gracious invasion of the world and trust that He's still in the saving business. He's a living Presence, and that is no less miraculous than parting a sea.

These "little miracles" are what we look for one day at a time and one moment at a time. The fact that we live in a noisy world is one of those things we both accept and can change. The world is not going to slow down. But we can, and when we do, we begin to see things in the days and moments that bless and sustain us.

One Frame at a Time

Life has three times, four if you count eternity. We have the past, the present, and the future. I've mentioned the ongoing pull and tug of the past and the future. Many people are burdened by a past they can't change and can't escape. Others are living with a suffocating anxiety about the future, unsure of their relationships, finances, health, etc.

We have already discussed the importance of forgiveness for handling a difficult past, and trust as the antidote for a fearful future. But what about the present?

Imagine a film strip. Each frame represents a single day. If I lay out about 100 years of film strip, that should cover more than what I can reasonably expect to attain. So, my whole life is rolled out on the floor. I can note the frame of my birth, my 16th birthday, my graduation from college, my marriage to Leslie. On other frames are other graduations and births. Still other frames contain darker memories. Granddaddy's sudden death. My brother's murder. The hazy frames of my alcoholism.

Then we come to the present frame, with a particular date. It's a single frame. Events are swirling around me. I'm precipitating some, like the writing of this book, and I'm acted upon by a phone call from my son, a text from my daughter, a conversation with my wife. This frame is fairly unremarkable up to the present moment. Of course, it's only about 10:15 a.m. The day could contain some wild swings.

The future frames are a mystery, a dream. I don't even know how many there are. Statistically, I'm due another 15 years, but there's no guarantee I'll make it to Thursday. If I imagine the frames stretching out the usual amount, I can fill them with fears or hopes. Frankly, most people fill them with fears.

Here's what people do a great deal of time with the film strip of their lives: they take all the frames from a burdensome past and pile them up on the present frame. They carry with them guilt, regret, and resentments.

Jean Paul Sartre in his play *The Flies* describes a town where everyone is forever burdened with their past sins. Annually, they are forced to relive the crimes of their past; they can never forget that they are forever guilty. One of the characters describes guilt in these words, "One day you too will commit an unforgiveable crime. At every step you will think that you are leaving it behind, but it will remain as heavy as before. Though you disown it time and time again, always it will be there, a dead weight holding you back. You will realize that nothing remains for you but to drag your crime after you until you die."

Some people spend their lives paying for their sins, a very sad and hopeless way to live. Most people are far better prosecutors than defense attorneys, and they win every case against themselves in a constant regret that they should have done better. Or they turn those prosecutorial skill on past offenders. The energy with which they tell you how they've been hurt leads you to believe the offense of years ago happened earlier that morning. Either way, they take all the burdens of the past and pile them up on the present day.

On the other hand, we have the "future trippers," who take all their worries and bring that pile of frames onto the present frame. My mother called herself a "world class worrier." She truly was, and I'm not sure she even regretted it. We cloak our anxieties with fine-sounding words like prudence, concern, even planning. One lady told me that she worries about everything so she can anticipate and plan. When I suggested that almost nothing she worried about happened, she suggested that was because she worried about them. It's kind of hard to work with that.

What's exasperating to me was completely anticipated by Jesus. He devoted a large section of the Sermon on the Mount to the topic of anxiety (Matt. 6:25-34). We must not overlook the significance of that. The Sermon on the Mount is the largest body of Jesus' teaching, taking up three chapters in the Gospel of Matthew (5-7). Some of the most memorable lines from the Sermon come from that section. The average person on the street will note a ring of familiarity in "the birds of the air and the flowers of the field." That's from The Sermon.

Jesus plainly said, "do not be anxious" (Matt 6:25). It's an imperative. The memorable lines of this section are all related to examples of how God takes care of His creation. Because human beings are at the pinnacle of God's creation, we can assume that since he has provided for the birds of the air and the flowers of the field, then we can rest assured that He'll provide for us.

The prohibition against worry pops up in other parts of the New Testament. Paul again flatly commanded us "to be anxious for nothing" (Phil. 4:6). Peter wrote that we are to "cast all your burdens upon God because He cares for you" (1 Pet. 5:7). Peter's command is not simply a call to "get over it." He clearly connects our potential to be anxiety-free with God's character.

We don't worry because in our obvious weakness we trust in God's loving strength. Frankly, the anxiety or fear that I feel is an indicator that I'm not trusting God completely. I don't want to allow my failure to become another thing I worry about, but I don't want to give up on the idea that I can avoid a tremendous amount of worry if I simply trust God to be God.

To get back to our film strip illustration, the point here is that we take all of the uncertain frames of our future and pile them up on today whenever we worry. The antidote, of course, is to remember that God was in every frame in the past, and because His character is constant we can rely on His presence in every frame in the future. That describes the source of a great deal of our base-line discontent: we imagine frames without God's presence.

The point here, however, is much more immediate. If we pile up the past and the future on the present, then we lose the present. It's impossible for us to live one day at a time because we're trying to live scores of days at a time by reliving the past and worrying about the future.

I believe if I could mandate a single verse for people to memorize from the Sermon on the Mount, a verse that would relieve a great deal of suffering and enable people to turn their attention to God, that verse would be Matthew 6:34: "Therefore do not be anxious about tomorrow, for tomorrow will be anxious for itself. Let each day's trouble be sufficient for the day." Notice Jesus didn't say we would be trouble-free. The unreasonable expectation that we'll be endlessly happy is one of the most common reasons we're never reasonably happy. Each day has some trouble, but God can be trusted one day at a time, because He is in one day at a time.

Interestingly, we find this principle in the writings of John when he wrote that we "have eternal life" through faith in Christ (John 3:16 and 1 John 5:13). Notice the tense of the verb. It's present. We have eternal life. Eternal life, therefore, is not something like an insurance policy that kicks in when we die. Eternal life is a present reality, already shaping and helping us become aware of God's many graces in each moment. As Jean-Pierre de Caussade noted "Every moment reveals God to us. Faith is our light in this life." (*Abandonment to Divine Providence*, Chapter II, sec. 1). That God is truly in every moment is a major theme of his book, and one that he picked up from the Scripture.

One of the most basic disciplines we must develop for reasonable happiness is to live one day at a time. We have to clear off of that day the wreckage of the past and trust it all to God's grace and mercy. We clear off the imagined wreckage of the future by trusting all things to God's gracious Providence.

Imagine what it would be like to give God all of your guilt, regret, worry, and fear. Nothing drags you down from your past, and nothing frightens you about the future. What would that be like? You would be left with a single day where you can encounter God in that frame. My Jesuit friends love to emphasize that God is always at work around us, and our challenge is to be attentive and responsive. When we simply accept each day as God's gift, leaving alone both past and future, then something truly miraculous happens. We discover the miracle in each moment.

On a very practical level, the ever-presence of God means that we can re-start our day at any time. We all have the experience of "waking up on the wrong side of the bed." A bad dream lingers. A dreaded appointment looms. We're churlish and anxious and have too long accepted these stresses as unchangeable, and we usually let everyone around us know how out of sorts we are.

Enjoying one moment at a time means that we can take hold of eternal promises that certainly transcend temporal challenges. We can mentally and spiritually redirect our thinking at any time. Faith enables this. We create the opening for God to come in and calm us. The change in our attitude and change in our day is a simple as a prayer, a quiet moment, a recaptured faith.

Any Bush Will Do

Some people call what I'm about to tell you "a great secret." It's actually no secret at all. It's a basic truth that we've simply neglected and forgotten. When reminded of it, most people respond with a relief that is like stepping out of a cold, dark cave into the sunshine of a beautiful day. The truth is this: God meets us only in the present moment. Lingering in the past or rushing ahead to the future only ensures that we're walking alone. Each day is composed of an endless series of single moments where we can meet God unobscured.

Elizabeth Barrett Browning captured this truth memorably with the words, "Earth's crammed with heaven, And every common bush afire with God, But only he who sees takes off his shoes; The rest sit round and pluck blackberries." God has tucked away a bit of Himself in every nook and cranny of creation, both micro and macro. If we live in these moments, we find God, but it's not easy.

David's first profession was shepherding. Later he would slay a giant, become a king, lead a nation to the zenith of its power and influence. But in his early years he watched sheep and spent many a night out under the stars. Perhaps that was his inspiration for the compelling words of Psalm 19 where David declares, "The heavens are telling the glory of God and the firmament proclaims His handiwork." He goes on to suggest that though there are no words, the voice of the heavens goes out through all the earth. These verses are one of the earliest and most profound arguments for God's existence from design and beauty. If you look up at the stars, you can't help but feel and even hear the presence of God.

I've made many trips to the Amazon River Valley and traveled far from the cities and other sources of light. On a moonless, clear night I've stood and watched the heavens. I swear sometimes I think I hear the words David wrote about 3,000 years ago.

Sometimes when I speak to groups of people, some of whom are not believers, I ask how many of them have seen the Milky Way. Less than 10% say they have. Many people have even asked me if the Milky Way is actually visible, thinking that it's something very distant instead of our home galaxy. The only reason they can't see the Milky Way is because the glare of civilization has wiped away what our forbearers beheld nightly.

Some people actually advance the notion that the rise of atheism corresponds to the development of the streetlamp. As cities brightened during the nights, fewer and fewer stars were visible. Today, if you live in a city, you're lucky to be able to see a score of stars. When I accompany groups to the Amazon, they're stunned by the first clear night sky they've ever seen. I have them point their binoculars to view the plane of the Milky Way, and the density of stars is breathtaking.

I don't know if streetlamps have contributed to atheism. I do know that we're increasingly cut off from the stars as well as Browning's flaming bushes. God clearly reveals Himself both in the beauty of nature and in its quiet. People do not look up as they used to, and perhaps that has led them to assume there's nothing worth seeing.

The Prayer, as well as the poem, suggest that every moment has something for us to enjoy. Out of habit, as I've suggested before, we typically only look for the aggravation of each moment, and the world in many ways conspires to present us with a dash of problems for each moment.

Living a reasonably happy life does not mean we eliminate unhappiness. Happiness and unhappiness are not binary, so that you only have one or the other. They're dualistic, existing often side by side within every moment. The presence of unhappiness doesn't mean we're faulty. Good, faithful, well-balanced people have a share of unhappiness. But what is the focus? We have the ability to choose. We can look at the aggravation and complain. Or we can look for God and rejoice.

As a teenager, I heard a minister say that if you ever feel down, read the book of Philippians. I did and found it very hopeful and encouraging. It's only four chapters long, so it doesn't take long to get the divine "lift" that the Scripture can give us.

I never forgot his words, and as I began my studies in seminary, I learned more about that little book that make its message even more powerful. Paul wrote it when he was in prison, facing a very uncertain future. Our best guess is that he did survive this imprisonment, later to be rearrested and executed. But when he wrote Philippians, he didn't know if he would make it out alive.

With that background in mind, look again at some of the words Paul wrote in the letter. "Rejoice in the Lord always!" Always? That sounds ludicrous. Paul anticipated our typical response, for he followed up, "and again I say rejoice" (Phil. 4:4). Remember that the word "joy" is built on the same root as the word for grace. Joy is a gift from God.

Was Paul happy during his imprisonment? Remember, I've suggested happiness is related to external events, so he may not have been happy. We're entitled to be unhappy when the events around us are difficult. But apparently, he believed in the absolute staying power of joy. Even in prison, he could find grace in the difficult moments.

Paul made this abundantly clear a few verses later where he wrote, "Whatever is true, honorable, just, pure, lovely, or gracious; if there is anything excellent and worthy of praise, think on these things" (Phil. 4:8). Paul knew that these wonderful qualities surrounded him, even in a prison cell. "Think" is an imperative. He meant that we can intentionally tune our minds to see these qualities. Anywhere and anytime. We must not allow difficult circumstances to obscure God's presence or silence His Providence.

We don't manufacture joy. It is a gift from God. We can choose our happiness, or at least the potential for it, even in difficult times, if we choose to look in the right places in the right ways. We can find the flaming bushes. We can hear the light, silent sounds.

The Voices Do Come to You

Years ago, I ran across George Bernard Shaw's play *St. Joan*, which depicts the life of St. Joan of Arc. She was an unlikely French military leader in the Hundred Years War and because of her faith and passion, she was later canonized.

In the play, as in real life, St. Joan claims to hear the voice of God, and with that conviction she inspires the men to follow her. The prince, however, is jealous of this young woman and her power to inspire. "Why don't the voices come to me? I am king not you!" he whines. Joan answers, "They do come to you, but you do not hear them. As soon as the angelus rings you cross yourself and have done with it. But if you prayed from your heart and sat in the field and listened for the thrilling of the bells after they stopped ringing, then you would hear the voices just as I."

I never lost my faith in God during the dark years of my alcoholism. He was always there. Nothing in my theological studies or the practice of my faith for decades led me to believe that He pops in and out depending on my performance for the day. I do know that I can wander off the path, though. I'd wandered quite a distance from that sure and certain path.

I've described our culture as noisy. The city sounds drown out God's quiet voice. We all face that challenge. I can assure you, however, that nothing is noisier than addiction, and all that noise is self-generated. The drug, whether alcohol or one of the scores of others, screams for attention and offers a solution to the pain and with a promise to bring peace. It's all a lie, but once you cross the line into addiction nothing else makes sense.

When I dragged myself into a treatment center, I couldn't hear God. I felt dark and heavy and empty. Of course, I had all of the training and decades of experience. I could parrot the words but could derive no real comfort from them. God was with me, but I couldn't hear and that only added to my despair. We were offered the opportunity to go to worship services on Sundays, but I didn't go. I really didn't know what was left of me or left in me.

The fellow who ran Palmetto was Darren Davis, in many ways an incarnation of north Louisiana where he born and raised. He was tough, absolutely no-nonsense, and if we could get around the privacy issues, would be a star in a reality show. In recovery himself, Darren combined personal experience, education, and an innate ability to peer into an addict's soul. He's a gifted healer.

One meeting, he talked about connecting with a Higher Power. Many folks enter treatment with a grudge against God, and many others don't believe at all or are unsure of what they believe. I had all the education, and I suppose some conviction, but I just didn't know what any of it meant anymore. Darren wasn't speaking to me exactly, but he said something that really impressed me. "If you don't know about God, that's all right. Just go out on that tennis court over there at night and just look up and say that you need help. That's all."

I was three weeks into my stay there when one evening at 10 p.m., I put on my jacket and went out to that tennis court. Everything was still and quiet. It was early December, and I could see my breath with every exhale on that clear, cold north Louisiana night at an addiction treatment facility in the middle of acres and acres of cow pastures. I looked up and saw the stars. Never more broken in my life, I prayed, "God, I know you're there. I don't half understand what's happened to me and how I got here. I don't know what's left of me or in me. I'm as confused as I've ever been, but I'm calling out to You because I know it's the right thing to do. I need Your help."

The heavens didn't open at that moment. No pillar of fire or dove descending upon me. I'd taken a suggestion and done everything I knew to do. I took all of my broken self and gave it to God as

I understood Him. I just kind of dumped my life at the altar. I left it all up to God and went to bed with a peace that I'd truly meant what I had prayed.

Three days later, standing alone beside a bayou that runs behind the property, I felt something that I can only describe as a breath. It was the light, silent sound of God.

Celtic Christians believed in "thin places." It's the idea that certain places are sacred, and that in those places, the distance between our physical world and the spiritual world is quite thin. The sacred places offer us the opportunity to look beyond the surrounding clamor of empty busyness and "see" what is true, real, and eternal. Thin places nurture our souls.

One of my thin places was that tennis court in a treatment facility. I believe there are definitely dependable and regular sacred spaces like our beautiful churches. But I also know you don't have to go to a certain place to be in the presence of God. You just have to bring the right mind along with the eyes and ears of faith. Give your attention to what God is doing right in front of you and trust Him to take care of the problems when they come, not before. Then you begin to see God one day at a time and enjoy Him one moment at a time. And that leads to a reasonably happy life.

Toward reasonable happiness:

- Time is a challenge for most people. We are dragged down by the past, burdened in the present, and frightened by the future.
- One of the most basic challenges in life is to realize the joy that is tucked away in each moment. We need help to do this.
- God created us to enjoy Him and the life He's given us. Inadequate images of God as threatening or angry prevent us from drawing close to Him.

- We focus on our discontent in life chiefly because we neglect to see how a good and loving God is blessing us in countless ways every moment.
- The world shouts. God whispers. We must create quite moments during the day to have a quiet mind to hear and see God.
- Enjoying one moment at a time doesn't mean we eliminate unhappiness. Happiness and unhappiness usually exist side-by-side. We simply look for the occasions of joy that surround us.

Thin places (and times) are opportunities to see how close the spiritual world is to our physical world. We must create thin places and times in our day-to-day lives.

CHAPTER SEVEN

ACCEPTING HARDSHIPS AS THE PATHWAY TO PEACE

"In the world you will have tribulation. But rejoice, for I have overcome the world."
John 16:33

"Although the world is full of suffering, it is also full of overcoming it."
Helen Keller

Anyone who has darkened the door of an AA meeting, or just about any 12-Step oriented meeting, will be familiar with The Serenity Prayer, but only the first three lines. When I work with people in early recovery, I often introduce them to the long version of The Prayer and ask them to read it and then share with the group a phrase that comforts and a phrase that challenges. The overwhelming choice for most challenging is "Accepting hardships as the pathway to peace."

It's not only people in early recovery who struggle with this idea. Anyone who has given any thought to God and spiritual matters wrestles with the idea of why bad things happen and what those bad things say about the God they're trying to understand. To suggest, as The Prayer does, that something positive can come from the struggles is not only a new idea but for many people an outrageous idea. Suffering, they suppose, is to be entirely avoided, and its presence is merely a problem to be solved.

The goal of life from a biological standpoint is to avoid suffering. This is the way our brains operate. In large measure, the brain is a survival organ designed to get us through life safely. That is the goal.

To complement this biological drive, we now live in an age where science and technology protect us from a great deal of hardship. The results have been dramatic, but we take them for granted. Until James Lind in 1747 discovered vitamin C as the antidote to scurvy, half the crews of lengthy naval expeditions died of scurvy. After the battles, prior to penicillin, doctors regularly amputated limbs from soldiers with relatively minor wounds out of fear of gangrene. Who thinks about scurvy and gangrene today? Plumbing, electrification, even laws holding manufacturers liable for poor workmanship have combined to create a terrific ability to avoid hardships that formerly were a regular and expected part of life.

Diseases are technological challenges today. Think of the incredible strides we have seen in the treatment of many cancers that only a few decades ago were death sentences. The record is so strong and confidence so high that some scientists speak of being able to create "amortals" within a century, people who will live forever barring an accident (thus "amortal" instead of immortal). Our technology in countless ways is meeting the biological drive we've had since the beginning.

But we cannot avoid suffering. The inevitability of hardships forces us to try to construct something helpful out of the difficult situations. It's hard, and we can make many mistakes in our attempts, but if we don't try, then we risk cynicism and despair. What good is being amortal if you don't have meaning?

This phrase of The Prayer takes us into the very deepest waters of spiritual truth and practice. If we only focus on the physical realities of suffering, then all we can do is strive to avoid hardships. While it's true that we're wired to do this and ever more successful at implementing successful technologies, we need more than mere avoidance to construct meaningful lives and attain reasonable happiness. We have to deal with the reality of suffering.

That's where the mind comes in. The mind is to the soul as the brain is to the body. The orientation of the mind, the way we think about things, gives direction to the soul. If we nurture the soul, then we find meaning in both good and bad. In fact, we can genuinely learn to stop thinking of events in this binary way, as either good or bad. They simply are. Our response, the way we think about them, either invites God more deeply into our pain or convinces us of something sinister. As throughout The Prayer, it's our response to the unalterable suffering that helps us transcend it and even grow through it.

I had a good seminary education. Excellent professors. I studied hard and enjoyed it very much. I learned good theology. The choices I made prior to those years and in the years afterward enabled me to live productively and happily for the most part. But some things you can't really learn in seminary until you face the real-life situations. Hardships have a purpose you can't comprehend in a classroom.

When I was fresh out of treatment for my alcoholism, a man who had many years "in the program" as we say, gave me a book of daily devotions for people in recovery. I use it to this day. Inside the cover he wrote, "God gave you a gift when he gave you alcoholism." Many people will stumble on the idea that God "gave" me alcoholism. That's a very hard concept, and we'll look at it more deeply later in this chapter. Don't let it stop you at this point. Just go with the idea that God certainly allowed me to have alcoholism. But that's not my main point right now. It's the idea that I was supposed to be thankful for it that really jolted me initially. When he first gave me that book, the pain was so recent that I had a hard time thinking that I needed to "be thankful for my alcoholism." Seven years later, I am, for through this gift of suffering God has brought me a peace that I simply had never experienced before and could not have experienced any other way.

The Importance of Getting This Right

The longest-range ballistic missiles take 30 minutes or more to reach their targets. They are powered for only the first few minutes of the flight. After the fuel is exhausted and the stages jettisoned, the remainder of the rocket flies along its path in accordance with well-established physical principles. It's like a ball being thrown. The accuracy depends on the initial, carefully calculated launch angle and speed. If you get that right, the missile hits the target.

Our thinking about the problem of suffering is one of the most crucial theological launch angles conceivable. Some people end up with a very comforting theology of suffering and have found peace in spite of, or even because of, their hardships. Others find suffering to be a final nail in the coffin of their faith. Their hardships simply confirm either God's inexistence, impotence, or insouciance. This theological fork in the road cannot be more consequential. We have to get it right. Yet we so often get it wrong.

Most everyone, when they think about God, begins with the idea that God is somehow involved in their lives. Further, they believe that God is able and willing to help them in some important ways. So, when they run into hardships, it's quite natural that they turn to God for help. When the suffering remains and the help doesn't show up in the expected way, then the deep questions arise.

This can happen to very faithful, orthodox believers. A man I knew quite well lost a child in an accident. That is a dreadful life experience that you would have to endure if you're going to understand how it impacts someone else. Those of us who've not gone through it simply lack the vocabulary. Imagining it brings pain, so we choose not to imagine it. This man, who had an apparently deep and meaningful faith his entire life, descended to the point where he was sure that God didn't answer prayer and was fairly sure God didn't have anything to do with day to day life. He couldn't reconcile the idea of a good and loving God with the fact of his child's death.

John Claypool was first a Southern Baptist pastor, then later Episcopalian. He experienced the death of his eight-year-old daughter Laura Lue to leukemia. From diagnosis to death took only 18 months. His book *Tracks of a Fellow Struggler* chronicle his journey from hope to questions and back to hope, though a more realistic hope. In the first sermon after her death, Claypool voiced a very understandable plea, "You owe me an explanation." (*Tracks,* p. 70)

Is this question bad, or, as some suggested when he first asked it, heretical? I don't think so. It may not be helpful, but it is honest and authentic. The main point here, however, is that if you dig down even a little bit under the surface of someone who either struggles with the idea of God or rejects God outright, you almost certainly will find the problem of suffering as the source of their doubts. It happens to all of us at some level, and for some the reality of hardships proves to be the shipwreck of their faith.

Charles Templeton for many years shared a friendship and religious zeal with Billy Graham. They made an evangelistic tour of western Europe, often rooming together as they journeyed from country to country. He later attended Princeton Seminary and hosted a religious television show on CBS called *Look Up and Live.*

After a long battle with doubt, however, he declared that he no longer believed in God. His book *Farewell to God: My Reasons to Reject the Christian Faith* sums up his intellectual problems with faith but also maintains that faith is often deleterious to individuals and society. Templeton's tone is often harsh. The faith that once gave him both comfort and purpose became an obsolete and destructive lie.

For his book *The Case for Faith*, Lee Strobel interviewed Templeton and asked, "Was there one event in particular that caused you to lose your faith in God?" Templeton answered that it was a photograph in *Life* magazine. He explained that the picture was of a Black woman in Northern Africa who was holding her dead son in her arms. The child had perished in the devastating drought that had ravaged the area. Templeton explained that he simply did not believe a good and caring God would not send rain to this region to help this poor woman and so many others like her. So, he decided, there was no such thing as a loving God. (*The Case for Faith*, p. 14)

Templeton's questions were neither wrong nor bad. He formulated in a very intelligent manner the question with which every believer has struggled at some level. His question revolved around a more global perspective. Why is there suffering in the world? Most people struggle with at the more personal level to understand why hardships are happening to them. Either way, the potential is huge, and it is to a degree understandable for a seriously questioning person to come away with the idea that God does not exist, much less give peace in the midst of hardships.

Sometimes, the problem of evil is treated as unassailable proof that God either doesn't exist or doesn't care. "After all," the reasoning goes, "if I had the power to relieve the suffering of another person then I would do it. Hence God either doesn't exist, doesn't care, or can't do anything about hardships and therefore can't be relied on or trusted."

This line of reasoning is common and persuasive to many people for obvious reasons. The presence of evil does raise considerable issues. However, people who so easily adopt this logic often don't seem to have looked at the other side of the coin. If evil proves the inexistence or inadequacy of God, then what does the presence of good prove? So, equally thoughtful, rational people can look at the same evidence, or a broader sampling of evidence and come away with opposite conclusions.

A. J. Gossip, a Scottish preacher who died in 1954, preached one of the most celebrated and memorable sermons, at least by title, in the history of preaching: "But When Life Tumbles in, What Then?" He delivered this sermon soon after the death of his wife. Hardship had hit. He summed up the fork in the road that he and all of us face: "I do not comprehend this life of ours. But still less can I comprehend how people in trouble and loss and bereavement can fling away peevishly from the Christian faith. In God's name, fling to what? Have we not lost enough without losing that too?" (*20 Centuries of Great Preaching*, vol. VIII, p. 235).

Templeton and Gossip. Two men of deep and demonstrable faith who faced the challenge of hardships. One flung away. The other held on. Their stories are endlessly repeated in the lives of ordinary people every single moment of every single day. Again, the stakes could not be higher, and so we must seek the truth carefully if we're ever going to see hardships as a pathway to peace.

God's Character Is More Important than Our Comfort

Up to this point, we've looked only at how difficulties and suffering may be a reflection on God. If God doesn't stop all suffering or merely stop *my* suffering, then maybe He's unable or unwilling to do so. Or more devastatingly, maybe He's not there in the first place. The point is, so far, we've only looked at the problem of suffering through one lens, the one aimed at God.

An even more malevolent idea arises when we turn the lens around and point it at ourselves. Hardships can cause not only doubts about God but doubts about ourselves. Are my hardships the result of *my* inadequacies? Unfortunately, many people feel this way because the idea is promoted by some Christians who should know better.

Without question, in this vital area of our thinking about God and life, we have some of the very worst ideas imaginable. In my early years of ministry, I was asked to speak to a young woman in the community where I pastored a small church. She had lost a baby to sudden infant death syndrome. The minister who conducted the service had said that God took her child in order to get her attention. Understandably, this young woman was in a mixture of confusion and despair when she came to talk to me. She also had an overwhelming guilt that perhaps her lack of faith and commitment had led to the death of her child.

Years later, a woman told me that when she was in the hospital for ulcers, a leader in her church came to visit and told her that her problems were due to unconfessed sin. She was confessing with her stomach instead of confessing with her mouth, he said. To her credit, she didn't embrace his idea and told me that a few years later she visited him in the hospital after he'd undergone bypass surgery. She said she resisted the impulse to suggest to him that he was obviously confessing his sins with his heart instead of his mouth. I admired her restraint.

These are just a couple of examples of the scores of such stories I've encountered over the years. Imagine how difficult it must be to reconcile those grotesque examples with the idea of a good, loving, and caring God. Instead of being the pathway to peace, hardships prove to be the shipwreck of faith. Again, the theological launch angle is wrong from the start, and it's no wonder that a great many people turn away from the only source of help that is consistent.

How does such an idea arise? If I were attempting to turn people away from God, the most effective way is not to approach them with a blatantly evil alternative. Anyone could see through that obvious ploy. No, the best way to convince people to turn away from faith is to take a good idea and twist it, even if only slightly, and then wait for it to take effect. Subtly, the virtue becomes a vice, and few people are going to even notice.

The disturbing idea that we're directly to blame for every misfortune comes from the biblical notion of blessing and curse. Moses said, "Behold I set before you this day a blessing and curse" (Deut. 11:26). Moses went on to explain that if the people obeyed God's commandments, they will be blessed. If they do not obey, they will be cursed. This very basic proposition underlies a great deal of the Old Testament, and it holds an important theological truth and a very practical application.

I have already noted that God dispenses blessings to all people regardless of their faith or lack of it. Jesus taught that God makes the rain to fall on the just and the unjust and the sun to shine on the evil and the good. God is good, so any good we enjoy is either directly attributable to Him or the result of the way He's constructed the interaction between the physical and spiritual worlds. God is love, and He is good. It's His nature to bless.

The idea is also pragmatic. It works in the real world. Drawing close to God brings you close to the source of love and goodness. Faith in God and adherence to His way has demonstrably better results in every significant metric of life. We avoid a great many dangers and dangerous ideas by being close to God. We're also able to be much more helpful to others, for faith in God comes with an imperative to love and help others. Very simply, faith is the way to make life work. As C. S. Lewis put it, "If you want to get warm you must stand near the fire: if you want to be wet you must get into the water. If you want joy, power, peace, eternal life, you must get close to, or even into, the thing that has them." (*Mere Christianity*, p. 153)

This biblical idea, especially as it plays out over the entirety of the Bible, is very simple and straightforward. We do better when we believe and are faithful to God's ways. We hurt ourselves and others when we don't.

I'll be addressing the biblical record in more detail in the next section, but I do need to emphasize here that the idea of God's cursing people today does not fit with the New Testament. We do find the "law of the harvest," the idea that whatever we so sow we also reap (Gal. 6:7), but again this is more of an expression of the way life works. To have an idea of God holding his finger over the smite button while He waits for us to trip up is cartoon fodder, but is not a fair representation of the full narrative of Scripture.

But let's get back to the distortion. It arises when we try to come up with reasons for the hardships we or other people face. It's fairly irresistible for people to think that they have had a hand in their own trouble, and it's even more deliciously seductive to try to come up with a theological reason someone else is in trouble. Thus, hardships for a believer can become the occasion for all manner of doubt and self-loathing. "I must have done something to offend God," goes the reasoning. Or when applied to others, "they must have done something to offend God." This latter line of reasoning is as old as Job, whose "friends" were sure he'd done something to earn the misfortune that had befallen him.

It's at this point "the distortion" has its full effect, for we begin to associate every misfortune with our direct responsibility and God's direct action. If I believe God is constantly grading, dispensing both blessings and curses depending on my actions and thoughts, then I've moved fully into the realm of performance-based theology and away from grace. Nothing truly good happens when I operate from that perspective, and a lot of very bad things inevitably will occur.

I worked for a time with a treatment facility for men trying to recover from addiction. I introduced them to spiritual principles and helped some of them begin to think about the idea of God and others to think more clearly about a God who can help them recover. When you give free rein for people to talk about their most serious theological questions and issues, the problem of evil always comes up. One common response was outrage that they had endured some very hard times such as the loss of a parent or a friend. These are events for which they have no culpability. They're hurt and angry that something bad has happened to someone they love. So, we talk about a God who can help us in those situations, who offers grace and love no matter what we face or what we've done.

The conversation then morphs into an often-vigorous discussion of why any bad thing has ever happened to them. They talk about not getting what they deserve. That's the key word that I look for, and it prompts me to ask this question: "Do you really want a theology in which you get what you deserve?" Their first response is a spirited "Of course!" Then a few of them will pause and say, "No...wait."

They realize that if we got what we deserved, then we'd all be in grave trouble. There is no grace in getting what you deserve. That's where I want to take them in our discussion, to grace.

The uniqueness of the Christian faith is that only here does redemption precede righteousness. You don't have to be good enough to come to God for salvation. With karma, you get what you deserve. With law-based theologies, you either pass or fail. With grace, you begin from a point of acceptance with God, and that becomes the deepest motivation for real change in our lives. Conduct emerges from love. Good works, which are always vital, grow from the soil of grace.

As long as we feel that God's response to us is based on our conduct rather than His character, we will never see hardships as the pathway to peace. Hardships simply become a verdict and play to our fears, guilt, and shame. God's intention to teach us the path of wisdom becomes so distorted through legalism that difficulty makes us either resentful of God or angry at Him.

God Is Good, Life Is Hard

When it comes to reviewing what the Scripture says about something as important and complex as hardships, it's vital to have a solid understanding of the nature of the Bible as God's revelation to us. The distortion I spoke of in the previous section arises out of the Scripture, but it's a distortion because it lacks a solid foundation. It highlights and takes out of context a few ideas we find in the Bible. It's persuasive because it appeals to our performance-based natures. It fails because it focuses on a few drops but ignores the current of the river. While challenging, it is deeply true that the Bible as a whole shows how hardships can be the pathway to peace.

Entire volumes address this topic, but I want to briefly touch on three ideas I think will provide a framework for looking at what the Bible has to say about hardships. The first idea we must keep in mind is that God is good. This sounds so basic, but the distortion can clearly lead us to places where we could begin to doubt that. God is not going to engage in anything that is bad. His goal is to save, comfort, and guide.

Second, the Bible is not flat. It rises in its revelation. Ideas that are introduced in the pages of the Old Testament find their full expression in the pages of the New. All of the Bible is inspired and valuable as God's revelation to us and a record of how people have understood and responded to God, but we don't treat all of the Bible as equally applicable. Many passages and stories are descriptive of certain events at a particular time in the story of redemption but not prescriptive in that they give us a complete insight into God's character or an enduring example of how we should conduct ourselves. In other words, there's a clear reason that Christians pass out copies of the Gospel of John at some events but not the Book of Leviticus.

Third, we should read the entire Bible through the lens, so to speak, of Jesus. His remarkable claim "if you have seen me you have seen the Father" (John 14:9) means that we find answers to what God is like by studying the life and teaching of Jesus. We find in Him answers to any questions or doubts we have. He's the ultimate arbiter. So, with these in mind, let's survey some important themes that help us understand hardships and suffering.

We begin with the fact that hardships are woven into the fabric of life. There is no escaping them. Jesus said, "In the world you will have tribulation" (John 16:33). Every follower of Jesus we know anything about in depth in the New Testament faced a very difficult path. God didn't even make it easy for His Son to be born into the world. Mary and Joseph traveled for a census when Mary was late in her third trimester. After His birth they had to flee to Egypt for their lives.

The Apostle Paul, who singlehandedly did more than any person in history to spread the gospel, was stoned, beaten, imprisoned, shipwrecked, and eventually executed for his faith. He wrote of feeling unbearably crushed and despairing of life itself during one particularly dark period in his life (2 Cor. 1:8).

Peter, the first Pope mind you, wrote, "Do not be surprised at the fiery ordeal which comes upon you to prove you, as if something strange were happening to you" (1 Pet. 4:12). He warned his readers because he knew how unpopular it was to be a Christian and how difficult life would become for them. The fiery ordeal eventually consumed him as well. According to tradition, he was crucified upside down because he felt unworthy to die in exactly the same way as his Lord.

Let's not forget that Jesus Himself did indeed die on a cross. Again, it was Peter who summed up what that means for anyone who follows Jesus today: "For to this you have been called, because Christ also suffered for you, leaving you an example that you should follow in His steps" (1 Pet. 2:21).

Nothing in the New Testament suggests in the slightest way that being a Christian protects us from hardships. To the contrary, Jesus and every writer who addressed the subject went to great lengths to tell us the truth. Life is hard, and being a Christian doesn't give us a pass. Harold Kushner said, "Expecting life to be fair to you because you're good is like expecting the bull not to charge you because you're a vegetarian." Neither the bull nor life are concerned about the quality of your faith or conduct. Good, faithful people get sick, have accidents, lose jobs and relationships, get addicted, and die. Faith is not an insurance policy against the winds of real life.

What faith does, however, is much more important than simply creating for us a pleasant arrangement of circumstances. Faith lets God into our lives so that what threatened to make us weak actually makes us stronger. We can count on this. In the same passage where Jesus assured us that we'll face tribulation, He added, "but rejoice for I have overcome the world" (John 16:33). The world doesn't have the final say.

Accepting the reality of suffering is plainly necessary. There's simply no need to continue wrestling with the unfairness of life. You can curse the darkness if you wish, but the sun will still set every day. The Scripture is clear, honest, and complete on the reality of suffering. We can't "saint" our way out of the reality of life. In fact, the main contribution of the saints is to show us that we not only must accept the presence of suffering, but we can understand it as a gift from God.

Suffering as a Gift from God

If the Bible only presented the reality of suffering and stopped there, then we'd have to confess that it's long on diagnosis and short on cure. It's hardly good news to be told you will suffer and leave the matter at that. But the Bible doesn't stop there. It presents a vision of what inevitable suffering can mean in our lives. This phrase of The Prayer arises from the very challenging idea that suffering is a gift from God.

That suffering can actually be a benefit to us is the ultimate understanding of suffering and one of the most concrete expressions of acceptance. It is also among the most difficult spiritual concepts imaginable. As I said, I honestly was not able to see my alcoholism as a gift. I understood it, accepted its reality, and believed deeply in the prospect of recovery, but I was not able at that early stage to see it that way.

How can we get there? Religious belief is a genuinely complex human behavior involving a great many ideas, understandings, and theological starts and stops. When faced with suffering, people have a variety of responses: denial, outrage, control, depression, acceptance, even joy are all on the table. It's tempting to set up stages of progress like the familiar stages of grief. But human behavior is simply not linear, especially when it comes to something as challenging as suffering. What we can accept one day, we challenge and resist the next. Still, our goal must be to glimpse and take an often slippery hold of the higher visions.

This phrase of The Prayer promises a *pathway* to peace that is paved with difficulty. The pathway implies a process. This is what Paul had in mind in the opening verses of Romans 5 where he stated that we have peace with God through faith. That is the end point of the journey, but he knew that getting there would be challenging.

Somewhat stunningly, he wrote that on this pathway we are to "rejoice in suffering," and then lines out the steps: "Knowing that suffering produces endurance, endurance produces character, and character produces hope" (Rom. 5:3-4). The word for suffering is one of the more aggressive words for challenge and difficulty in the New Testament. It's derived from words that mean to crush and break. These are hardships of the highest order, and a reminder that in The Prayer it's not moderate discomfort that leads to peace. The pathway is paved with the hardest of hardships.

The initial faithful response to suffering, therefore, calls for endurance, a Greek word that implies patience. Endurance is leaning into the wind, not giving in to it. Endurance is the key to not allowing hardships to wreck our lives.

Character refers to something that has been proven to be dependable and true. Enduring suffering with faith and patience both reveals character and builds it. Suffering does not have a neutral effect on the life of the sufferer. It will leave you stronger or weaker, better or bitter. In keeping with the tone of The Prayer, the difference lies in the manner of our response. For the Christian, this means keeping Christ in the center and clinging to Him in the midst of the storm.

Ultimately, this process leads to hope. Think of hope as vision that enables us to see the sun above the storm and to trust that dawn will follow the darkness. Our English word for hope is too weak for this sturdy Greek word. In English, we can hope for all kinds of things that will not happen. I hope my situation will improve in some way, but I don't know. The hope Paul wrote of here is grounded in the promises of Christ. There is no doubt. We're here anticipating the powerful promise of the later phrase of The Prayer where we can fully trust God to make all things right.

This amazing spiritual principle explains why some of the biblical writers penned astonishing words like, "Count it all joy, my brethren, when you meet various trials" (James 1:2). Paul wrote that he "all the more gladly boast of my weaknesses" (2 Cor. 12:10). Why? How? Because God has made clear throughout the scripture and in the lives of countless saints that "My grace is sufficient for you, for my power is made perfect in weakness" (2 Cor. 12:9).

This is the way forward. Jesus said we will have tribulations in the world (that's the plain reality). He then added that we can rejoice because He has overcome the world (that's the hopeful solution). We see pain as a problem. God sees and uses it as an opportunity to help us grow stronger.

Stephen Colbert, one of America's most popular comedians, suffered the loss of his father and two brothers at a young age. Reflecting on that grief and the other sufferings of life he said, "What punishments of God are not gifts?" He was drawing on words from a J. R. R. Tolkien letter in which he states, "A divine 'punishment' is also a divine 'gift,' if accepted, since its object is ultimate blessing, and the supreme inventiveness of the Creator will make 'punishments' (that is, changes of design) produce a good not otherwise to be obtained." (*The Letters of J. R. R. Tolkien*, p. 286)

Is my alcoholism a gift? I've raged against it. Doubted myself. Questioned God. Was it a punishment from God? I'm sure I should put the word "punishment" in quotations marks as Tolkien did, but I simply lack the full perspective. But I have now fully accepted it and believe God has blessed me and made me stronger through it. Anything for my eternal benefit is, in fact, a gift.

I've devoted quite a bit of extra space to this survey because, as I maintained earlier, it's essential we get this right. Because so many people who get this wrong use the Bible to support their positions, it's vital to present a biblical approach that paves the way for us to accept hardships as the pathway to peace. The fact that difficulty comes to all people, faithful or unfaithful, is the first key that we must accept in this phrase of The Prayer. Understanding that God both draws near to us and enables us through Christ to draw near to Him assures us that that Source of Peace is with us to help.

Is the Problem Pain? Or Pleasure?

Good, faithful people make the mistake of assuming their faith should prevent all hardships. When trouble comes, they're often at a loss as to how to respond, or worse, they decide that God is unable or unwilling to help them. The problem arose because they had the wrong presuppositions. Their expectations set up a cascade of failure as they sought a life of ease that is simply not promised in the Bible.

Ironically, people who have no interest in faith at all are making a similar mistake. They want a life of uninterrupted comfort. When anything gets difficult, medically, emotionally, vocationally, relationally, they're as unaccepting of hardship as people of deep faith can be.

This common ground extends beyond the shared unrealistic expectation that life should be easy. Both sides think the issue is the problem of evil. It's a natural mistake. We're hardwired to avoid pain and to seek comfort. We believe that if we can eliminate pain, evil, suffering, hardships, then life would be grand. That becomes the goal: the elimination of hardships. We're seeing these efforts all around us, and frankly we're pretty good at it but often with disastrous results.

The steep rise of opioid use in America is one of the most direct expressions of our warped expectation of a pain-free life. Scientists have created versions of opioids, each succeeding generation with much higher potency. They're effective because they bind directly to opioid receptors in our brains and mimic much more strongly the natural opioids our bodies produce. Most people have heard of endorphins, one of the "feel good" hormones the brain releases when the body is stressed. The name is a contraction of "endogenous morphine." Our artificially created opioids are simply much more powerful versions of the natural opioid that relieves our pain and reduces stress.

The availability of these opioids skyrocketed from the 1990's on, as patients became aware of them, and doctors increased prescriptions. It's a multi-faceted issue and beyond the purpose of a book about The Prayer, but the point here is that we're able to alleviate pain to an historically unheard-of degree. The medications, while effective, have been hugely overprescribed, often due to a demand from patients who don't need that level of intervention. One oft-quoted and staggering statistic is that Americans consume 99% of the world's hydrocodone, a commonly prescribed opioid. Are we really in that much pain as Americans? Or do we have a wildly distorted expectation of both pain relief and an ability to take a medication that simply makes us feel good whether we're in pain or not?

The rise in marijuana use, and rapidly changing laws making it widely available, highlight the same issue. I regularly address the problems this shift represents and portends as manufacturers promote a wide range of brightly colored gummies, colas, and other edibles in addition to the simple pure weed that has tremendously high concentrations of THC, the main active ingredient that produces the high in all cannabis products. I can count on a question/response that runs along the lines of why I'm opposed to the legalization of marijuana. My response is that is not my point at all.

I'm asking people to consider a much more basic question of why they want to get high in the first place. Again, what is it about life that is leading more people to want to escape? Is the stoning of America really the answer?

People genuinely and deeply want to discuss the problem of evil. More insidious, however, is the problem of pleasure. In many ways, we are blessed to live in a culture that can relieve a great deal of suffering that our ancestors regarded as common. Drought is a problem only because we can't water our lawns or fill our swimming pools. Famine doesn't worry us. Many don't eat right or well, but the problem often is more along the lines of consuming the wrong kinds of calories than not having access to food. Medically, we can work wonders, and it's in this arena that we see the wrong question most clearly. What is the spiritual facet of this problem? What are the spiritual dangers we're barreling into? That's my main concern.

This contrast between the problem of evil and the problem of pleasure is well-illustrated by two dystopian novels that are on the reading lists of most high school students: *1984* and *Brave New World*. George Orwell published *1984* in 1949, warning us of a tyrannical government that threatened and bullied its population with Big Brother, thought police, and other forms of government overreach. Aldous Huxley wrote *Brave New World* in 1932, describing a society consumed by pleasure and amusement, where every citizen took their daily dose of soma to forget all care and eliminate all pain. One focuses on the problem of evil, the other on the problem of pleasure. Which was more prophetic? Which one applies more to our present culture?

Neil Postman reflected on this very idea in his book *Amusing Ourselves to Death*. "What Orwell feared were those who would ban books. What Huxley feared was that there would be no reason to ban a book, for there would be no one who wanted to read one. Orwell feared those who would deprive us of information. Huxley feared those who would give us so much that we would be reduced to passivity and egoism. Orwell feared that the truth would be concealed from us. Huxley feared the truth would be drowned in a sea of irrelevance. Orwell feared we would become a captive culture. Huxley feared we would become a trivial culture, preoccupied with some equivalent of the feelies, the orgy porgy, and the centrifugal bumblepuppy." (Foreword, p. 38)

Aldous Huxley reflected on his work nearly 25 years after its publication in *Brave New World Revisited* (1958). He'd seen the type of tyranny Orwell warned of and that Solzhenitsyn would later address, yet he saw a greater danger. Those who opposed tyrannical and oppressive governments "failed to take into account man's almost infinite appetite for distractions" (p. 92, from ch. IV). The Roman emperors understood this and pacified the unruly mobs with bread and circuses. Today, we have a seemingly infinite number of apps, websites, and, most frighteningly, increasingly potent drugs to provide artificial pleasures and mute the angst our highly connected world creates. Addiction, and behavior not on the level of addiction, is very much a huge distraction from the real business of living life, enduring life, and finding peace through hardships.

To sum up, Orwell conceived of a culture that would control its population by inflicting pain. Huxley feared a culture that exercised control by inflicting pleasure. As Postman observed "In short, Orwell feared that what we hate will ruin us. Huxley feared that what we love will ruin us." In a culture increasingly consumed by the pursuit of pleasure, which vision has proven more accurate?

Without question, I think, we are loving and pursuing the wrong things in the delusional belief that we can achieve heaven on earth. The culture of pleasure itself is an extraordinarily powerful drug that has both its distractions and false promises. Numbing ourselves to challenge and hardship may feel good for the moment, but like a drug it always prevents us from becoming truly strong and content.

Managing Expectations

The problem of hardships, or the more insidious problem of pleasure, presents a huge challenge to any thoughtful person and perhaps especially to the thoughtful Christian. After all, an inadequate answer to these questions has proven to be the stumbling block for many people of faith. Of course, it is also the most basic and difficult challenge from people who scorn faith. In their self-certain moral clarity, they would never allow suffering, and of course the examples of suffering are limitless.

We obviously must find and formulate an answer, while at the same time realizing we are incapable of coming up with a final answer. I suggest a single word that may serve as a solid foundation for a helpful response: expectations. When it comes to the problem of hardships, what are we expecting from God? From life? From ourselves?

The book of Job delves deeply into the problem of hardships. It wrestles with this great mystery for forty-two chapters that are eloquent, insightful, heart-wrenching, occasionally humorous, and eventually hopeful. People who know little about the Bible know the story of Job, or at least think they do. I've heard many people say something along the lines that Job answers the question of why there is evil. Really? It's not as much of an answer as it is a very helpful response.

Job, a thoroughly righteous man, has enjoyed a fruitful life in every way. Unbeknownst to him, he becomes a pawn in a celestial wager. Satan, whose name in Hebrew as I mentioned actually means adversary or accuser, suggests that Job become a test case for faith. Satan is certain Job's righteousness is based solely on a quid pro quo. As long as life is easy, Job will believe. But what would happen, Satan suggests, if he faced hardships?

Then the hardships come. Brutal, repetitive, soul-crushing hardships in which Job loses his family, his servants, his fortune, and his health. To make matters worse, his friends come to him with words that are more condemnation than consolation. They are sure he's done something to deserve this brutal turn of events. He must have offended God. Job steadfastly maintains his faith and refuses to "confess" something that is simply not accurate.

The book of Job is full of the why questions we all ask. Why is this happening to me? Why is God silent? Why did God take my family member? Why is my faith inadequate? Why has my service to God been inadequate? But here is where the book of Job fails to live up to its popular characterization of being the answer to the problem of suffering. Frankly, it offers no answer. It offers a response.

Job and his three friends wrestle with the mysteries of life and suffering through chapter 37, and for all of that time God remains silent. Finally, in chapter 38, God shows up in a whirlwind, an F-5 swirling response to all the questions, accusations, doubts, and pain. God's answer? "I'm God, and you're not." Throughout the next four chapters, God does all the talking, and the subject is examples of how God knows and understands all things.

This response is exceedingly inadequate if the mind of the questioner is seeking a straightforward A + B = C formula. Frankly, that's where most of us are. We have a distorted and self-centered view of life combined with an exaggerated confidence in our ability to understand great mysteries. This common amalgam is toxic to faith, for it leads to the certainty that we could do a better job than God.

The why questions are understandable. God doesn't condemn us for them any more than He shut down Job during the first forty-one chapters of the book. But the why questions are ultimately fruitless.

Take any tragedy as an illustration. Suppose a woman has lost her husband. She mourns his death, and the grief eats away at her, robbing her of every former joy. She goes to bed with it, faces it during the dark watches of the night, and wakes with it. Grief is that kind of companion especially in the early days, months, or even years after a great loss. Understandably, she circles around to the why questions regularly.

Now suppose that God sits at her kitchen table across from her and says, "You want to understand why. I'm going to explain the answer and give you the capacity to understand my words. Here goes..." At the end of God's explanation, the woman has what she wanted. She knows why. But she's still without her husband.

An answer to the complex problem of hardships does not provide a solution or a way forward through hardships. The Prayer promises that accepting hardships is the pathway to peace, NOT that having an answer to the problem of evil is the pathway to peace. We simply must discard the expectation that we deserve an answer or that we could comprehend an answer.

We must also discard once and for all the idea that life should be easy. It simply is not, nor can it be. We all live on the threshold of calamity, and the more people we have close to us, the higher the likelihood that calamity will strike. It's an inevitability and key to understanding so much of the central purpose of the prayer. This is where acceptance comes in, and it's the second time the word has been expressly used, though it's implied in every phrase.

Finally, let's be done with the idea that God's purpose is to make our lives easy. This idea truly borders on heresy, and not just because it's a bad idea. It hurts people deeply and drives them away from the very source of peace and comfort they need so badly when calamity hits.

The most revealing scene in scripture regarding hardships is Jesus in the Garden of Gethsemane just before His arrest and subsequent crucifixion. He knew what was coming, and He clearly wanted a way out. His prayer to "let this cup pass from Me" was not a charade, and neither was it a test of God's faithfulness. No human can possibly comprehend the horror the Son of God was about to endure, and not just on a physical level. Many people had been scourged and crucified. This punishment was standard fare in the brutal Roman system. It was both terrible and terrifying, but it was not unusual.

The real pain Jesus experienced came from taking on Himself in some mysterious way the collective sins of all humanity. Words fail here because the human mind is insufficient for such a horrifying reality. Jesus was the agent of creation. Nothing came into existence apart from Him (John 1:3, Col. 1:16). The beauty of all creation and every life itself bears witness to the love in which it all has been conceived. Now the creation was about to turn on the Creator. It's not overreaching to state that they were about to kill God. Who can imagine such pain?

Anyone can understand why He asked for a way out, but the Father did not grant it. Why? Because the hardships are the pathway to peace. This truth works in every degree of reality from the most exalted divine to the most common mundane. God secured our peace through His ultimate hardship.

The Son did not get the answer He wanted from the Father that night in the Garden. He did get the answer He needed. Because He trusted Himself to the Father even when life was excruciatingly (a word derived from the Latin word for pain and the cross) painful, God gave Him not a way out, but a way through. Jesus rose from that prayer with a renewed commitment to the Father and an assurance that He was not alone. Even on the cross when He asked why God had forsaken Him, that was the human cry of a man who felt alone but actually never was.

He was never alone. And neither are we. The "answer" we find
in the book of Job, and indeed throughout the Scripture, is that
God is with us. Remember the C. S. Lewis quote about how you
must get close to, or even into, the source of joy, power, peace,
and eternal life if you want to experience these things? The
greater truth is that the source of these wonderful blessings
stands close to us and even abides in us.

God With Us

I may be completely wrong about what I'm about to write, but I
don't think so. The topic is Psalm 23, which may be the single
most familiar Scripture of all. Nearly everyone could finish the
sentence "The Lord is my _____." It is the most requested
passage at funerals. I normally use it at gravesides because of its
special familiarity and comfort. The Psalm is well known
because it addresses some of our most fundamental needs and
desires. Let me tell you what we know with certainty about this
most famous Psalm. Then I'll tell you what I think is true about
it. It's in this latter part that I could be wrong, but I don't think
so.

The psalm was written by David, who is introduced to us first in
the Scripture as an overlooked youngest son whose big brothers
got all of the attention and treated him like an irritating little
brother. Everyone knows the story of how, with God's strength,
he brought down the giant with a slingshot. Before that, he killed
lions and bears as a boy shepherd.

For all of his strength, David also possessed a rare humility and
patience. Most readers will not know that he was anointed to be
the second king of Israel at a very young age, before he met
Goliath in fact. Yet he kept that secret and served Saul, the first
king, faithfully even when Saul felt threatened and tried to kill
him. David would not even take advantage of the opportunity to
kill Saul quietly. He waited for God's timing.

When he finally did become king, David took Israel to the zenith of its existence. He was an inspiring leader and a brilliant military strategist, possessing an incredible bravery and an extraordinarily deep faith in God. Half the Psalms bear his name. He had the rare combination of the heart of warrior and the soul of a poet. God called him a man after His own heart. David was a truly great man.

And David also was capable of great evil. People forget the incident with Bathsheba. She was a rooftop-bathing-beauty that David ogled and then seduced. She became pregnant, and to cover up the affair and its consequences, David recalled her husband Uriah, one of his soldiers, from the front. He hoped that he would sleep with his wife and then assume the child was his. Uriah, however, did not cooperate. He refused the comfort of his own home because his comrades remained at the front.

The intrigue takes an even more sinister turn when David devised a plot in which Uriah would be at the point of attack, and then on a secret signal everyone would withdraw, leaving Uriah to battle alone. He died believing in God, king and country. David then married Bathsheba so that he could claim the child as legitimately his own. He believed his deeds were secret, but his sins were exposed in a most public way and David suffered terribly for them. The man after God's own heart also possessed the most fragile feet of clay.

All of this is indisputably from the Scripture. I'm just quoting facts at this point. I can't be wrong. We know this much to be true about the author of Psalm 23. He was a man who was capable of great nobility and despicable abuse of power. He was both an inspiration and a warning.

Now here's what I think is true, but I can't say with certainty. I believe David wrote Psalm 23 late in life. He had lived the highs and the lows. He'd summitted mountaintops and descended into the very worst of valleys. He knew life at its best and its worst and was often alternately responsible for both. As an older man, he looked back over the often-unpredictable sine curves of life and noted one dependable thing in all of life. With all of the variables, David saw the truth that whatever he faced, the Lord was his shepherd.

Interestingly, in the Hebrew text, Psalm 23 has 57 words. Right in the middle of the psalm are the words "I will not fear." Right after that are the words "for Thou are with me." All the assurances of the psalm, as well as the frank admission that there will be valleys of shadow and death, rest on the fulcrum of God's assurance that we do not need to fear because He is with us.

As Matthew began to relate the story of Jesus' birth in his Gospel, he quoted Isaiah 7:14 where the prophet said that the Messiah shall be called "Emmanuel." Matthew translates this Hebrew term for us: God with us. The meaning of the literal physical birth of God into the world is that He is with us. What God has always offered crystalized on the first Christmas. We are not alone. We never have been, and we never will be.

That is the ultimate "answer" to the problem of hardships. It does not take them away, nor does it line up a series of causes and events that bring us to the present expression of the problem. As I stated earlier, that simply would not help. What God offers is to live with us and in us as we invite Him. No hardship will overcome us because that would mean the hardship would need to be stronger than God.

Even more miraculously, God's presence transforms the suffering into a means by which we become stronger and even more aware of His love and grace. In this way, that which threatens to break us actually makes us stronger. It all boils down to our willingness to stay close to God when the shadows tempt us to run from Him. This deep and abiding assurance transforms our outlook on life, even to the point that we do not regret a painful past nor even wish to alter it. For the pain became the pathway to peace.

In Greek mythology, there are five rivers that run through Hades. Most readers probably will have heard of Styx, the river that forms the boundary between Earth and the underworld. One of the other rivers is called Lethe, from the Greek word "to forget." Troubled souls could drink from Lethe and forget their earthly lives. All their troubles would disappear. If such a river existed, and such a result possible, would we be tempted to take a drink?

John Erskine's poem "Actaeon" depicts Actaeon, a Greek mythological figure who suffered a terrible setback and a tragic death, standing beside the river Lethe. He watches troubled souls rush by to rid themselves of their painful memories. Actaeon, perhaps tempted to follow, thinks instead of the consequences: "One draught of Lethe for a world of pain? An easy bargain; yet I keep the thorn, to keep the rose."

Reasonable happiness is never more challenged than when hardships come. As in every aspect of life, our response to these painful and often unalterable events makes all the difference. We can resist them by trying to forget them, change them, explain them, defend them, and eventually be consumed by them. Or we can accept them. That means bringing God into all of our mourning, regrets, persecutions, and even our trauma, and letting Him wash His grace over all our wounds.

Acceptance is never more challenged than when we face challenges. It sounds like resignation. Instead, acceptance, especially in the most difficult circumstances, means that we are trusting that the challenge is part of God's providence. He's working it into the fabric of our lives to make the tapestry even more beautiful. Acceptance is not resignation. It is a courageous trust.

Grace pools in our wounds. What once were ragged and bleeding gashes heal slowly but inexorably so that one day we have scars whose stories tell of a God who was with us and brought us through the hardships to a greater and eternal strength. He was in the sunshine and the storm, the light and the darkness, the valleys and the hills. In Him, never in the circumstances, we found peace and reasonable happiness.

Toward reasonable happiness:

- We are biologically wired to avoid suffering. This is a survival instinct that creates in our modern world the expectation that we *can* avoid *all* suffering.
- The inevitability of hardships, however, challenges this distorted expectation.
- If we wait for our lives to be free from hardships so that we can be happy we will never be happy. The real challenge is not to avoid suffering, but to create meaning out of suffering.
- We make a huge step forward when we focus on God's character rather than our comfort. He is good and loving. He wills good for us in spite of suffering and often *through* suffering. Thus, hardships become gifts and opportunities for spiritual growth.
- Drugs and alcohol enable us to manipulate our experience of pleasure, but with disastrous repercussions. We can end up relying on a substance instead of God.
- The Bible does not promise a life free from suffering for the believer. Rather it presents a God who enters into our suffering. His presence is our joy. We are never alone.

Hardships do not prove the absence or impotence of God. Hardships illustrate the necessity for God.

CHAPTER EIGHT

TAKING AS HE DID, THIS SINFUL WORLD AS IT IS, NOT AS I WOULD HAVE IT

"Jesus did not trust Himself to them, because He knew all men...and He knew what was in man."
John 2:25

"You'll never reach your destination if you stop and throw stones at every dog that barks."
Winston Churchill

The Prayer has certainly presented us with some challenging ideas to this point, but the challenge mainly has been in the arena of implementation. It's very hard to accept what we can't change, change what we can, and discern the difference between the two. Enjoying days and moments is a challenge, but it's accessible. We've all had the experience of a moment so sublime that we are drawn to quiet gratitude to God. Accepting hardships can be enormously difficult, but the idea is clear. So, while it's hard to do all these things, they're not hard to understand.

With the next phrase in The Prayer, however, we come to an idea that is challenging to the point of being offensive for some people. We're supposed to just "take" this sinful world as it is? Setting aside our personal rights is, well, personal. But when we witness so much devastating impact of the evil of this world, how can we simply "take it" and remain morally responsible?

It's good to remember here that Reinhold Niebuhr, the author of at least the first three lines of the Prayer, was a leading voice in the social justice movement of the 20th century. As an elderly man, he was arrested while protesting American involvement in Vietnam. Even if he did not author this line, he did certainly author the line that has a similar idea of accepting unchangeable things.

Even more puzzling is that Jesus, the "He" of this phrase, hardly let the world go on its merry but destructive way. We'll have ample time to delve into this a bit later, but for the present let's admit that the author of our faith and the focus of this phrase of The Prayer was a world-changer as no other in history.

The soul of The Prayer consistently focuses on our perspective and our responses to unalterable realities. While we certainly can and must be agents of change in the world, we must also realize that at best we are going to be rather small links in that great change. What do we do, how do we respond when we run up against those limits? That is the point of The Prayer, and the sole focus on this phrase of it.

While we're going to be revisiting some important themes in this chapter, we'll also have the opportunity to dive deeply into some fascinating theology. Some of it may sound dark, but only if you forget the unconquerable Light that shines in the darkness.

Is This Really a Sinful World?

Many years ago, I read a brief letter to an editor of a news magazine that said the world was getting better and better in every way. The writer believed in the advance of technology to solve many of our health and security concerns as well as politics to solve social inequities and other problems. I don't think this is a common hope anymore, though I can't be sure. Some people have an optimism that strains the definition to the point of absurdity. The Enlightenment is being "rediscovered" by a whole new generation that trumpets its undeniable advances as something akin to the law and prophets of the religious realm they wish to extinguish. Still, I can't say that I find the present times particularly hopeful.

It's not always been so. Buoyant optimism was the rule of the day at the beginning of the 20th century, corresponding roughly to the end of the Enlightenment Era. Influential writers like H. G. Wells were confident in the advance of science and the capability of the human mind to lift the whole race out of its various problems. Interestingly, theologians joined in enthusiastically. The magazine *Christian Oracle*, begun in 1864, changed its name to *Christian Century* to reflect the editors' confidence that faith and science together would transform humanity into a harmonious fellowship in the coming new century.

The "Christian" century, however, produced two world wars, numerous genocides, weapons of mass destruction, the rise (and partial fall) of governments that resulted in the deaths of millions of their own citizens, and a general decline in faith. Wells lived long enough to witness the Second World War, and the title of his last book, *Mind at the End of Its Tether*, is particularly revealing. He did not think the human race would survive much longer and even advanced the possibility that a whole new species, possibly extra-terrestrial, would replace humanity. His human-focused hope disintegrated against the reality of the human capacity for evil.

Aleksandr Solzhenitsyn was born in 1918, during one of the great upheavals of the 20th century. The previous year had brought the overthrow of the Russian monarchy, and 1918 saw the beginning of the Russian Civil War between Lenin's Bolshevik Red Army and a loose confederation of opponents that comprised the White Army. The Bolsheviks won, and the Soviet Union was formed in 1922.

Solzhenitsyn was born into a heady time of hopeful empowerment and grew up to embrace the vision of a world-transforming revolution. He lived on a collective farm during his formative years, studied mathematics and physics at a university and took correspondence courses in philosophy, literature, and history. The course work was heavily ideological, of course, but he did not question the grand experiment and believed with the conviction of a convert. He even served in the Soviet Army during World War II, rising to the rank of captain.

His outlook began to change soon after the war. He criticized Stalin in private letters that did not remain private, even insinuating that a change in leadership was necessary. He was tried for anti-Soviet propaganda and sentenced to eight years in the gulags where he saw the inevitable result of the brutal Soviet vision. He had no way of knowing at the time that Stalin would be responsible for the deaths of tens of millions of Russian citizens, but his experience in the gulags was enough to convince him of the evil that had overtaken his homeland.

The Gulag Archipelago is Solzhenitsyn's most famous work. In it, he recounts stories of the barbaric behavior of his captors and weaves through the lengthy narrative a spiritual vision born of his Eastern Orthodox faith. The *Archipelago* was not merely a political commentary. Solzhenitsyn anticipated that some would take it that way and warned, "So let the reader who expects this to be a political exposé slam its covers shut right now." The problem is not so simple, he continues, and the source is much closer to home. "The line dividing good and evil cuts through the heart of every human being." (pp. 361-62). He would later add that the line oscillates.

Thus, we are all capable of wondrous dreams and terrifying nightmares. We are victims and perpetrators all. Though we have by volume certainly avoided the scope of Stalin's crimes, Solzhenitsyn's insight is we are all capable of the same generic sin. The idea that the world will get better is illusory, and dangerously so, for it rests on the notion that humanity will conquer the spiritual bent that caused the problem in the first place. The gravity of self-centeredness, or the "flesh" as Paul put it in his letters, is simply too great. It proves the ruin of any vision that leaves God out, marginalizes Him, or, perhaps worst of all, seeks to meld Him into a union with human vision.

The danger of trusting in a good world, apart from God, is the essence of Solzhenitsyn's message. He was uniquely gifted and then placed in an uncomfortable position to make his observations with a stunning moral authority.

In his Templeton Address of 1983, Solzhenitsyn summed up his central moral and spiritual critique of the terrible 20th century: "Over a half century ago, while I was still a child, I recall hearing a number of old people offer the following explanation for the great disasters that had befallen Russia: 'Men have forgotten God; that's why all this has happened.' Since then I have spent well-nigh 50 years working on the history of our revolution; in the process I have read hundreds of books, collected hundreds of personal testimonies, and have already contributed eight volumes of my own toward the effort of clearing away the rubble left by that upheaval. But if I were asked today to formulate as concisely as possible the main cause of the ruinous revolution that swallowed up some 60 million of our people, I could not put it more accurately than to repeat: 'Men have forgotten God; that's why all this has happened.'"

Will humanity improve? Will we solve our problems and live as one? I wish it were true. God would be no less God if we were able to lift ourselves out of our historic darkness. God certainly has put at our disposal wondrous gifts of discovery and compassion. If we truly harnessed all the potential, I doubt anything is beyond our reach. As optimistic by nature as I am, however, that unity and success will never happen for the simple reason that the solutions to our most fundamental problems are not scientific or political. They are spiritual. My observations are not pessimistic but simply realistic. The human will to self-centered power is too entrenched. Nothing short of faith in Christ, Who without partiality is able to bring disparate people together, will make us truly one.

Unfortunately, even that vision is not realized under the umbrella of those who follow Christ. A good friend of mine, a monsignor, was asked one time "what question would you like to address any historical figure?" This influential leader in the Roman Catholic Church replied, "I would like to ask Luther, 'Did you mean for it to go this far?'"

Ironically, the very fractured nature of the Christian community demonstrates not the inadequacy of Christ, but the absolute need for Him. In Christ, we are called to combine a depth of conviction with a breadth of sympathy. At the very least, that means that I regard with understanding and patience my brothers and sisters in Christ who differ from me in some points of theology and practice. For those of differing faiths or no faiths at all, Jesus' message means I respond to them with the same patience and understanding. We simply must move beyond the limbic tendency to always judge and assign people to our various cubicles. The harshest among us succeed only in creating a hundred rebels for every convert. Acceptance works in the church as well as outside of it.

Now if this section seems dark, I conclude it with a most hopeful note. It is plain reality that the world is broken, and that brokenness is merely an expression of the brokenness of the human soul, as Solzhenitsyn so memorably put it. The Bible reflects the egalitarian nature of sin. No one is immune or protected from its ravages. The alternative to naïve optimism, however, must not be either blindness or despair. We can't deny the obvious, nor do we lose hope. We need only look to God's response for help in navigating this sinful world.

God Responds to a Sinful World

If someone were convinced that God was inclined to anger and punishment, then reluctance to think about sins and brokenness would be understandable. If a cure for my disease was not available, I'm not sure I'd want to talk about my symptoms and pain. What would be the point? It would be an exercise in hopelessness.

The Bible is unsparing in its description of the plight of humanity. The fact of sin is explicit or implied on nearly every page. We can't make the Bible say something different simply because it offends some sensibility, or we've substituted some vocabulary. I once heard someone describe the Bible as a very pessimistic book, and I suppose this man only had in mind the diagnosis that is so very clear in its pages. But to describe the Bible as pessimistic, or to be fearful of God because He's against sin, is to miss the whole current of the biblical narrative.

Long ago, I learned that we should read the entire Bible through the lens of Jesus. In other words, I must let His life, teaching, and example guide me as I think about the whole Bible, and especially those difficult, frustrating, and even frightening parts. He claimed to be God, a fact so clear both in the Scripture and in early church history that we can't seriously think that the idea of His divinity was created by power-brokers with a political agenda. When He said, "Anyone who has seen Me has seen the Father" (John 14:9), He meant that we can understand God more deeply by looking at and listening to Him. So, what did He have to say that might help us understanding how God feels about this broken world?

God has chosen to love the world. One of the most famous verses in the Bible, the gospel in a nutshell according to Luther, is John 3:16. It begins, "For God so loved the world." He doesn't hate the world, as twisted as it is. Isn't He angry with the world? I'm not sure that's a good way to think about God and His love. Am I truly loving someone if I first have to remind them at every turn how disappointed I am in them? The nature of unconditional love is that it's truly unconditional, and that is a quality that simply goes far beyond our human capacity to understand.

As if to dispel any lingering questions about His purpose on earth, we find clearly in the next verse that Jesus did not come into the world to condemn the world. That's not His purpose. At the very least, this means that anyone who feels condemnation when they think about God is not getting a clear message from God.

In his first letter, John twice wrote "God is love" (1 John 4:8, 16). Nowhere in the Bible do you find anything like God is anger, condemnation, disappointment, or disgust. Does the Bible present a God who is hostile to sin? Of course, but in the same way that I'm hostile to the staph infection that sickens one of my grandchildren.

To the passages that explicitly speak of God's love for the world we can add the many stories and passages about grace. Truly, these are some of the most puzzling and challenging teachings in the entire Bible, and literally were at the root of a major division early in the church.

The Parable of the Prodigal Son perhaps comes first to mind. It's better named the Parable of the Loving Father for he truly is the central character and the point of the story. With both the wasteful son who lost his identity in addition to his wealth and the elder brother whose careful obedience was devoid of grace, the loving father responded with an offer to forgive and accept.

In the same vein, the Parable of the Laborers in the Vineyard presents an irrational business plan. Workers hired for one hour receive the same full day's pay as the laborers who worked the entire day. It's an astounding illustration of what God offers each one of us, from the very worst to the very best.

I've taught about grace for more than forty years, and it's not unusual in a teaching setting (thankfully not during a sermon on Sunday morning), to have someone aggressively take the side of the elder brother and the workers who labored all day. When I point out how upset both parties are, more than one person has exclaimed "Well, I don't blame him/them!" Honestly, most of us can admit to similar feelings at some point. We're accustomed to earning and crave recognition. This response points out the beauty of Jesus' teaching method. He highlights both God's truth and our need for it.

Beyond particular verses or parables, we can look at the way Jesus related to people as a clear indicator of how God feels about the world. He called common men and women to follow him. They were not the elite. An exception is Nicodemus, a ruler who was genuinely curious about Jesus (John 3), defended him before other Jewish leaders (John 7:51), and even helped prepare His body for burial (John 19:39). Jesus called simple fishermen who likely struggled for a living, and a tax collector (Matthew) who was likely quite wealthy. Jesus' appeal crossed all normal lines that separate people from people.

The simple statement "He eats with sinners" sums up a great deal of the radical nature of Jesus' life and ministry. In a culture that valued ritual cleanliness about all things, Jesus took the religious risk of associating with all manner of unclean sinners. He allowed a prostitute to touch Him, and He touched lepers. So egregious was His behavior in the eyes of the religious leaders that they leveled what they thought was a devastating accusation against Him: "He is a glutton and a drunkard" (Luke 7:34). For Jesus, all of this vitriol was simply an affirmation that He was doing what He came to do. He associated with sinners because God loves sinners. That is remarkably good news for all of us.

Finally, let's spend some time with an obscure teaching from Jesus that may best fit what we're aiming for with this line of The Prayer. In the Sermon on the Mount, Jesus said, "Do not resist one who is evil" (Matt. 5:39). Again, on the face of it, this statement sounds practically offensive. When we dive a little more deeply into the word for resist, the problem gets even thornier, for it means to not oppose. We're not supposed to oppose evil? That sounds like a recipe for cowardice and even anarchy. Do we even have a need for police or armies if we're not going to oppose evil?

Understand that Jesus was addressing matters of personal relationships, not broader social, national, and political issues. He was speaking to people who were occupied by a foreign army, and they were very interested in how to get those soldiers out of their country. A beleaguered little nation like Israel had no chance against the power of Rome. The occupation was an unalterable fact of their existence, and no amount of military power they could muster would change that.

In this context, Jesus' teaching in the verses make more sense. You turn the other cheek, give up your cloak, go the extra mile because in small ways that is what God has chosen to do with highly resistant humanity. He did not come bringing a heavenly military invasion. He came bringing love and grace. Why? Because those are the only ways to truly change anyone for the better.

Law pushes. Grace attracts. Law, with its strictures, is like the concussive force of an exploding shell. Things change when it goes off, but if not handled wisely the damage can be huge. Grace, by contrast, is more like gravity. It pulls us and draws us to something higher and better. All expressions of power and manipulation can have the appearance of changing people, but until you get to the heart and soul, no one really changes. That's why only grace will lead us home.

Jesus taught these things to us because they are the plan that God has always had in place. God has always made the sun to shine on evil people and good people, and rain to fall on the unjust and the just (Matt. 5:45). Why? God is love. Lavish blessings, even those that are completely unacknowledged by people who couldn't care less, are in His nature.

We live this life along two axes, vertical and horizontal. The vertical axis describes our understanding of God. It is primary. Until and unless we get that axis or view of God right, we have little chance to find joy in life, much less to be reasonably happy. In other words, the horizontal axis, our ability to live productively in this world and with other people, is terribly compromised if we do not first understand that God is love. The powerful current of the Bible leaves no doubt about this truth. People of faith, very wise and good people, have been assuring us of this truth for thousands of years. Yet we forget, and when we do, we forfeit the peace and joy we were created to have.

Wrestling with the World

Jacob's name in Hebrew means "one who strives" or "one who usurps." His story begins in Genesis 25 and is a great example of how the Bible provides unvarnished insights into the heroes of our faith. Jacob was striving from the day of his delivery, holding onto his twin brother Esau's foot in an attempt to keep him from being the first-born son. Life for Jacob began as a competition in a race down the birth canal. He lost that race, but he never stopped striving and conniving.

He cheated Esau out of his birthright. He later participated in a scheme hatched by his mother to deceive his elderly and blind father Isaac. He dressed in Esau's clothes and allowed his mother to glue sheepskin on his arms and neck so that he would feel hairy like his twin brother. Isaac was fooled and pronounced the blessing on him. Jacob ran for his life when Esau found out. He had a very rocky relationship with the uncle he fled to. It was a complicated family dynamic.

Jacob believed he was being clever, but he left behind him a string of ruptured relationships. Many years later, he decided to return to his ancestral home and face his brother. Overwhelmed with fear and anxiety, he spent an entire night wrestling with God. He came out of that match with a limp and a new name. Israel.

Jacob wrestled with the world from the day of his birth, not ever quite being satisfied with the arrangement of things and certain that he could change things to suit himself. Frankly, he was fairly successful at it. He did end up being the "firstborn," he got the wife he really wanted, became wealthy in the face of unfair challenges from his uncle. He was a "success," but it left him anxious and uncertain of his place in the world or God's will.

In many ways, Jacob could be the patron saint of wrestlers, that is those of us who wrestle with the world. We live in a wrestling culture. The signs of struggle and discontent surround us. Writing in the middle of the COVID crisis, I've watched people morph from somewhat alarmed but willing to cooperate to very angry and demanding to return to life as it was previously. The mask-shamers rain down judgment on anyone who chooses not to use a mask. Both sides vilify the other.

I'm truly astounded by the social media bent to criticize and complain. Frankly, I regularly scrub my "friends" list to include pretty much only those people who are showing me pictures of grandchildren, dogs, and pretty sunsets. Am I being naïve and ignorant? I don't think so. I just don't want to see how clever and insightful you think you are for a blistering post about some politician. I don't need to watch your latest wrestling match.

Every generation, particularly as it ages, tends to think that succeeding generations are ushering in the end of the world. Remember Mr. Dale yelling, "We're going down! That's where we're going! We're going down!" It seems in addition to being assured of our three score and ten, we've become contractually obligated in our later years to become prophets of doom. And each generation, seduced by its own unerring sense of uniqueness, believes it is right without also realizing that it has become hopelessly unhappy.

"It's getting worse" is the refrain of all the professional world-wrestlers. If you're always fighting, then you do tend to believe that fighting is the only appropriate response. Are things getting worse? Leaving aside the absolute impossibility of measuring such vague statements, we need to remember that the world has always been terribly troubled.

As he began to describe one era in history, a historian prefaced the chapter with these words "I am entering upon the history of a period, rich in disasters, gloomy with wars, rent with seditions, savage in its very hours of peace. . . . All was one of delirium of hate and terror." That was Tacitus (d. 117) writing about the first century A.D. Delirium, hate, and terror. That terrible trinity sounds right at home in the 21st century.

We cannot seriously imagine that the world is getting worse when everyone who came before us thought the same thing. If that were true, at some point we would have surely hit bottom and the apocalypse would have come.

Don't mistake the previous lines for endorsing a rosy outlook on life. What made H. G. Wells and his optimistic fellows wrong at the beginning of the 20th century is the same thing that makes such optimism wrong in the 21st century. Frankly, the world has always been a mess, and if we set our hope on things of the world, then we will inevitably become hopeless and angry.

We're asking the world to do something for us that it simply cannot, and when it acts as it always has, we resist it with every fiber of our being. Take this sinful world as it is? Impossible! But wrestle with it and all you'll do is come away with a limp and a hopeless outlook.

Yet we continue to wrestle and don't understand why we're not happy about it. I live in south Louisiana where miles and miles of levees keep the rivers bounded and enable us to live with some semblance of safety. Still, there are plenty of places where people build homes in low-lying, flood-prone areas. Every so often, the torrential rains for which we are famous in the coastal states bring a deluge that floods those areas. Inevitably, some poor soul complains to the reporter about their home being flooded. They seem just as genuinely surprised by this flood as they were during the last one.

When you live in low-lying areas, you risk getting flooded. If you live in tornado alley, you risk a tornado. If you live in Minnesota, you risk a blizzard. If you live on the West Coast, you risk an earthquake. The world has been flooding, freezing, blowing, and shaking for as long as it's been around. And people have been conniving, vindictive, controlling, and unfaithful since the Garden. For all the chaos this broken world brings, we should admit that at least it's predictable.

After the remarkable miracle at the wedding feast at Cana, Jesus went to Jerusalem and many people believed in Him. Most anyone would treat this as a sign of great success and growing popularity. Things were rolling! Jesus' response, though, was surprising. He didn't trust that initial wave of positivity. He didn't think it was the harbinger of better things. Why? John tells us that Jesus "knew what was in man" (John 2:24).

The same Jerusalem crowd that cheered and accepted Jesus at the early point in His ministry would later mock Him as He hung on a cross. Jesus knew not to place His hope and trust in a fickle humanity. He was not cynical, for He still loved everyone. But He was realistic. He was not surprised when opinions turned against Him. That's the nature of humanity and the world. Wrestling with it will not change it.

While Jesus' words here may sound discouraging, they actually point the way forward. Whether we're hurt by the impersonal forces of nature or hurt more deeply by the very personal nature of relationships, we make no progress by criticizing and complaining about a world that is not going to change.

The stakes are very high and soul deep. Many times, I've seen adults even late in life continue to talk about their parents' mistakes as if they happened last year. Everyone is wounded in some way. Life breaks us all. But the evil we encounter can become the evil we adopt. Remember the line of good and evil that Solzhenitsyn described does indeed oscillate, and if unchecked it shifts inexorably into caustic spiritual habits. We become what we hate.

While wrestling is a common response to the brokenness of the world, no one wins that match. We will end up bruised and bleeding, full of anger, fear, resentment, and self-pity. We have to find a better way, or reasonable happiness is a cruel illusion.

Wrestling Moves

"Terry, can you see the color of these flowers?" I was in the second grade, sitting near the back of the classroom. Apparently, I had exhibited some trouble seeing the board, and my teacher had picked up on the possible problem. I'm not sure why she asked me about the color of the flowers as I've never had any trouble with color. I simply remember not being able to make out much of anything about the flowers, color or otherwise.

Of course, that all led to the rather typical experience of a child going to the eye doctor, getting glasses, and in the car on the way home remarking, "I can see leaves!" This precipitates a great deal of anguish on the part of the mother, who believes this episode constitutes at least careless inattention and possibly neglect. It's neither, of course, but moms do tend to feel these things very deeply.

I didn't know that my eyesight was bad. Patients with a variety of maladies often are not aware of any problem until the symptoms get very bad. High blood pressure is called "the silent killer." In the cognitive and emotional realm, I've often worked with people who, after a few months of recovery from addiction, remark that they simply didn't know how impaired they were. Feelings of well-being are new and so remarkable that we sometimes refer to this as the pink cloud. It's a spiritual awakening augmented by a physiological healing. I remember it quite vividly. It truly was as if the scales had fallen from my eyes.

Taking this sinful world as it is means, of first order, recognizing our own wrestling moves. These are the patterns of our mind that lead us to take an aggressive and exhausting stance in the first place. We need someone to ask us the same kind of question my teacher asked me, but with a spiritual bent. "Do you see the colors of grace?" Chances are, most of you, if you're honest, will answer no. It's hard to see beauty when you're in the middle of a fight.

Recognizing your wrestling moves is absolutely vital. The mind is to the soul as the brain is to the body. The brain sends signals, and the body responds accordingly. The mind sets a spiritual tone and trajectory for the soul. If it's consumed by negative spiritual emotions, then the soul is troubled, and reasonable happiness is impossible. With practice and intention, we can become aware of those caustic emotions and make a healthy change. Let's take a look at a few common wrestling moves.

Complaining. Complaining is a negative spiritual emotion. We touched on this earlier when discusssing changing the things we can. Some of that bears repeating briefly here, however, because it is so common. Complaining affects the soul and thus our connection with God and appreciation for the better and ennobling things of life. Complaint is the polar opposite of gratitude. When we're complaining, we're focusing on what we perceive is wrong, and while we may be right about what is wrong, we need to ask whether our complaining can really change anything, or is it simply useless wrestling?

Complainers and criticizers tend to think very highly of themselves. It's impossible not to when you're passing judgment on an endless variety of subjects. Complaining, therefore, becomes a very self-centered exercise, though the complainer is very unlikely to see it that way. Notice that the chronic complainer is almost never open to seeing things differently or to a change of mind. That would mean they must alter their perceptions, and that would be a devastating blow to their ego. When I complain, I don't pray well, and frankly I don't think well. So, I'm not open to seeing things from a different perspective, and that simply perpetuates complaining and criticizing.

Comparing. Comparing inevitably leads to discontent, for the mind will search incessantly for something it perceives to be superior. That precipitates complaint and self-pity. Take the Evil Queen in "Snow White" as an example. She had to be the fairest of all, not just pretty fair, or "fair for your age." Coming in second was simply not enough. Second of all the women in the world is surely not a bad thing, but she poisoned #1 just to keep her standing.

Whatever metric you choose, comparing is disastrous. If you happen to be on top, then you're likely to be worrying, like the Evil Queen, about the competition. That hardly leads to serenity or reasonable happiness. I see this in high-performing students who may achieve the highest GPA, but instead of feeling satisfaction and accomplishment, they only feel an exhausted relief that they've proved themselves one more time. In other instances, finishing at the top produces a winner with insufferable pride. Neither result is admirable or rewarding.

More common are the people who compare themselves and feel that they never measure up. Except for the most narcissistic, all people go through periods when they feel they don't fit in. Interestingly, most of these people will be sure others do not feel this way. I've never worked with anyone very long or deeply that DIDN'T have feelings of awkwardness combined with the conviction that everyone else is entirely comfortable with every facet of life. Comparing simply belittles us to the point that we're sure everyone else is superior.

On the other hand, comparing sometimes leads to the bizarre phenomenon of finding someone worse off than you in order for you to get relief. The most common expression of this is something along the lines of "I wept because I had no shoes until I met a man who had no feet." Finding personal relief through someone else's misfortune hardly sounds admirable. Additionally, this strategy forces the unfortunate soul who gave you this twisted relief in turn to find someone even more unfortunate.

Comparing is just a form of wrestling that means you're unwilling to accept where you are in life. The world is not going to be fair to you when you begin looking at how you fit in. None of us are truly competent to compare ourselves for we lack the proper perspective. Only God can give us a genuine sense of value and worth that relieves us from the grinding sense of inadequacy and meaninglessness.

Cursing. A friend of mine recently made me aware of this wrestling move when he said that he finds himself swearing the more he starts worrying. I'd actually never thought of cursing in this way. I'd always known there are some words I just shouldn't say, and when I say them, I feel that somehow I've crossed the line. But there's more to it than simply breaking a verbal rule.

In seminary, I learned that the Hebrews believed that words had an energy about them. When a word was spoken, it released good or ill in the world. That's why they took the notion of blessing so seriously. When a parent pronounces a blessing on a child, for example, it changes the course of the child's life. Having worked around many people who didn't have that blessing, I can see in their adult lives what they've missed, and often they're completely unaware of it.

Going back to my friend's experience, cursing reveals more than worry. Jesus taught that our words reveal our heart. Words have a positive or negative energy about them that is directly connected to the spiritual state of our souls. What a dramatic and revolutionary way to look at our vocabulary! Words, patterns of speech, are not neutral. They add to our personal sense of well-being or foreboding.

Cursing is not merely the use of that handful of words we were all taught are not appropriate. It can manifest itself in the form of a hostility to the world or being convinced that the world is out to get you. A flat tire may precipitate not only a few curses, but also a reinforcement of the idea that the world is against me. When I start looking for ways things can go wrong, it seems that I find that things go wrong more often. So not only do I find what I look for, but I seem to create what I expect.

It's a simple spiritual checklist to survey how much you complain, compare, and curse. These are great indicators that you're not taking this sinful world as it is. In fact, this phrase of The Prayer offers a useful and easily accessible polarity. Taking the world as it is means you're not wrestling, and that's a good thing. Demanding that it be "as I would have it" means you're forever tilting at windmills that are not going to stop being windmills.

Most of us don't realize how much we've been fighting. We've been angry for so long that it seems natural to us. But there is a better way, and it starts with a simple decision to stop fighting. God can't put grace into a closed hand. When we put down our fists and open our hands, then God can give us a gift that really helps us embrace the wisdom of this phrase of The Prayer.

A More Excellent Way

Some people criticize The Prayer for being too passive. More than once, I've heard something along the lines of "what are we supposed to do? Just give up and let things happen?" Well, that's simplistic, but not far from the truth if we've entrusted our lives in this world to the care of a loving God. He is our Creator, and in Him we find rest and peace, along with mission and purpose. Nothing about the latter has anything to do with giving up. It just means we've learned Who fights for us.

Jesus taught us to be wise as serpents and gentle as doves (Matt. 10:16). He first spoke these puzzling words to the disciples He was sending into the world for the first time. Notice He didn't suggest that it was going to be easy or that world was a nurturing and safe place. Quite the contrary. He told them they were going to be unwelcomed in some villages, arrested and flogged by authorities, and fleeing from one town to the next. You had to be tough to be a disciple, and you were certainly under no illusions that the world is a sweet and pleasant place.

Once again, we run up against the insistent idea that life is hard. The Christian response is not full-out retreat, but rather a wise engagement where we clearly understand what we can expect from the world and refuse to be outraged when the world reacts in a thoroughly predictable manner.

"Dogs bark" is one way of putting it. We can't expect a dog to stop being what a dog is or doing what a dog does. We take on the attitude of Jesus who "knew what was in man." He understood. So should we. That's the being wise as serpents part. Serpents seem to have a knack for survival. Even though they are a very unpopular family of critters, they know how to exist in a hostile world.

Being gentle as doves reflects the compassion of Jesus we are to have as well. As discussed above, for all of its evil, God chose to love the world. That doesn't mean He loves all the actions of individuals in the world. He would not be moral if He did. But He has chosen through love to redeem the world, and that is the mission we're all to embrace. Frankly, it's one that many of us as Christians could do better.

The Christian mission is never helped by anger. Never. Gentleness and anger simply don't go together. Nevertheless, some Christians, and some segments of Christianity, have made anger a central theme. Ironically, I've felt a rise of anger when I witness angry Christians. Of course, I'm likely to justify my anger with the idea of righteous indignation. The problem is, I've never talked to any angry Christian who didn't think their indignation was righteous.

Anger may sway some but I'm not sure the direction of the sway is positive and helpful. Sometimes anger produces a hundred rebels for every convert. I don't think the gospel, or good news, would have swept the globe if anger had been the theme. Instead, love is.

It is hard to love. It's risky. And it often hurts. That's why the idea that The Prayer is too soft or easy is simply ludicrous. Jesus loved the world to such a degree that He allowed it to put Him to death. It's hard to take the world as it is. He, Who could have called down legions of angels to defend Him, chose to remain silent before His accusers. He even loved the religious authorities who reviled and accused Him and the Roman authorities who pronounced and carried out His death sentence.

He loved the soldiers who pressed the crown of thorns on His head and the ones who drove the nails through His hands and feet. Yet while He hung on the cross, He pronounced forgiveness for every person responsible for putting Him there which, lest we forget, includes each one of us. And we're to take this sinful, awful world as He did?

Even more pointedly, Jesus very carefully told us to love others as He loved us. The Greek language has the advantage over English in many ways, and one of the clearest is in its available vocabulary for the word love. *Eros* is romantic and sensual love. *Phile* refers to friendship. *Storge* has the idea of fondness in it that could apply to loving children or even pets.

Agape, the fourth word, is the richest and most theologically significant. All the other loves are conditional and subject to change. Romantic love may diminish and couples divorce. Friendships sour and people become memories. Dogs bite and may get sent to a new owner. Every one of these "loves" has a condition attached to it.

Not so with *agape*. It's entirely selfless, without any concern for what the "lover" receives in return. *Agape*, therefore, is also immutable. No circumstances or conduct alter the lover's commitment to love. Finally, *agape* is engaged. The lover is committed to bettering the life of the object of *agape*.

The New Testament was written in the first century in Greek, and to really understand the depth of meaning of a Greek word in the New Testament, you need to look at how the word was used before the New Testament was written. What was the word's meaning to the Greek moral philosophers? This background is important because it helps us understand how a

Greek writer in the first century would have understood and used the word.

When we look at the pre-biblical use of *agape*, we find that the word certainly did have the idea of being not self-seeking. It also tended to be used to describe the love of something higher for something lower. Thus, a ruler may love his subjects in this manner or a god his worshipers. However, Greek writers tended to use the words for sensual love and friendship love almost exclusively. *Agape* was seldom used.

In the New Testament era, the word *agape* gained its footing, being used 215 times in its noun and verb forms. By contrast, the word for friendship love is used 21 times. The words for sensual love or fondness are not used at all.

This etymological shift is huge. Christianity essentially gave the word *agape* its currency and theological richness. But why? What made the word so very appropriate in the Christian vocabulary?

The answer lies in the very heart of the gospel message. The love that God showed by sending His Son, who willingly came and gave His life in a brutal torture and execution, needed a new word. That *agape* was not self-seeking gave the first Christian writers a foothold. In a sense, they baptized it and made it so uniquely Christian that people today who have only a slight knowledge of the faith are likely to have heard of the word. People widely know this word is special.

God loves us without any precondition because love is His nature. Recall that God is love (1 John 4:8, 16). We don't have to be good enough, have the right theology, or engage in certain practices to beloved by God. God is fatherly in His attitude toward all people. Certainly, we can experience personally God's love by embracing and nurturing certain beliefs and practices in the same way that we can experience the current of a river by moving out into the middle of it. But the current is there whether we acknowledge it or not. God's love is a simple and fundamental fact of the spiritual world. Faith enables us to leave the bank and step into the deep.

In a sense, the New Testament writers shaped the word *agape* to fit the story they had witnessed. They were often aware of their own shortcomings. Paul referred to himself as the chief of sinners, a confession echoed in many ways by other writers and characters in the New Testament. Yet they saw Jesus' commitment to them and to all people, even asking the Father, from the agony of the cross, to forgive the very people responsible for putting Him there. This love went beyond any of the other "loves" available. God loves us no matter our moral standing.

There is another very important nuance of *agape* that helps us understand God's nature and the hope we have in Him. *Agape* includes compassion, that is, a commitment to action. Empathy is feeling another's pain, and God certainly understands our struggles and difficulties. Compassion, however, goes beyond empathy. Compassion attempts to relieve the suffering.

If I were to say, "God is love," you'd be entirely justified in replying, "Well, that's great but what good does that do me?" The answer is that God came personally into human history, loved, taught, and healed everyone He came in contact with. He then died on a cross and in a mysterious way secured our healing for the deep spiritual malady that afflicts us all. "And what good does that do me today?" you would be right to ask. The answer is that Jesus was raised to life and offers to come into the life of anyone who has faith to ask Him.

This *agape* love of God is the foundation of grace, and grace is the action of *agape*. So, God is able to enter our lives and relieve our spiritual suffering in every way conceivable. Grace, therefore, becomes the means by which we can make real changes in our lives. It's an inside job. God within us, loving, forgiving, guiding, motivates us to make the deep changes that conformity to an external love can never accomplish.

God is not saying to us "I love you in spite of..." or "I love you anyway." He's simply saying, "I love you." In Christ, He showed us how much and assured us that nothing can possibly separate us from Him and His love, not any of the external threats or the more dangerous internal threats of fear and doubt.

I've devoted considerable space to the idea of God's love because without understanding it, the idea that we are to look at the world with love is simply ludicrous. We've got to get the vertical axis right before we can talk seriously about the horizontal axis. If God loved this sinful world as it is, and if He loves us with all of our darkness, then we have an example to follow as we try to take this sinful world as it is. We do "as He did."

Loving the World

Taking this world as it is brings us again into the very heart of acceptance. Remember that in acceptance we don't have to agree or approve. We simply accept that circumstances can be hard and disagreeable and so can people. Taking on God's love and grace as our own enables us to find the collateral grace in a difficult world and love people.

Jesus anticipated our struggle to love people. One of His most memorable teachings concerns our need to love our enemies. Again, people only slightly aware of the details of Christian faith will have heard of "love your enemies." They also are likely to speak of "going the extra mile" and "turning the other cheek" not knowing that these sayings come directly from the Sermon on the Mount. Jesus used this vivid language because He knew it would get attention, and He wanted to draw attention to the power of love.

Here is the great challenge. Remember the different words for love. *Agape* is God's love for us. We accept that and celebrate it. We also know that the command to love one another is sprinkled throughout the New Testament. Again, vividly, we're told to "love our enemies and to pray for those who persecute us" (Matt. 5:44). Here's the kicker: the Greek word for love here and throughout the New Testament is *agape*. We are to love others as God loves us.

God doesn't command anything for which He does not provide us the strength and courage to accomplish. He knows that our best recourse to living in this broken world is love, especially love of enemies.

Loving your enemy neutralizes them not by changing them, but by removing their hold on you. Whether they change or not is frankly none of your business. Love must become our nature as it is God's. And to dispel any doubt about the extent of this love, to mute our tendency to come up with qualifiers and exceptions, Jesus ended this important section of the sermon with "You must be perfect, even as your heavenly Father is perfect" (Matt. 5:48).

Leo Tolstoy wrote a little book entitled *What Men Live By*. The story is about an angel named Michael who lost his heavenly standing because he did not trust God. He was sentenced to live on earth until he discovered the answers to three important questions. A shoemaker named Simon finds him naked, huddling against a chapel. Simon, though burdened himself, takes him in.

Over the succeeding six years, Michael smiled only three times. When the poor family took him in, and the wife served him a meal, he smiled. Years later, a surly nobleman demanded boots of a very high quality and threatened Simon that if they didn't wear well he would have him arrested. Michael smiled as he watched the unpleasant scene. Finally, a woman came in for shoes for two little girls, one of whom was crippled in one foot. The woman explained that the little girls were not hers by birth, but she adopted them when their mother died in bed with her daughter and crushed the foot of one of the babies. Hearing this story, Michael smiled for the third and final time.

After the woman left, Michael came to Simon and fully revealed his true nature and the reason for his presence on earth, and that now he could return to heaven and his work for God. He knew the three answers.

The kindness of the family that rescued him, clothed him, and gave him a place to live made him realize that men are capable of extravagant love. The episode with the self-important baron revealed that often men do not know what is really needed for their physical well-being. Then, as he watched the woman who took in the two babies, raised them, and loved them as her own, he realized the greatest lesson. "I learned that it is only in appearance that men are kept alive through care for themselves. In reality, they are kept alive through love."

We will keep wrestling with life until we realize that we were created to receive God's love and to share it even, and perhaps especially, with a sinful broken world. Our very existence is the result of God's love. That love flows through our veins, quickens our spirits, and brings joy to the deepest parts of our souls.

Paul wrote that there are three great words: faith, hope, and love. These are the "theological virtues," each one a gift from God. Each has a rich and limitless capacity to enrich our lives. But, he added, the greatest of these is love (1Cor. 13:13). The challenges of life reveal the reason.

"Taking, as He did, this sinful world as it is, not as I would have it" is a call to accept the difficulties of life without feeling that the world is out to get you or focusing on the unfairness of life. Life is hard and unfair. When you run up against this broken world, you have a choice to make. Do you complain, compare, and curse? Or do you choose to respond in a loving, trusting, and forgiving way? One choice multiplies the misery. The other enables you to be reasonably happy.

———————

Toward reasonable happiness:

- Reasonable happiness requires a frank admission that we live in a broken and sinful world. We must accept life as it is, and life is messy.
- "The line of good and evil cuts through the heart of every human being." We cannot always cast stones at the brokenness of the world without realizing our own participation in this brokenness.
- God responded to the sinfulness of the world with love, sacrifice, and the offer of redemption.
- If we charge into the world trying to control and change evil at every turn, we're adopting a strategy that Jesus manifestly rejected. He chose the way of grace.
- We wrestle with the world when we complain, compare, and condemn. Fighting in this way always leads to soul bruises and lacerations.
- Love is the most excellent way, even though it exposes us to rejection. We are called to love this broken world.

We can "let the world win" and respond with love, as Jesus did. This divine strategy is the means of healing this sinful and broken world.

CHAPTER NINE

TRUSTING YOU TO MAKE ALL THINGS RIGHT IF I SURRENDER TO YOUR WILL

"For I know the plans I have for you, says the Lord, plans for welfare and not for evil, to give you a future and a hope."
Jeremiah 29:11

"Let God have your life. He can do more with it than you can."
Dwight L. Moody

The typical phone call I get as an interventionist comes from a wife, mother, or sister who begins the conversation with "I was given your name by_____." I know what to expect. They're calling because someone in their family has a problem with drugs or alcohol. They fear, or they know, it's addiction.

The stories are so very similar. For all of the chaos and confusion addiction creates, the disease is remarkably predictable. Fear is the overarching emotion. Families are scared when they call me. They're also angry and hurt, but mainly afraid. They're afraid of losing their loved one. They're afraid of doing something they fear will only make things worse. They're afraid of losing jobs, homes, status. They envision the worst, and their fears are not unfounded. Their struggling loved one has already begun to show the signs of the inner disintegration and spiritual void that gives rise to all the outward manifestations like legal problems, broken relationships, illnesses, accidents, etc.

I tell them I'm so glad they called. I get out a pad of paper and say, "Tell me about your loved one." I listen, jot down notes, and ask a few questions over the next 45 minutes or more. At the end of the tears, the anguish, the frustration, and fear they're exhausted. They've told the story so many times. I say, "All right. Are you ready for me to talk now?" The question is very intentional. I need to know and have them affirm that they're ready to listen, because my first words are, "I want you to have hope."

They need to hear that word: hope. They're looking down a tunnel that is so full of darkness and dread they can't envision anything worthwhile. They've heard so many broken promises from their loved one and have seen so many squandered opportunities. Efforts to talk, just talk, always degenerate into loud storms of accusation, shame, blame, and guilt.

"Trusting You to make all things right if I surrender to Your will" contains more of the essence of The Prayer than any other phrase. It follows quite naturally the previous two commitments to accept hardships as the pathway to peace and to take the world as it is. Once we know that something good can come out of suffering and that we don't need to fight, we want assurance that there is a plan. Peace from hardships promises victory in the individual battles. Trusting God to make all things right means we know God wins the war. We've got to know that chaos doesn't win.

This phrase of The Prayer, also like the previous two, holds the most extravagant promise but also raises the most serious questions and objections. The wrongness of our lives and the world is very loud and obvious. It creates a *prima facie* case against the notion that there is a plan and someone, or something, is in charge. Yet, we're praying for trust that God will make all things right. How different life would be if we knew that somehow everything turned out all right. We could endure the deepest darkness if we knew the certainty of dawn.

In Lexington, Kentucky where I grew up, basketball was in the air. I was a Wildcat fan from my earliest recollections, listening to games on the radio, keeping statistics, and even playing along with a coat hanger bent into a rim and a Nerf ball. Like any boy who closely follows a sport, I could name all the players, knew their numbers, and their averages. I literally would cry when they lost, and sometimes I still do. The word "fan" is derived from "fanatic," you know. Being a fan means being delightfully crazy. I was and often still am.

Back in those distant days, the game would be broadcast live on the radio, and Caywood Ledford, "The Voice of the Wildcats," would paint a vivid picture of the action. I can still "hear" his tone, tenor, and phrasing. Later, at 11 p.m., if I recall correctly, the game was replayed on tape delay. I was thrilled when I finally was old enough to stay up and watch the game.

If it was a close game, I was a nervous wreck while listening to it. The outcome was uncertain. It looked bad. It was getting worse! I sometimes turned off the radio because I simply couldn't bear to listen to my Cats lose. I can't claim to have changed much over the years. But if we won the close game, I could later watch the replay with utter calm and confidence. I knew the outcome.

This phrase of The Prayer calls for that same kind of confidence. Yet it's *very* difficult, and we don't have the benefit of knowing ahead of time the ebbs and flows of the score as the game is played out. Frankly, I struggle with this phrase because I anxiously struggle to trust in a God who prefers to work subtly, quietly, and often in the background.

Those family calls come from people who are looking into the abyss of addiction. All the promise they had for their loved one hangs in the balance, and when they call, they're full of doubt and dread. In fact, about 75% of the family members I work with are absolutely convinced that their loved one will not accept help. They have no hope. They're calling out of desperation, wanting to try "one more time" to get through to their loved one, but certain it will do no good.

Trusting God to make all things right? The record for these families is full of a thousand broken promises. Many of them have given up and let go. This phrase sounds wonderful in theory, but in real life it looks ridiculous and nonsensical.

But what if it's not? What if we know the outcome of the game? What if we can rise above the sine curves of life and look down on all of it from a divine perspective? That would change everything, wouldn't it?

Meaninglessness and The Death of Hope

The idea that God will make all things right is called Providence. Providence means God has a plan and no amount of chaos will derail that plan. In fact, Providence means God will use the chaos itself to bring about His ultimate goal for all creation. Billy Graham is credited with saying "I've read the last pages. Everything turns out all right." That's Providence, and it's the most hopeful of all theological concepts.

This hopefulness, however, quickly runs into some harsh realities that seem to destroy the notion that God will make all things right. Frankly, very few people, in my experience, have that level of trust. I went through a time when I knew about God's Providence as a theological proposition but wondered if it were really true. My world had turned to ash.

One of my favorite Christmas carols reflects this rhythm of hopefulness and doubt. "I Heard the Bells on Christmas Day" tells a story, as all really good hymns do. Henry Longfellow authored the poem that was put to music, and in the first stanza he described hearing "the bells on Christmas day, their old familiar carols play, and wild and sweet, the words repeat of peace on earth, good will to men." The refrain reminds us of that first heavenly choir of angels who sang of the bright hope ushered in by the birth of Christ. Wonderful!

In stanza two, Longfellow reflected on how this message has rung clearly through the centuries. This is the enduring hope that echoes throughout the ages. The hopeful strains are always there!

In the third stanza, reality hits. "And in despair I bowed my head, there is no peace on earth, I said. For hate is strong and mocks the song of peace on earth good will to men." Longfellow wrote this poem in 1863 when the United States were not united. Surrounded by stories of death, destruction, and loss, Longfellow wrote what many of us have felt at some point in our lives. Providence is a fantasy. Despair is the bleak reality. When it was in the grips of cold evil, C. S. Lewis described Narnia as a place where it was always winter but never Christmas. We've all spent time there.

The fear that life has no purpose or meaning is a very common by-product of addiction. Neurologically, the brain is damaged. This produces a spiritual void full of darkness. The brain is basically a survival organ. It monitors and modifies countless bodily functions, keeps us safe from environmental dangers, and tries to ensure that we make it through short and long periods of time alive and well. Much of its work is autonomic.

Things change when we get to the prefrontal cortex. It operates on a much higher level. In this area of our brains, we anticipate consequences, weigh decisions, and have higher spiritual experiences and higher forms of love. It is the seat of wisdom. This part of our brains makes us more human, enabling all of the higher functions that separate us from lower creatures. The prefrontal cortex of our brains is truly the intersection of heaven and earth.

Perhaps not surprisingly, in this fascinating part of the brain we have the development of the "idealized future self." This is how we think about ourselves in the future. We envision the improvement of our lives. A young man recently told me about applying to law school and what he hoped to do with that degree. In his prefrontal cortex is a picture of himself as a successful and influential lawyer. You've had a similar experience when you were about to get married, have a child, change jobs, etc. We envision things getting better, and those visions aren't necessarily rational. The old saying that "the grass is always greener on the other side of the fence" is a classic prefrontal cortex statement, but it's patently not true. It simply expresses a hope that life will improve, and hope is a very powerful survival tool.

Interestingly, in addiction, the prefrontal cortex goes "off-line" so to speak, a phenomenon called the dysexecutive syndrome or hypofrontality. Other, more primitive parts of the brain take over and direct thinking and actions. Families are often mystified by the plainly destructive behavior of their addicted loved ones. "What are they thinking?!?!" is a common question. The answer is they're not thinking, or at least not thinking with the parts of their brains that enable them to make wise decisions.

So, what happens to the idealized self in addiction? It's gone. Addiction truly is the death of hope. The addict is full of darkness and despair. They likely will ignore any evidence to the contrary, so the addict almost certainly has a badly distorted view of God or no belief in God at all. They truly do not believe "things will get better." Their solution is the drug. Any thoughts of the future are either gone or take the form of some ludicrous notion like winning the lottery.

The death of hope is not reserved for addicts only. Carl Jung described meaninglessness as the general neurosis of our time. That was back in the 1950's, and no one can seriously suggest that things have improved. A meaningless worldview envisions no better future and considers all events to be part of an over-arching chaos.

When I was a doctoral student in seminary, I also worked as a cabinet maker. Nothing too fancy, but I did carve out a niche in specialty bookcases and cabinets for libraries and reading rooms in people's homes. On one job, as I was removing books from the old shelves that were to be replaced, I ran across a book of poems. I don't recall anything about the title or the author, but something intrigued me. I opened it and found an inscription the man had penned to his wife. He'd obviously given it to her on some special occasion. The inscription stunned me. It read, "I hope this helps you through this hell we call life."

I couldn't help but speculate briefly on the cheery occasion for such a gift. "Merry Christmas, honey. I though this might help you through this hell we call life." Quickly leaving aside such musings, I felt deeply sad that anyone regarded life as a hell to endure. And this was a fairly well-to-do family in the New Orleans Garden District. I was in my mid-20's at the time, and wondered how this man who had so much also had an emptiness in his soul. Years later, I read Victor Frankl, who said that we have the means but no meaning. Meaninglessness has no demographic boundaries.

The advent of "new atheism" has given rise to some very eloquent and persuasive expressions of meaninglessness, though many who follow this path would say otherwise. Young people hear things like we're "dancing to our DNA" and somehow find that liberating without recognizing its sad limits and dangers. The universe, we're told, is simply the random result of time, matter, and chance. If the same applies to human beings, as it must logically from that foundation, then are we merely a random accident?

In *Sapiens: A Brief History of Humankind*, Yuval Harari surveys human development in ancient history and pre-history. He's very much interested in human happiness and the pursuit of meaning. He's also extraordinarily forthright in claiming that meaning is an illusion. "As far as we can tell, from a purely scientific viewpoint, human life has absolutely no meaning. Humans are the outcome of blind evolutionary processes that operate without goal or purpose….Hence, any meaning that people ascribe to their lives is just an illusion." (Chapter 19, "And They Lived Happily Ever After," in section The Meaning of Life). His viewpoint is bleak, but well-written.

Where do such propositions leave us? We seem tuned to find meaning in life. It appears that we need a sense of coherence and purpose to live well in a world that offers so much chaos and uncertainty. Christopher Hitchens, one of the leading voices in the new atheism, summed up the challenge: "It could be that existence is a pointless joke. Yet it's impossible to live one's everyday life as if this were so." It's a mistake to think that all atheists are constantly bordering on mayhem. They would object strenuously and, to my mind, rightfully, that they have created through some admirable pursuits a meaningful life. I'm certainly not in a position to deny this for them. What I can say from my personal experience and observation, however, is that such an approach to life and meaning is profoundly unsatisfying to vast numbers of people. They want more.

People yearn for meaning. They seek it, sometimes wisely and sometimes unwisely. But the gist of this phrase of The Prayer appeals to a fundamental need in the human psyche to bring order to an often very harsh reality. Something(s) is wrong, and we want it to be right. If we believe we have no opportunity to improve our lives, then we live without hope.

Is Life a DIY Project?

Living without hope is genuinely a dismal choice, but humans seem to be created with a fundamental need for hope and belief in a positive future. Again, our neurological framework leads us to envision a better tomorrow. We have to believe in something good that pulls us into the future. Hope is essential to living well. The question, therefore, very basically is where does this hope come from?

When I worked with young men who were early in recovery, I would often hear them express a variant of the idea that all of life is up to them. They create their own happiness, meaning, and even their own god. The only story they could embrace was the story they created for themselves. It's a subtle form of idolatry. They've created a god in their own image but are completely unaware of their utter self-absorption. They still long for hope because they were created to do so, but they have taken on the responsibility for creating it. Ironically, few of them had any hope (remember addiction is the death of hope), but sadly too few of them were willing to make the changes necessary to awaken it.

Life for many people today is a DIY project. They're taking on life on their own, writing their own stories, creating their own meaning. While it sounds encouraging and courageous to believe that you're master of your fate, as I've already noted, this idea is a distortion and ultimate failure. If we are created by a transcendent being, and if that transcendent being offers to care for us, guide us, and save us, then the very worst thing we can do is trust in ourselves and ignore the transcendent. Yet many people do, and if the surveys are accurate, more and more people are treating life as if it is all up to them.

Christians should tread carefully here. We shouldn't paint all unbelievers as hopeless narcissists pursuing a self-centered life of meaninglessness. We'll never convey the beauty of the gospel while at the same time trying to convince unbelievers that they're sure to become like Lenin, Stalin, Mao, or Marx. Our best approach, I think, is to avoid trying to convince anyone their lives are meaningless, but at the same time presenting the meaningful life we can find in Christ. Positive construction of the truth is much better than negative destruction error. Let the message of Christ be our goal.

So, how would Jesus respond to the DIY culture? The Sermon on the Mount gives us several illustrations. Jesus said there are only two ways in life, one leads to destruction and the other leads to life. He taught that all lives have a foundation, either of sand or of bedrock. The former will fall when the storms come, the latter will stand. He taught that if we put God first in our lives, then our worries will diminish, but if we rely on our own insights and strength then we only multiply our anxieties.

Perhaps most clearly, Jesus taught that we must deny self in order to follow Him. If we seek to save our lives, that is to form and create our own meaning and live in our own strength, then we will lose the very thing we're trying to create (Mark 8:34-35).

Again, our task as Christians is not to convince someone else of the meaningless of their lives. Life itself will convince them. The 2 a.m. questions simply will not be silenced by the idea that "I've just got to do better." Only God can give the richest, most satisfying, and eternal answers to those insistent questions. Lives built by our own hands will fall painfully. This is not an opinion or careless condemnation, but the core of what Jesus taught. It's spiritual physics. We are not created to be self-sufficient. Yet the popularity of "I will make my own meaning" persists.

Anthony Bourdain was the ultimate new millennium bon vivant. An accomplished chef, popular author, television star, and world traveler, he led a very colorful life. He also dealt with the very dark shadows of addiction and the various hangovers a Bohemian lifestyle inevitably leaves. In one of his more popular books, *Kitchen Confidential*, he wrote what could be a succinct summary of his approach to life: "Like I said before, your body is *not* a temple, it's an amusement park. Enjoy the ride."

Whether you like Anthony Bourdain or not, just notice how starkly these two sentences contrast with the teaching of Jesus and the New Testament where we're taught that our bodies *are* temples, and we are to be both accountable and grateful to God for the lavish gifts He bestows on us. One approach to life makes your own unbridled passions the ultimate arbiter of how you will live. The other approach to life makes Christ the center and seeks to live in resonance with Him who claims to be the author of life. The first approach to life is very popular today and many people take it. The other approach to life is much less popular and is perhaps trending even more that way. And relatively few people take it. One way markets easily. The other can easily be made to appear obsolete.

In June 2018, a friend found Anthony Bourdain dead in his hotel room. He'd hung himself. Suicide is rarely simplistic. Bourdain's sad ending was probably the result of a number of factors: depression, incomplete recovery from mind-altering substances (he continued to drink and smoke marijuana after he beat an addiction to heroin and cocaine), and the multiple heartbreaks life brings.

But the spiritual dimension bears mentioning, especially in this very mechanistic and hedonistic culture. If you treat your body as if it is an amusement park, what do you do when life is not amusing? If the sum and apex of your resources are the meaning you make, then what happens when you can't formulate sustainable meaning?

Stanley Hauerwas is credited with saying that the motto of the reigning philosophy of this present day is "The only story I have is the story I make for myself." That neatly sums up the individual, isolated, and self-centered approach Jesus warned us against. It does not offer enduring answers to the most important questions of life because it has a self-imposed limit.

The Christian answer to the search for meaning is that God is the author of our lives, and He has written us into His story. Life, therefore, is definitely not a DIY project. We have different answers to the problem of what to do when life ceases to be amusing, and these answers are revealed to us by a loving God.

To be fair, of course some people who commit suicide are Christians. Christians get depressed, addicted, arrested, sick, and experience any of the other countless pains life can inflict upon us and that we can inflict upon ourselves. Sometimes life does overwhelm us. But never because the answers God provides are inaccurate or inadequate. In a very sad way, the despair of a DIY life is predictable and even inevitable when we find the self unequal to the task. We cannot generate a sustaining hope that weathers any storm. The answer God gives is an invitation to trust Him to make all things right, especially when those "things" are beyond our control or comprehension.

Does God Have a Will?

That God will make all things right is an extraordinarily comforting idea. I've witnessed many people visibly relax in the assurance of the words that "God's got this" or "He will take care of you." They cling to these promises as if they are a lifeline, and they certainly are. In a chaotic, unpredictable, and cruel world that can only give us foundations of sand, we long for something solid and dependably good. We want to believe God can fulfill the promise He's created in us.

Once we embark down this hopeful road, we immediately encounter two important questions. First, does God really care?

And what's He done, or what is He doing, to show that care? The first question addresses God's character, and that is the focus of this section. The second question addresses God's involvement in the particulars of our lives, and we'll look at that question in the next section.

For many people, the jury is still out on both questions, and that includes many people who believe in God and claim they are Christian. In *America's Four Gods*, Christopher Bader and Paul Froese, both sociologists, surveyed thousands of Americans about the two questions I posed in the previous paragraph. Their findings shed very important light on how people think about God and whether God is willing and able to help them in their lives. They discovered about 55% of people believe God is highly involved. That means, of course that nearly half of all people believe God is not involved, and that includes the 5% of people who were atheists.

The study contains many fascinating insights, but for this particular section let's note that not believing that God is involved in our lives makes this phrase of The Prayer impossible. Believing in a distant and uninvolved god is the functional equivalent of believing in no god whatsoever. We are back at square one where everything depends on the self.

Belief in an uninvolved god is hardly new. In the first century, Christianity proved very attractive to Greeks because of its message of a good and loving God who knows and cares for each person individually. This was a stark contrast to the idea of gods and goddesses either too busy for the commoner or tucked away in the lofty isolation of Mt. Olympus. The more modern version of this idea is represented by the Deists who were very influential in the late 18th century. They and their theological descendants believe God created all and put laws into place but then retreated to heaven to become an observer only. So, God does not really have a will in the sense that He orders and directs and intervenes in our daily lives. Again, this strain of belief is rather common.

It's important to emphasize that not only atheists or agnostics have given up on the idea of an involved God, and not by a long shot. Again, many believers in God doubt that He is involved in their lives, and that accounts for about 40% of people according to the America's Four Gods study. The point is, belief in God and belief in God's involvement are two different topics and they create dramatically different approaches to faith. Believing that God is involved in your life is obviously a definite prerequisite to trusting Him to make all things right.

So why would anyone believe in an uninvolved God? Clearly, one reason is that believing in an involved God can interfere with personal agendas. Defiance is as old as the Garden of Eden, and it remains deeply woven into every human will. One of the quickest ways to eliminate critical thinking about personal choices and the notions of right and wrong is to get rid of any pesky belief in transcendence or make the transcendence so distant that it hardly matters. Get rid of an involved God, or get rid of God all together, and you're relieved of the messy burden of self-examination, accountability, and hard choices that bring you more in line with the Creator.

Also, many Christians give up on an involved God because of disappointment. They have faced pain or a loss of hope and cannot reconcile that with the idea of a good and loving and involved God. The question is simple and important: "If God is good and involved, then why did I lose my _____?"

We've already looked at the problem of evil, so we won't rehearse all that again. Our question here is even more basic. Does God have a will for individuals, the world, and all of creation? If He doesn't, then the question of evil is solved but hopelessly so. If He is involved, then we have a bit more work to do, but the answer is much more encouraging.

The biblical revelation is unequivocal. God is definitely in the business of making all things right. Remember the three great epochs of theological history: The Creation, The Breaking, and The Restoration. The end of The Restoration is God's final re-creation of all things, a new heavens and new earth in the biblical phrasing (see Isa. 65:17-19, 66:22, Rev. 21:1-5). God ended the first great epoch by pronouncing all of creation "very good." He will have the same pronouncement at the end when once again all of creation will be returned to its Edenic perfection and splendor.

This idea of a theological movement in history is very important. We are not going around in circles. We are moving toward a consummation that is filled with hope. Pain and loss are not the final verdict. The end of all things is not the result of a sad spiritual entropy.

While the mystery of God's will does prove to be the shipwreck for many Christians, it doesn't need to be so. Again, and not surprisingly, believers who struggle with the idea of an active God, or who outright dismiss the notion, do often arrive there after a bitter disappointment. Life itself is a kind of theological Rorschach where we tend to find what we look for. If someone at any point sought God's will and things didn't turn out the way they expected, then they can begin to see the prevalence of chaos and ignore the patterns of grace.

This is where the connection of God's will and God's character is vital. His will is an expression of His character, and God is love. Love is God's fundamental essence and power. All attributes and activities derive from that foundational starting point. So, God's will is not a mechanistic grinding machine, nor is it an infinitely complex equation in which we all are just minor variables. If God is love, then He must have a will for us and be intimately and lovingly involved in our lives.

The alternative to this hope is a bleakness that needs to be highlighted and recognized. Carl Sagan in his book *Pale Blue Dot* stated, "Our posturings, our imagined self-importance, the delusion that we have some privileged position in the Universe, are challenged by this point of pale light. Our planet is a lonely speck in the great enveloping cosmic dark. In our obscurity, in all this vastness, there is no hint that help will come from elsewhere to save us from ourselves." (Chapter 1, "You Are Here"). The implication is clear. It's all up to you. The individual is the final arbiter and is responsible for creating his or her own meaning, purpose, and happiness. In this scenario, each individual life is clearly a DIY project.

What an incredible contrast this phrase of The Prayer offers! Christian thought teaches us that God created both the vastness, the pale blue dot, and every creature on that dot. Further, He loves each person individually and deeply. Not only are we not lonely, we are accompanied by the Creator. And "no hint?" The hints are all around us and are echoes and reflections of The Great Hint when God became flesh and dwelt among us. God does have a will. Now we turn our attention to how we can become part of it.

Going with the Flow

If God is good and caring, then the question naturally arises: To what degree? How is God involved in the day-to-day, even moment-by-moment human efforts to know and live by His will? Not surpassingly, as with all God-questions, the answers people give span a broad spectrum.

Then there are believers who claim to know God's will for their lives in the smallest detail, minute by minute. A man once told me that God directed him as to what color socks to wear in the morning. While I can't claim anything close to that degree of knowledge, nor even a desire for God to direct my clothing choices, I can't dispute that maybe God does reveal His will to that man in that way. Perhaps he needed that level of direction. Or perhaps he was simply trying to integrate God's presence and will into the very smallest details of his life, and that is admirable.

In case you think this unusual, let me assure you as a son of the South that many prayers are offered up every Saturday in the fall on behalf of a favorite football team. I'm sure our region is not unique in this regard, but when people talk about sports being a religion, they're not far off in the states I've lived in. Don't mock the man who seeks God's will for his sock color if you're occasionally asking God to make an opponent's field goal attempt veer wide right.

Frankly, I seriously doubt God is deeply interested in either socks or football scores. Though some people are oriented to that, I can certainly warn against making that level of God's involvement normative. It's a sure setup for disappointment. Though I wish it were so, it's not ludicrous to imagine that some people have lost their faith over a last-second loss.

Other Christians reserve God's will only for the big questions of life, such as career, spouse, or health. Again, while this too is admirable and does recognize that certain decisions in life are of much greater impact than others, it actually suffers from the same generic mistake of limiting God's will to a game-show level where we simply need Him to fill in the blank. Viewed in this way, God's will becomes little more than a cheat sheet to an unending life-quiz.

As tempting as it is to think of God's will only as a way of figuring out answers to questions, the more fundamental problem is that people make God's will needlessly complex. If our goal is to figure out what God wants us to do in every particular, then we're constantly trying to fit pieces of the puzzle together and endlessly speculating about how an event, usually an unpleasant event, fits into the overall plan of God.

I've known many people like this, and they often become exhausted, frustrated, or even give up on the idea that God has a will. I've discussed the latter group but it bears mentioning here that simply because something is difficult doesn't mean it's useless or an illusion. I found calculus to be very frustrating and never was very good at it. But it never occurred to me to question its validity or to mock people who both believed in calculus and were very good at it.

God's will is something much more fundamental than reading the signs or always trying to determine which course to take. We are in God's will right now, surrounded by it, immersed in it. Thomas Aquinas wrote that God is in all things, and intimately so. All things. *The Baltimore Catechism*, used mainly to instruct Catholic school children until the late 1960's, picked up on Aquinas's insight, and in the 15th Question asked, "Where is God?" The answer: Everywhere. And more specifically regarding God's will, Pierre de Caussade in *Abandonment to God's Providence* repeatedly states that we are to welcome everything in life as the expression of God's will.

At first, the idea that God is in everything and everything is an expression of God's will rankles us terribly. In what moral sense could God be in the very worst of circumstances, the vilest crimes, and the most heinous chapters in history? Frankly, we make the problem much worse by trying to categorize events as "in" or "out" of God's will. We don't gain a richer vision of God by limiting the scope of His activity. Acceptance, which is the heart of The Prayer, means stepping down from the judgment seat.

Not for a moment does this mean that we give evil a pass. The world has plenty that is terribly wrong. Setting everything in the context of God's will simply means trusting that evil doesn't have the final word and that God is still at work.

In what is probably the most cherished and familiar of all verses concerning God's will in our lives and His presence during our sufferings, Paul wrote, "We know that in everything God works for good for those who love Him and are called according to His purpose" (Rom. 8:28). Notice first that it is God who works. Often, we hear "things will work out." Things never work. Things are inanimate. They have no purpose any more than the flood has a purpose. It just inundates and destroys. But if God is at work in, and in spite of, the flood then the equation is changed entirely.

The fact that God works for good reminds us of the first principle of the foundation I suggested for reading and understanding the Bible. God always has our ultimate good in mind, and because He is all-powerful, God will not let any bad event become our ultimate undoing. God is into transformation. He took the cross and wrought the salvation of humanity. He can take any crushing event and bring something good out of it. He wastes nothing, even the dark times that come into our lives from our own hands.

Finally, in this verse we see that the good that God works is for those who love Him. This simply means what Lewis referred to in a quote I cited earlier. If you want good to come from your challenges, then you need to stand with The One who can bring the very best outcome imaginable (redemption) out of the very worst event conceivable (humanity rejecting God and nailing His Son to a cross).

God's will is like a vast river, moving everything along inexorably to an appointed end where He will make all things right. This "general will" of God is at work all around us, and God invites us to surrender to the current. The Bible is quite clear that salvation history includes a time when the restoration of all creation will be complete. In the future, God will again say of all creation that it is very good. It is in this sense that we can understand that everything in life is in the will of God. We're all in the river.

The river includes dangerous swirls and eddies. Some we see and swim away from. Others we still have the infuriating habit of paddling right into. Sometimes we see them from a distance, and they look terrifying. Sometimes the channel narrows, the waters deepen, and the current increases. Perhaps other times the river flows over dangerous rapids. Sometimes we futilely try to swim against the current and with extreme effort and an early burst of energy we convince ourselves that we've found a better way, but the current always wins. Other times we may stand on the bank, afraid of where the current may take us.

As we become more aware of this current and decide to move with it, life becomes clearer. Then at times when we are faced with important decisions we can pause and pray and watch. God's answer comes in a problem solved, an inspiration or insight, a word of wisdom that seems to come from beyond us, or a person who comes into our lives to help. The order is important. First, accept the vast general will of God of which all things are a part. Second, pray for guidance and recognize that God's will for a particular event in your life may only be realized through your engagement with Him in prayer.

Going with the flow does not mean we are either uninterested, uninvolved, or overlooked. We're part of a flow governed by the love of God which is beyond words yet also individually personalized for every soul. Being in the will of God is much vaster than trying to determine who to marry, for example. Augustine said we are created for God and long for Him in ways that we can only partly understand. The river of His will takes us home. There we will find eternal rest in the Eternal Answer who takes all of our wrongs and make them right.

The Centrality of Trust

If we are presented with the possibility that a good and loving God cares for us and has a will for us, then what are the obstacles to such a wonderful reality? This phrase of The Prayer contains two especially challenging words for the seeker who may not yet be a believer but is intrigued by the Christian faith: trust and surrender. However, the hesitancy is not only for those who have not yet taken the step of faith. Trust and surrender are twin and fatal blows to an assertive ego. They are the ultimate "no" to lingering vestiges of the DIY life. We'll deal with trust in this section and surrender in the next.

Diana is a wonderful and classic example of a young person struggling with the need for trust. She is gifted and successful in many areas of life and open to trying to pin down some of these important spiritual concepts. At an early age, she earned a doctorate in a specialized area of neurosciences. She teaches, is very analytical, and carries some difficult memories of a religion that either failed to challenge her or she failed to investigate deeply. As in most cases, it's probably a combination of both.

Many young people in her situation have never given ten minutes of serious consideration to the most important matters of life. As children or early teens perhaps, they had a negative experience with religion, or a misunderstanding, or battled with parents, etc., and they gave up on the idea of God and certainly the church. No one should live the rest of their lives based on often distorted adolescent perceptions, but people often do this with matters of faith and spirituality. Diana is rare in that she's willing: willing to ask good questions and willing to listen to suggestions. She needs a religion of the mind, in addition to a religion of the heart, and the Christian faith has a very rich intellectual history that proves interesting to her.

As we were discussing God's will and how He operates in our lives and offers to guide and care for us, I could see the questions

percolating. She was being challenged to trust, and that proves
to be an honest and understandable obstacle to someone steeped
in the scientific method and committed to empiricism. She
blurted out, "I want to see the plan! That's my problem. I want
to know how this is supposed to work. I can't, and so I end up
fighting with God."

Well, God loves those wrestling matches. He truly does. What
Diana and others like her struggle with is the unnecessary
tension between science and faith. At its extremes, a very
science-oriented person will believe that smart people can't
possibly believe in God and that it would be immature to do so.
A more reasonable approach, I think, is to accept that science
can provide wondrous explanations for many things, but it
certainly can't explain everything, and it absolutely cannot
prove the inexistence of God. Moreover, science offers a way to
some very important knowledge, but not all knowledge. When
all is said and done, we still have a tremendous amount of
evidence that the universe has a beginning, and because it
appears so finely tuned for us, then it must have a cause, and,
therefore, a Causer.

This isn't the book to address these important questions. What I
want to highlight here is that if we approach the matter of faith
with only half our brain, which is largely the scientific approach,
then we've obviously left out half our brain. Trust is a right-brain
phenomenon, and God gave us a corpus callosum for a reason.
Trust will prove very difficult for anyone who is unwilling to
complement the honest accumulation of evidence with a
willingness to go down a metaphysical path that evidence points
to. We must not eliminate the need for trust simply because we
cannot. We're programmed for the centrality of trust.

God's will is a mystery. We may think we want the certainty of
God's finger writing on the wall, the pillar of fire by night or
cloud by day to guide us. We read these stories in the Bible and
others like them and come away with the impression that God

reveals His will in undeniable and often dramatic ways. We forget that the Bible actually doesn't present these stories as normative at all. We also fail to recognize the miraculous revelations are rare and often come years or decades apart.

Faith is a challenge for many people, but it doesn't need to be. I wonder if part of their problem is that these folks assume "faith" is a packet of settled issues. While the Scripture and the rich history of theological thought provides many proven and helpful answers to the most important questions of life, they cannot remove the need for trust. One facet of faith *is* trust. So, perhaps an exchange of those words would be helpful. Theologically and etymologically, that is sound.

Whatever we may say about the degree to which God intervenes in the details, we need not be afraid of uncertainty. God is not a dime store author whose plots you can pick up from the cover of the book. God, because He is God, will always have a certain elusiveness because of His overwhelming transcendence. He is vastly different from us, and the fact that we struggle to know His will at times does not mean He is either distant or uncaring. God's nature calls us to have faith, not doubt. We can certainly confess to a degree of uncertainty, for humility demands it. But let our uncertainty be reverent and still trusting.

Are there times when we struggle, or miss out, or get God's will wrong? Of course! We are fallible humans and prone to make mistakes. And are there times when things don't work out as we wanted? Again, of course! Life, because of the echoes of The Breaking, will always be a mixture of what we want and what we get. But these troubling events never dam the river. They are exceptions, inevitable exceptions that take the form of struggle and pain. We simply must not live by the exceptions. The King is always in residence, and His river still flows.

In the opening chapter of this book, I referenced my calling to be a minister at age 19 in August 1977. In the darkness of that room, late at night, I had an encounter with God. There was no audible voice, for that would have been less impressive than the whisper I heard in my heart and soul. I knew in that moment an important part of why I had been born. A few months earlier, I told God I was willing to do whatever He wanted of me, and if there was a part that remained unwilling, I was willing for Him to make me willing. In that simple prayer, I gave God all of myself as I understood myself to God as I understood God. I was born and called to be a minister.

I've had many times of struggle since then, but what has helped me is to go back to that moment of clarity. As the biblical patriarchs would pile stones at the site of a significant act of God to remind them in the future of how God had acted, that August evening has proved innumerable times to be that spiritual marker for me. Is it always that clear? Of course not, but I have to hold onto that moment. It has been enough. I've trusted my way through some very difficult times, and even at the bottom, I've found through trust that I'm not alone.

Trust is central to believing God will make all things right. The stakes are very high, for the opposite of trust is loneliness. If we only use half our brain, then we risk losing meaningful contact with the God who offers to accompany us and guide us on the river. Existential loneliness may be one of the main general neuroses of our time. Additionally, we've multiplied distractions to such an absurd level that we don't have the spiritual space to recognize our estrangement from the God who made us.

Diana, and others like her, is much closer to the kingdom than she realizes. She simply needs to combine her commitment to science with a commitment to trust. The good news is that God created her with both. Stepping into the Kingdom is simply a matter of accepting the centrality of trust and taking the steps where the evidence leads. We can trust in a very trustworthy God.

Surrendering a Losing Position

If trusting proves to be difficult to the modern psyche, surrender proves to be laughingly impossible. Who wants to surrender to anything? Especially in our self-assertive and self-confident world. But this phrase of The Prayer has an inescapable condition attached to it. If we want all things to be made right, we must surrender to His will.

The enduring struggle, one of the classic "battles that don't stay won," is the desire for self-assertion. Our natural and usually first instinct is to try to make all things right in our own strength. We're very adept at pointing out the deficiencies in other people and situations and render our verdicts and proposed solutions readily. Even deeply committed Christians struggle with this. The desire to control always crouches at the door and is ready to spring.

Jesus understood this, of course. In one of His clearest descriptions of what it means to be a Christian, He said, "You must deny yourself, take up your cross, and follow me" (Mark 8:34). Denying yourself is the catch for most people. It sounds as if God desires our obliteration. Taking up a cross seems to verify this. The cross in this teaching is not a burden, challenge, or unpleasant situation. The cross Jesus had in mind here is not a difficult spouse or an unfulfilling job. The cross was a symbol of death. You take up a cross to carry it to the place of your execution. Jesus' call is for nothing less than the death of self. No one likes the sound of that.

Thomas Merton differentiated between the true ego and the false ego, or we may say the true and false self. God is very personal and has created us individually with various gifts, interests, and talents that He certainly doesn't want to be obliterated. God's goal for us is not that we become absorbed into Him and lose our identities. Each image God has placed in every human being is an image He crafted and chose. That true self is what Christ died to restore. The false self is the self-directed and self-assertive part of us that interferes with our relationship with God.

Surrender, therefore, means agreeing with Jesus that parts of us need to die. Our resistance to this is a direct expression of the self that rightly feels threatened. That false self wants to live, and in doing so keeps us in bondage.

It's a fact that we all surrender to something. Jesus said we will serve one of two masters, God or mammon. He didn't give a third option to serve neither. Mammon includes the false self with every expression of its self-centered pursuits. That service results in the actual obliteration of self, the true self God created us to be.

Jesus also said the truth will set you free. The freedom He had in mind was freedom from the tyranny of the false self. We resist the idea of surrender because our false self knows that it cannot survive. The truth will set us free, but first it will make us mad. The false self wants to control.

Assuming at some point a person decides to surrender to God's will, what exactly does that look like? The third step of Alcoholics Anonymous is: "Made a decision to turn our will and our lives over to the care of God as we understand Him." Countless times, I've been earnestly asked, "But how do I do this? What does this mean?" Like Diana, there's something drawing them, but they don't know exactly what to do with it.

It would be so much easier if there were some paperwork you fill out, have it notarized and then you have officially surrendered. Or perhaps it would help if there was a specific sacrifice you make. Get an unblemished whatever, offer it up on an altar, and there you have completed your surrender. But it's not that simple and contractual.

The surrender happens with will, expressed in words, accompanied by actions. The will is the volitional part of our mind. It is what we have decided we want. Let's use the illustration of marriage. Marriage is initiated by the shared desire of both parties to unite. Two becoming one starts with the will of the two to become one as they feel led by God into the sanctity of marriage.

Will alone, however, is not nearly enough. The words of the ceremony are vital. Recall the Hebrew understanding of the importance of the spoken word. Words create. I always underscore this for couples exchanging their marriage vows. What makes them "married" is not a document they signed at the clerk of court's office. The marriage is the result of spoken words of love and commitment. The ring is a visible symbol of a sacred event in which both parties promise love and devotion as long as they live.

But that's certainly not the end product, by any means. The words set a trajectory that is fulfilled and sustained by the actions of marital commitment. Love is expressed in fidelity, in good times and bad, in sickness and in health, etc. I sometimes add that marriage is proven just as validly in taking out the trash and paying mortgages as it is in purchasing rings and dresses, and planning rehearsal dinners and receptions. The actions of marriage confirm and strengthen the relationship over the succeeding years.

Surrender to God begins with a decision, an openness and willingness to try a lifestyle and adopt a world view that is radically different. My young friend Diana may want to "know the plan," but she also realizes that's not the way God works. Her mindset at these early stages, however, is still vitally important and wonderful! She has the will to say yes to Something she doesn't understand but wants to believe in and trust. I think God is delighted by this "coming to herself" as the prodigal son did in the parable before he began his journey home. It's an act of will.

Following this is a simple prayer, a verbal commitment to God to turn from the false self and turn to Him. It can take many forms. "Take up my cross and follow You." "Please give me Your grace through Christ." Or very simply, "Thy will be done, not mine." When the words are a sincere expression of the heart (even without understanding the complete plan), a whole new soul-trajectory has begun, and a person moves more closely toward the heart of God.

This step of surrendering is completed by a lifetime of inviting God into the details of life and committing to follow His will. The great mistake many people make is fencing off God to a weekend commitment, if that. The works Jesus and the writers of the Bible referred to so often are the daily kindness, walking in humility, turning even moment by moment from the infernal tug of the false self, and in trying to the best of our ability to understand, live, and share the message of Jesus. These are the good works God created for us to perform and live in.

Even at the start, however, we will begin to see a change, and that is the ultimate "proof," the "knowing" of the plan." It's in the results. Very quickly, people who make this surrender begin to notice a change in themselves, their circumstances, and even in the people around them. Those very pragmatic results are the faint foreshadowings of the ultimate end of history when God will make all things right. At this point, you have entered into the will of God every bit as much as you are doing the will of God.

Surrender, frankly, is a humiliation, but a humiliation of the very parts of ourselves that have disabled and corrupted the self that bears the image of God. We're surrendering a losing position. The battle could not be won except by choosing to side with the God who has chosen in grace to side with us.

Guarding the Center

City Slickers came out in 1991 and provided all of us young preachers at the time a wonderful illustration about what is most important in life. Mitch (Billy Crystal), an aging yuppie, is beginning to come to grips with the fact that his busy life is increasingly meaningless. With two equally confused friends, he goes on a two-week cattle drive in the hope of figuring out life.

The trail boss for the cattle drive, Curly (Jack Palance, a man so craggy you'd think he was the offspring of a butte and a mesa), is accustomed to these aging, empty baby boomers coming out west to "find themselves" in two weeks. They spend 50 weeks a year getting their lives all tied up in knots and think that a cattle drive will help them untie everything.

As Mitch and Curly ride together chasing down a stray, they have the talk that gave rise to "the illustration." Curly stops and asks the confused Mitch, "Do you know what the secret of life is?" Mitch, intrigued and hopeful, responds, "No. What is it?" Curly holds up one finger and says "This...One thing. Just one thing...Stick to that and everything else don't mean ____." You can fill in your own word for dung there.

Mitch wants the answer to a question he can't even form yet. Curly has an answer that Mitch probably can't hear yet. So, when pressed about what the one thing is, Curly replies, "You've got to figure that out for yourself."

What would Jesus say to Mitch?

He might respond with some words from the Sermon on the Mount about priorities. "If your eye is single, then your body will be full of light. If it is not, then your whole body will be full of darkness" (Matt. 6:22-23). Jesus was talking about focus. You have to be focused on "the one thing" or else other things will overwhelm and frustrate you. This is the language of surrender.

He may include, "Seek first the kingdom of God and His righteousness and everything else will be added to you" (Matt. 6:33). In other words, once you figure out the priority of "the one thing" everything else begins to make sense.

So, Curly got a lot right. Everyone needs "the one thing." It's unquestionably the case, that if we find the north star, we will be able to navigate through life better. Find a foundation on which to build. Get an axis around which everything revolves. Do these things, and life will improve. Focus helps you shed a great many unhealthy attachments.

But that general principle is NOT the ultimate answer from a Christian perspective. Jesus made Himself "the one thing." He repeatedly said we need to follow Him (nearly 90 times in the Gospels), put Him first, forsake everything else, lose your life, take up your cross, learn of Me, etc. He IS the one thing. He is the Creator of all things and in Him all things hold together. We don't get to decide that. We can only accept that.

Of course, a comedy about confused baby boomers is not the place to make a highly Christocentric point, but let's give Curly his due and recognize how right he gets it within the limits afforded him. You've got to find the one thing. But let's firmly establish the next step Christianity offers: find the best thing and everything else makes sense for eternity.

Also, Curly is not quite right when he said, "everything else don't mean ____." Everything else matters enormously. All the parts of our lives are important. Our families, work, relationships, sexuality, speech, finances, etc., are vitally important. It's just that when we allow any of those things in the center, we eventually end up confused and empty but unsure why. For example, it seems I've been hearing since the 60's that if you had more and better sex, then you'd really be happy. I don't want to attempt to imagine what more sex would look like in this sex-saturated culture, but I'm certain we've overdone it and missed the point.

In my office, I have a picture of the north rose window of the Notre Dame Cathedral. Thirty-three feet in diameter, it's one of the most beautiful windows in any cathedral anywhere. I can't imagine what it would be like to stand before it, bathed in the graces of those wonderful colors. The window captures a little bit of heaven and gently bestows it upon us.

It depicts scores of scenes and saints and kings and biblical events that would be overwhelming in its complexity if not for the wonderful coherence of its design. In the middle of the rose window is Jesus being held by Mary. The message is clear: the beauty of the window, its harmony, all depend on Christ at the center. The stories make sense as long as Christ is the one thing. The same is true for us.

Søren Kierkegaard, 150 years or so before Curly, said a saint is someone whose life is about one thing. He went on to say that a saint's life is "gathered." The will of God seeks to gather us.

Our distorted insistence on creating our own meaning, our own happiness, our own lives has only created confused lives full of noisy fractures and loose threads. Life is simply not a DIY project, and it never was meant to be.

I think Jesus' message to us today is captured in the rose window. When we search for meaning, happiness, and coherence in life, Jesus would not say, "You've got to figure that out for yourself." He'd want us to put Him in the center and strive to keep Him there. That's when you really begin to understand the mystery, promise, and wonder of God's will.

Creating your own meaning and happiness sounds so attractive and empowering, but we're unequal to that task. God will do for us what we cannot do for ourselves. And all those other things? They do matter, but we trust Jesus to add them to our lives in ways that bring order out of the chaos.

The Meeting of the Waters

I've traveled on the Amazon River perhaps a dozen times for mission trips. We fly into Manaus, board a boat that serves as our home for the next couple of weeks, and travel for days to reach villages and tribes that have limited access to medical and dental care and to the gospel. They are wonderful and hard trips.

As we leave port in Manaus, we very soon run into a fascinating sight called The Meeting of the Waters. The Amazon, also called the "Solimoes" west of Manaus, flows from southwest to northeast. The Rio Negro flows from the northwest to the southeast. The rivers meet but they do not merge. Due to differences in temperature, density, and current, the black waters of the Rio Negro flow side by side with the cream-coffee-colored waters of the Amazon. Both rivers maintain their identity for miles. Eventually, however, the waters begin to mix, and the mighty Amazon absorbs the Rio Negro and together they flow toward the Atlantic.

This major tourist attraction reminds me of my struggle with the will of God. I can try to maintain my independence, but the track record of that self-centered approach is not encouraging. Or I can surrender to a greater flow, a mightier current that will take me where I really wanted to go all along. Every molecule of the Rio Negro continues to exist, but it has a new identity and a more defined destiny. Jesus prayed that we would become one with Him and the Father, and surrendering to His will means finding our true identity and destiny in this unity.

Reasonable happiness cannot possibly mean living forever on the uncertainty of self-created swirls and currents. Some very important things we can know, but only if we trust and surrender. When faced with a tough time, it's common to hear, "You will make it through this." That's true but only if you go *through* whatever it is. That means dropping the obvious avoidance behaviors like drinking and drugs, or the more subtle ones like embracing fear, anger, resentment, and giving up. They all falsely promise to allow us to check out of the challenge. Trusting God to make all things right means putting our trust in the only Person who makes sense. He can get us through whatever we face. Not everything will go our way. Not by a long shot. But we do know that in the end, it will be good. Very good. And our present confidence in that future reality brings us reasonable happiness.

Toward reasonable happiness:

- This phrase contains the fundamental essence of The Prayer. No phrase is more important.
- We're wired to expect imminent danger and often read into mildly challenging events an out-of-proportion sense of alarm. We often feel that the world and our lives are spinning out of control.
- Human beings are meaning-seeking creatures. In the face of an apparently hazardous life, we strive to hold on to some sense of meaning.
- We can treat life as a DIY project, each one writing their own stories, creating their own meaning. This approach is the source of great unhappiness.
- Or we can trust that a good and loving God wants to write us into His Story. This trust leads to a meaningful life.
- "Surrendering" to God's will is a direct challenge to our DIY default setting.

We can choose to believe that God's will is an inexorable movement to an ultimate and eternal good. We can then relax in trust that God will take care of us.

EPILOGUE

One of the most endearing qualities of the Bible is the way God constantly called and used highly dysfunctional people to bring His grace to a highly dysfunctional world. Jesus said He came not to call the righteous but sinners. He addressed that memorable line to the murmuring Pharisees who were scandalized that He would eat and drink with tax collectors, commoners, and possibly even a prostitute or two. The delicious irony of Jesus's response, of course, is that the Pharisees needed grace just as much as the very worst sinner. In fact, in God's economy there truly is no "worst." Sin is very egalitarian, but thankfully so is grace.

The examples are legion, but Jacob qualifies as one of the more notable dysfunctional heroes of the faith, and he came by it honestly. His father Isaac and grandfather Abraham had issues. Yet they with Jacob form a kind of Old Testament trinity. Many prayers today begin by addressing the God of Abraham, Isaac, and Jacob. This is the family God chose to work through.

Jacob raised the level of dysfunction to a whole new level, however. His burly twin brother Esau vowed to kill him after an appalling deceit. Jacob fled for his life. On that trip, he dreamed of a ladder between earth and heaven. Angels ascending and descending. God can be fanciful, and perhaps this was His way of saying the divine connection between heaven and earth is still intact. Jacob did not fall so far as to be forever separated from his God. When he awoke the next morning, he set up a stone, anointing it to indicate the sacredness of the place. He called it

Bethel, which means house of God. He encountered God there, and it changed his life forever.

The Prayer came to me after a period of time so very dark that I wondered if I could ever find my way back to God, or even if I wanted to. One of the great misconceptions about the spiritual world is that we must find our way back to God. Spiritual awakenings are always about discovering the ways God has found His way to us.

I anointed The Prayer the day I found it. I made it sacred. It was a constant companion, encouragement, and a challenge for me during my early recovery. It remains a spritual "place," a house of God, where I go and meet the God who restored my soul. I touch this stone and remember. Life gets a little bit clearer when I pause and say The Prayer.

More than anything, The Prayer helps me manage my expectations. When I become too full of requests, which are little more than polite demands, I find my soul shifting into self-centeredness. Like Jacob, I'm trying to run my life and only end up ruining it. The essence of genuine spirituality is a cooperation with God in which I constantly acknowledge His wisdom and try to align my life with His.

All of this must be cloaked in grace. From first to last. If I try to run the show, even a little, then I risk giving into the pride that tells me I accomplished this or that task. When I take charge, I become a lot more like Jacob and a lot less like Jesus. Even the Son of God as He walked the earth consistently spoke of His reliance upon the Father.

Many years ago, I read an interview of Mother Teresa in which the interviewer asked her what it meant to her to accomplish the remarkable ministry in Calcutta and have a world-wide influence. Mother Teresa replied simply, "I don't think like that." Undeterred, the reporter pressed that it must be an extraordinary experience to be a woman who has achieved this level of fame and impact. Again, Mother Teresa replied, "I don't think like that." Then she added something that has stayed with me for decades now, "I am a pencil in God's hand. He does the writing. The pencil can only make itself available to the author."

The Prayer helps me remember that I am a pencil, a bit chewed upon, and perhaps more of a stub at this stage of life. No matter the limits or the battered history, I can take the pencil of my life and place it in God's hands. The Prayer helps me remember to let Him do the writing.

Trust that with this book go my prayers that you too will find The Prayer to be a sacred touchstone you can have with you every day. When you become aware of the heavy press of life, I hope you will remember to pause and say The Prayer. God doesn't make the relationship with Him too hard or complicated. He will help.

May God bless you with a reasonable happiness in this life.